JAPANESE COOKING RECIPES

英語で作る
料理の教科書

はじめに

この本は、日本料理にご興味のある英語圏の方や英語の勉強をしたい方に、日本料理への理解を深めていただくと同時に、日本料理を通して海外でよりよいコミュニケーションができるようとの思いを込めて作りました。

日本料理、特に代表的な家庭料理がほぼ網羅されており、細かい手順写真を加えて、日本語と英語での説明をわかりやすく掲載しています。おいしさの面だけではなく、本格的な器具を使わずともできる作りやすさなども考えて作りましたので、普段の家庭料理としてもご活用いただけます。

世界一の長寿国である日本は、食生活の面からも、世界から大変注目されています。特に、日本料理の基本的な調味料である味噌や醤油、伝統食である発酵食品が体によいとされています。おいしく、健康面にもすぐれた日本の家庭料理が世界に広まり、みなさんが健康で幸せに暮らしていただければと願っております。

川上　文代

Preface

I wrote this book for people who are interested in Japanese cuisine, and for Japanese people who want to study English. My hope is to increase awareness and accessibility of Japanese dishes while also promoting fun communication through cooking.

This book addresses major Japanese dishes with an emphasis on everyday home meals. Detailed photographs showing the step by step process with explanations in both English and Japanese will help guide you through these classic yet delicious dishes. Also, as I would like more people to enjoy these meals more often, I created"doable"recipes. No special equipment is needed to prepare these dishes.

As one of the countries with the longest life expectancy, Japan's diet attracts considerable attention from health-conscious people around the world. Its traditional seasonings such as Miso or Shoyu play a key role in the cuisine's flavour and are considered a healthy alternative for any diet.

I hope more people enjoy happy, healthy lives through delicious Japanese dishes.

Fumiyo Kawakami

Contents 目次

Contents 目次

第3章 Part3 — 洋風&中華風のおかず……123
WESTERN AND CHINESE DISHES

第4章 Part4 — サブになるおかず……169
SIDE DISHES

第5章 Part5 ごはん&汁物&漬物······199
RICE & SOUP & PICKLES

コラム Column

写真撮影／大内光弘、永山弘子　Photographer ／ Mitsuhiro Ohuchi , Hiroko Nagayama
デザイン／中村たまを　Designer ／ Tamao Nakamura
編集・制作／バブーン株式会社　Editor ／ Baboon co.,ltd
協力／高木忍、児玉尚子、谷章子　Special thanks ／ Shinobu Takagi , Naoko Kodama
　　　　　　　　　　　　　　　　　Shoko Tani

第1章
Part 1

日本料理の基本
Basis of Japanese food

これさえあれば
「日本のごはん」は作れます

ESSENTIAL COOKING UTENSILS
FOR JAPANESE CUISINE

調理器具は無計画に買うと、場所を取る
ばかりであまり使わない、なんてことに
なりがち。はじめは最低限の調理器具だ
けをそろえて、不便を感じたら少しずつ
足していくようにしましょう。ここで紹
介したほかに、ピーラー、すり鉢、すり
こぎ、うろこ取りなどもあると便利。必
要に応じて少しずつ集めてください。

Don't buy cooking utensils needlessly. You might not
use all of them, taking up too much space in your
kitchen. Start with the basic essentials and add
utensils one by one as you need them. In addition to
the utensils listed below, a peeler, an earthenware
mortar, a pestle and a fish scale remover are also
useful.

① ボウル
Bowl
切った野菜を入れたり、和え物を作ったりと使い道はいろいろ。大きさ違いでそろえておこう。

Bowls can be used for various purposes such as keeping cut vegetables and marinating ingredients. It is convenient to have bowls of different sizes.

② フライパン
Frying pan
鉄製のフライパンは長もちしますが、焦げつきにくいフッ素樹脂加工のものが使いやすくておすすめ。

Although cast iron frying pans are long lasting, fluorocarbon resin coated non-stick frying pans are recommended to of use easily.

③ 片手鍋
Saucepan
直径18〜20cmほどで、ある程度深さのある鍋があれば、たいていの料理は作れる。

A saucepan of 18-20cm diameter and some depth is useful for almost kinds of cooking.

④ ざる
Strainer
洗った野菜やゆでた麺の水気をきったり、スープをこしたりと大活躍。

Strainers can be used in many ways, such as drying washed vegetables, draining boiled noodles and straining soup.

⑤ お玉
Ladle
丸いタイプより、楕円形に近い注ぎ口のあるタイプがスープを注いだり、汁物を移したりするのに便利。

The elliptical type with a pourer rather than a round shaped ladle is convenient for serving or removing soup.

⑥ 包丁
Kitchen knife
まずは刃渡り21cmほどの万能包丁（三徳包丁）があれば大丈夫。とぐ必要のない、セラミック製のものでもよい。

The 21cm general-purpose kitchen knife (santoku bocho) is good for beginners. Ceramic kitchen knives, which require no sharpening, can be useful.

⑦ へら
Spatula
木製のものは炒めものを混ぜるときに、ゴム製のものはボウルに残った具材を取るときに便利。

Wooden spatulas are convenient for stir-frying and rubber spatulas are useful for removing ingredients remaining in a bowl.

⑧ 菜箸
Kitchen chopsticks
長い調理用の箸。揚げ物を返すときや盛りつけをするときなどの細かな作業に使う。

Long chopsticks for cooking can be used for detail work such as turning deep-frying food and placing food on serving dishes.

⑨ まな板
Cutting board
手入れをしやすいのはプラスチック製だが、木製のほうが刃あたりがソフトで疲れにくい。

A plastic cutting board is easy to maintain, but a wooden board absorbs shock when cutting, thereby preventing fatigue.

⑩ 泡立て器
Whisk
ドレッシングなどを混ぜるのに便利。ワイヤーと柄のつけ根がしっかりしているものが望ましい。

Useful for mixing dressings etc. Choose a whisk with wires securely fixed to the end of the handle.

⑪ 計量カップ
Measuring cup
金属製より透明なタイプのほうが計量しやすい。耐熱性のものなら、なお便利。

Transparent types make measuring easier than metal types. Heat resistant types are more convenient.

⑫ 計量スプーン
Measuring spoon
大さじ、小さじ、小さじ1/2のセットがほとんど。すりきりがつくタイプも。

Mostly available set is with tablespoon, teaspoon and 1/2 teaspoon. Some spoon sets are equipped with a leveler for exact measurement.

⑬ おろし金
Grater
プラスチック製、金属製、陶製と素材はいろいろ。ボックスタイプもあるが、板状のものが一番使いやすい。

Various material's of graters are available: plastic, metal and ceramic. The flat type is easier to use than the box type.

これがあれば「日本のごはん」作りはもっと便利になります

OTHER USEFUL COOKING UTENSILS FOR JAPANESE COOKING

日本料理を作るのに必要な道具のなかには、木製やステンレス製のものがあります。木製のものは、使い終わったらすぐに洗ってきちんとふいて乾かすなど、手入れをしっかりすることが大切です。

Some Japanese kitchen utensils are made of wood or stainless. Wooden utensils must be carefully maintained, for example, by immediately washing and drying after used.

❶ 土鍋
Clay pot

土焼きの鍋。保温効果が高く、料理が冷めにくい。炊飯、鍋料理などに向いている。

Earthen pot. Since clay pots effectively retain the heat of cooked food, they are ideal for cooking rice or for hot pot dishes.

❷ 圧力鍋
Pressure cooker

密閉して蒸気を閉じ込め、普通の鍋より高温高圧で調理するため、短時間で食材に火が通る。

With a pressure cooker, which can be air tight, not allowing steam to escape, food can be cooked at higher temperature and pressure, faster than with ordinary pots.

❸ 揚げ鍋
Deep fryer

鉄や銅でできた揚げ物用の鍋。油の温度を保つため、厚手で深さのあるものを選ぶとよい。

Iron or copper pots designed for frying food. A pot with a certain thickness and depth is recommended to keep oil temperature.

④ 落としぶた
Drop-lid

煮物を作るとき、食材を水や湯にさらすときなど、用途はさまざま。

Drop-lids are used in many ways, for example, when cooking food in a pot and when soaking food in water or hot water.

⑤ 盆ざる
Round bamboo strainer

水分の吸収がよいので、ゆでたての野菜を置いて冷ますときに使うと型くずれしにくい。

A round bamboo strainer absorbs moisture well, so it is useful for cooling boiled vegetables to keep the shape.

⑥ 飯台
Round, flat-bottom wooden tub

寿司飯を作るための道具。湿らせてから使用し、使用後は、よく乾燥させてからしまう。

Used for making sushi rice. It should be soaked before use and dried well before storing.

⑦ 巻きす
Bamboo mat

巻き寿司を巻いたり、卵焼きの形を固定したり、青菜などの水きりに使う。

Used for making rolled sushi, rolled omelet or draining green vegetables after washed.

⑧ 揚げ網
Deep fry strainer

小さな揚げ物をすくったり、揚げかすを取り除いたりするのに便利。料理中のアク取りにも使える。

Convenient for picking up small fried and removing residue from oil. Can also be used for skimming off the scum.

⑨ すり鉢、すりこぎ
Mortar and pestle

材料をすりつぶすときに。すり鉢の下にぬれぶきんなどすべり止めをしき、安定させて使うとよい。

Used for grinding ingredients. To keep the mortar stable, place a slip stopper such as a wet kitchen cloth under it.

⑩ はけ
Brush

食材にたれをぬるときや、粉類をつけるときなどに使う。

Used for coating food with sauce or powder.

13

包丁の使い方の基本を
きちんと覚えましょう

LEARNING THE BASIC USAGE OF KITCHEN KNIVES

食材が上手に切れない、下ごしらえが手早くできない……、これは包丁の扱い方が原因かもしれません。切るときの姿勢や包丁の握り方を正すことで、作業のスピードがグンとアップします！

Is it hard to cut ingredients? Does it take a long time to prepare ingredients? These problems could be due to your way of using a kitchen knife. Learning the appropriate posture for cutting and the correct way to hold a knife will significantly improve your working speed.

包丁の種類と用途 TYPES AND USES OF KITCHEN KNIVES

万能包丁 General purpose knife

これ1本でいろいろ使える
Can be used in many ways

三徳包丁のこと。魚、肉、野菜、堅いものなど、すべての食材に対応する。最初に購入するならこれ。

A general purpose knife is also called a Santoku bocho. This knife can be used for all kinds of ingredients including fish, meat, vegetables and firm others. This is the basic knife for beginners.

出刃包丁 Pointed carving knife

魚・肉の下ごしらえはおまかせ
Exclusively used for preparation of fish and meat

堅い魚をおろすときなどに使う。重量感があり、刃元が厚いため、魚は骨ごと簡単にぶつ切りにすることができる。

Used for cutting firm fish. This knife is heavy and the section of the blade near the handle is thick, so you can chop fish with bone into chunks easily.

薄刃包丁 Vegetable knife

野菜の皮むきやカットに
Used for peeling and cutting vegetables

刃先が薄く幅が広いため、野菜の繊維をこわさずに切ることができる。関西では、切っ先側の背が丸みを帯びた鎌形薄刃が主流。

Because the blade edge is thin and wide, vegetables can be cut without breaking their fibers. In the Kansai region, the kamagata (sickle-shaped) style variation, which has a spine that curves down at the tip to the cutting edge, is popular.

ペティナイフ Petit knife

細かな作業をこなす
Used for detailed work

小さな野菜やフルーツの皮をむくとき、切っ先を使って野菜のヘタを取るとき、飾り切りなど細かい作業をするときに役立つ。

Useful for peeling small vegetables and fruits, to stem ends from vegetables (using the edge of the blade), and detailed work such as decorative cuts.

基本の握り方
Basic way of holding

親指と人差し指で柄を軽く持ち、残りの指で柄を包んで、下側を支え、しっかりと握る。

Lightly hold the handle with thumb and index finger and wrap the other fingers around the handle. Grasp securely to support the lower part of the handle.

人差し指を背にかけてもよい。この握り方はとくに、細かい作業をするときに向いている。

You may place your index finger on the top of the blade. This way of holding is particularly useful for detailed work.

細かく切りたいとき
How to chop or mince

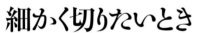

柄を軽く持ち、背の切っ先側から3分の1くらいの位置をもう一方の手で押さえながら、包丁を上下に動かす。

Lightly hold the handle and support the spine of the blade with your free hand (about 1/3 the way along from the tip end). Then move the knife up and down.

✕ NG!
刃の下のほうを持ってはダメ
Do not hold the lower part of the blade.

刃の下に指を置くと危険。指は柄の内側に丸め込む。

It is dangerous to place your fingers under the blade, so curl your fingers beside the handle.

✕ NG!
先端を押さえてはダメ
Do not hold the tip of the blade.

押さえる手の位置が切っ先に近すぎると切りにくい。

If your free hand position is too close to the tip of the blade, you can't move the knife freely.

包丁のとぎ方
How to sharpen a knife

1 砥石を水に浸しておく。砥石に包丁の刃先を60°傾けてあて、背を少し持ち上げ、包丁を前方に動かす。

Soak a grinding stone in water. Place the cutting edge of the knife blade at a 60° angle to the stone. Raise the spine of the knife slightly and slide it ahead on the stone.

2 角度を保ちながら手元に包丁を動かして元の位置に戻す。これを何度も繰り返す。

Keeping this angle, move the knife towards you until it reaches the original position. Repeat the sliding motion several times.

お手入れを ラクにする方法
Easy Maintenance

包丁は毎日とぐのが一番です。最近では、手軽なとぎ器もあるので、難しければこちらを使うのも一案。また、セラミック製の包丁はとぐ必要がないので、お手入れする時間のない人におすすめです。

Ideally, a knife should be sharpened every day. An easy-to-use simplified sharpener is now available for beginners. Ceramic knives are recommended for busy people because of unnecessary to sharpen.

日本料理の基本

Basis of Japanese food

切るときの姿勢 Posture When Cutting

①包丁を持つときは、肩の力を抜きましょう。まな板に近づきすぎず、こぶし2個分ほど離れて立ちます。

① Relax your shoulders while holding a knife. If you are too close to the cutting board, you can't do well. Leave a space of two fists from the cutting board.

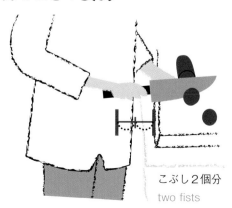

②次に足を肩幅に開き、利き手側の足を後ろにひき、体を約45°に開きます。

② Leave a space equivalent to your shoulder width between your feet. Move your dominant leg back so that your body angle is about 45° to the cutting board.

こぶし2個分

two fists

野菜の切り方を
マスターしましょう

LEARNING DIFFERENT CUTTING METHODS
FOR VEGETABLES

野菜は種類や形によって切り方が変わります。また、長時間火を通す料理は厚くて大きめに、生で食べたりさっと炒める料理は薄めにと、調理法によって切り方も工夫しましょう。

Cutting method varies depending on the type and shape of vegetables. It also differs depending on cooking style. For example, vegetables should be cut into large thick pieces for extended cooking times but should be thin for salads or light stir-fries.

基本 1 BASIC CUT 1

くし形切り Cutting into semi circular shapes

トマトや玉ねぎなど、球体の野菜を放射状に切る方法。厚みがあるので、煮物や鍋物といった煮込み料理に適しています。

This is a method to cut round vegetables such as tomatoes and onions into a radial pattern with thickness. This is good for boiling and stewing vegetables.

1 野菜を縦半分に切る。平らな面を下にして置く。

Cut the vegetable in half lengthwise and place face down on the cutting board.

2 芯を中心に放射状に包丁を入れて、等分する。

Cut the vegetable into equal radial patterns, keeping the vegetable core as the center.

基本 2 BASIC CUT 2

せん切り Julienning

野菜を細く長い形に切る方法。食感を残したいときは繊維に沿って、包丁を入れます。

This is a method to cut vegetables into long thin strips. If you want to keep the crispy texture of the vegetable, cut it along the fibers. If you want to blend the taste cut across the fibers.

1 繊維の方向を確認して置き、なるべく薄くなるように切っていく。

Check for fiber direction and cut the vegetable as thinly as possible.

2 ずらしながら重ねて横に並べ、1mmほどの幅になるよう細く切る。

Stack the sliced pieces and cut them into about 1mm width.

乱切り Cutting into triangular bite-sized pieces

ごぼうや大根など、棒状の野菜を同じくらいの大きさに切る方法。切り口の面積が広いので、火の通りがよくなります。

A method for cutting rod-shaped vegetables such as burdocks and carrots evenly into bite-sized pieces. you can cook rapidly because of wide surface of vegetables.

野菜を少しずつ手前に転がしながら、ななめに包丁を入れて切る。

Cut the vegetable crosswise and at an angle while rolling it gradually towards you.

ひと手間かけてもっとおいしく
Extra effort on tasting good

面取り Chamfering

切った野菜のかどを薄くそいで、形を整える。かどをなくすと、調理中に野菜同士がぶつかってもくずれにくい。

In order to prevent vegetable blocks from breaking up when boiled, chamfer the blocks to give them a rounded shape.

隠し包丁 Hidden cut

火の通りと味のしみ方がよくなるよう、裏側の表面に格子状や十字の切り込みを入れること。

In order to cook more quickly and allow flavor to blend into ingredients, make shallow cuts (lattice-pattern or cross-pattern) on the backside.

輪切り Cutting round slices

大根やれんこんなど、太めで切り口が丸くなる野菜を端から切る方法。調理方法や火を通す時間によって、厚さを調節しましょう。

This is a method to cut thick rod-shaped vegetables into round slices. Adjust the thickness to the cooking style or time.

野菜を横向きにして置き、一定の厚さに切る。切り口がななめにならないようにする。

Place the vegetable parallel to you and cut evenly. Cut surfaces have to be parallel.

半月切り Cutting half-moon shapes

輪切りを半分にした形。厚めにしたいときには、輪切りにしてから2等分しましょう。

This shape is a half cut of the round slice. For thick slices, cut the vegetable in round slices, then cut them in half.

薄めに切る場合は、縦半分にしてから切り口を下にして置き、切っていく。

For thin slices, halve the vegetable lengthwise and place the cut surface down on the cutting board before cutting half-moon shapes.

いちょう切り Cutting into gingko leaf shapes

半月切りをさらに半分にした形。いちょうの葉の形に似ていることから名づけられました。

This shape is exactly a half cut of the half-moon shape and named because of the similar shape of a gingko leaf.

野菜を縦に4つ割りにし、好みの厚さに切る。

Quarter the vegetable lengthwise and slice into the desired thickness.

日本料理の基本

Basis of Japanese food

拍子木切り Cutting long-sticks

祭りや歌舞伎で使う拍子木に形が似ていることから、名前がつけられました。四角柱の棒状に切ったもので、揚げ物によく使います。

The Japanese name is "hyoshi-gi-giri" as the shape resembles Japanese wooden clappers used for festivals or Kabuki theater. The square sticks are often used for fried foods.

4〜5cmの長さに切った野菜を繊維に沿って1cmほどの幅に切る。

Cut the vegetable in 4 – 5 cm length and then cut them along the fibers into 1cm thickness.

ねかせて置き、棒状になるよう1cmほどの幅に切る。球形の野菜の場合は、両端を切って端から1cm幅に切ったあとにねかせて置き、さらに1cm幅に切る。

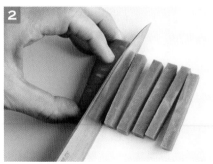

Stack the pieces and cut into 1cm width to look like sticks. For round vegetables, first cut off both ends of the vegetable and slice into 1cm thickness. Cut thes slices into 1cm width.

角切り（さいの目切り）Cutting in cubes

拍子木切りをサイコロのような立方体に切ったもの。

This is a method to further cut long-stick cut vegetables into dice-like cubes.

拍子木切りした野菜を横にして置き、1cm幅に切る。

Place long-stick cut vegetables parallel to you and cut them into 1cm width.

色紙切り Cutting in thin square pieces

拍子木切りを繊維に対して直角に薄く切り、紙状の正方形にしたもの。

Slicing long-stick cut vegetables crosswise into thin squares.

拍子木切りにした野菜を横向きにして置く。1〜3mmほどの幅に切る。

Place long-stick cut vegetables on the cutting board parallel to you. Slice them into 1-3mm width.

短冊切り Cutting into rectangles

1cm幅に切った野菜を、縦方向に薄くカットしたもの。炒め物や汁物など幅広く使えます。

Cut the vegetable into 1cm thickness and then cut them lengthwise into thin pieces. This cutting is commonly used for stir fry or soup.

1cm幅に切った野菜をねかせて置き、さらに、1〜2mm幅に切る。

Place 1cm width cut vegetable one beside others. Cut each of them into 1-2mm width.

みじん切り Chopping finely

野菜を細かく刻む方法です。野菜の旨みを出したいときや薬味に使うときに最適な切り方です。

This is a method to chop vegetables finely. Good to add the vegetable flavor in cooking or using as spice.

4〜5cmの長さに切った野菜を、1〜2mm幅のせん切りにする。

Slice the vegetables cut in 4-5cm length into julienne of 1-2mm width.

せん切りにした野菜を横向きにして置き、1mmほどの幅に刻む。できるだけ細かく刻むようにする。

Place the cut vegetable parallel to you on the cutting board and cut in 1mm width. Cut as finely as possible.

玉ねぎのみじん切り Chopping onion finely

球体の玉ねぎは、葉野菜や棒状の野菜とは違う方法でみじん切りにします。

Round onions require a different method from leaf vegetables or rod-like vegetables for chopping finely.

1 玉ねぎを縦に2等分し、切り口を下にして置く。芯を残し、繊維に沿って1〜2mm幅に切り込みを入れる。

Halve the onion lengthwise and place the cut surface down. Make incisions 1-2mm apart along the fibers leaving the core part uncut.

2 手で玉ねぎを押さえながら水平方向に3〜4本切り込みを入れる。

Press down on the onion with your hand and make three or four horizontal cuts parallel to the cutting board surface.

3 玉ねぎを包むように手で押さえ、細かく刻む。**1** の切り込みを粗くすると粗みじん切りになる。

Support the onion with your fingers and chop finely. If you chop roughly in step **1** above, the result is semi-fine chopping.

4 芯近くは芯を上にして置き、同様に繊維に沿って切り込みを入れ、芯に向かって刻む。

To chop the area near the core, place the piece so that the core is away from you. Similarly make some incisions along the fibers and chop towards the core.

細切り Cutting into sticks

せん切りよりもやや太めに切ることです。太さはだいたいマッチ棒ほどで千六本とも呼びます。味噌汁や和え物に向きます。

This is a method to cut vegetables slightly thicker than julienne. The thickness is almost the same as a matchstick. In Japanese this method is called "senroppon" and is suitable for miso soup and cold dishes mixed with dressing.

4～5cmの長さに野菜を切る。縦にして置き、3mm幅にスライスして薄めの長方形にする。

Cut the vegetable in 4-5cm length. Place the cut pieces lengthwise and cut in 3mm width to make thin rectangles.

切った野菜を、何枚か重ねて置く。さらに3mmほどの幅に切る。

Stack several cut pieces on top of each other and cut them into about 3mm width.

葉野菜のせん切り Cutting leaf vegetables into julienne

葉野菜のせん切りは、つけ合わせやサラダに使います。刻んだあとは水にさらしてシャキッとさせましょう。

Used for relish and salads. Soak cut vegetable pieces in water to make them crisp.

汚れた葉をはがし、4等分して芯をそぎ取る。内側の葉と外側の葉に分ける。

Remove the outermost leaves. Quarter other leaves and cut off the core. Separate inside leaves from outside leaves.

外側の葉は、軽く上から押して平らにし、1～2mm幅に薄く切る。内側の葉は、繊維を縦にして置き、同様に切る。

Lightly press the outside leaves to make them flatter and cut into 1-2mm width. Place inner leaves lengthwise in fiber direction and cut them in the same way as for the outer leaves.

青じそのせん切り Cutting green perillas into julienne

青じそは薄くて切りにくいので、小さく丸めると切りやすくなります。できるだけ細かく刻み、香りを出しましょう。

As a green perilla is thin, it may be difficult to cut. Roll it into a thin tube. Cut it as fine as possible to add the flavor.

青じそをくるくると巻き、細い筒状にする。何枚かある場合は重ねて巻くとよい。

Roll a green perilla into a thin tube. For more than two perilla leaves, place one on top of the other and roll them.

包丁の先のほうを使い、1mmほどの幅に細かく刻む。

Use the tip of the knife to cut into 1mm thin slices.

ごぼうのささがき Cutting burdock into long thin shavings

ささがきは、鉛筆を削る要領でそぎ切りする切り方です。切り口が広いうえに薄いので、火が通りやすく、炒め物に向いています。

Shave a burdock in the same way as sharpening a pencil. Because cut surface is wide and thin, you can cook quickly. Good for stir-fry.

1

ごぼうはたわしでよく洗い、泥を落とす。縦に何本か切り込みを入れる。

Wash a burdock well with a scrub brush to remove soil. Make several incisions lengthwise.

2

包丁をねかせ、ごぼうを転がしながら薄くなめに切り、手早く酢水につけて変色を防ぐ。

Holding the knife blade quite flat, cut a burdock in thin slices while rolling it. Soak in vinegar water to prevent from discoloring.

白髪ねぎ Cutting a white part of scallion into long fine strips

ねぎの白い部分だけをせん切りにするので、このように呼ばれています。煮物や麺のトッピングにしたり、薬味にしたりと広く利用できます。

This cutting method called Shiraganegi (white haired onion) in Japanese is to slice a white part of scallion into fine strips. Commonly used as garnish for stews or noodles, and as spice.

1

ねぎを4～5cmの長さに切る。動かないように手で押さえながら、包丁で、縦に半分まで切り込みを入れる。

Cut a scallion into 4-5cm length. Press them with your hand and make an incision lengthwise up to half the length.

2

切り口を開いて、内側から緑色の芯を取り出す。

Open the incised part to remove the green core from inside.

3

白い部分を軽く上から押さえて平らにしながら、繊維を断って細く切る。

Lightly press a white part to flatten it out and cut into fine strips by splitting the fibers.

4

せん切りしたものを水にさらしてシャキッとさせる。

Soak the strips in water to make them crisp.

日本料理の基本

Basis of Japanese food

野菜の下ごしらえをきちんとすれば
日本料理は失敗知らず

VEGETABLE PRETREATMENT IS ESSENTIAL FOR SUCCESSFUL COOKING

野菜の下ごしらえは、食べられない部分を取り除く、汚れを落とす、アクを抜くのが基本です。野菜ごとに正しく下ごしらえをしないと、失敗の原因になるので気をつけましょう。

Basic vegetable pretreatment includes removing inedible parts, dirt and astringent taste. Note the various of pretreatment the vegetables.

キャベツ Cabbage

キャベツの芯は硬くて火が通りにくいので、調理前に取り除きます。

Since the core of a cabbage is hard and difficult to cook, remove this part before cooking.

1 芯の根元に包丁を入れて、一周切り込みを入れ、芯をくりぬく。

Stab the root of the core with a knife and make an incision around the core to remove it.

2 ボウルに水をため、芯を取ったキャベツを沈める。水の重みで葉を1枚ずつていねいにはがす。

Soak the cabbage in water in a bowl. Carefully remove each leaf by utilizing the buoyancy of the water.

レタス Lettuce

サラダに使うレタスはシャキシャキ感が命。下ごしらえは水に浸して行ないます。根元にたまっている汚れに注意しましょう。

Lettuce for salads should be crisp. Pretreat by soaking lettuce in water. Carefully remove dirt from the root.

1 芯の根元に切り込みを入れ、芯をくりぬく。

Make an incision at the root to remove the core.

2 ボウルに入れて水を加え、葉を1枚ずつはがす。

Put the lettuce in the bowl and pour water into it. Then remove leaves one by one. remove leaves one by one.

ちんげん菜 Chinese cabbage

根元を落として、4つ割りにしてから洗います。火の通り方が違うので、茎と葉は分けて切ります。

Cut off the end and quarter before washing to remove all dirt. Cut the stems from the leaves to separate them because of different time to cook.

根元に十字に切り込みを入れ、手で裂き、4等分する。水をためたボウルでふり洗いする。

Make a cross shaped incision at the end of the Chinese cabbage. Quarter it by hand. Wash it in water in a bowl.

ほうれん草 Spinach

シュウ酸というえぐみ成分を多く含むので、1%濃度の塩を入れたたっぷりの湯で下ゆでします。

As spinach contains lots of oxalic acid, which has a harsh taste, boil the spinach in plenty of water with 1% concentration of salt before cooking.

根を落とし、根元に十字の切り込みを入れる。

Cut off the root end and make a cross shaped incision at the end of it.

水をためたボウルに根元をつけ、しばらく置いて葉をシャキッとさせる。

Soak the end in water in a bowl to freshen the leaves.

たっぷりの湯で塩ゆでして、水にさっとさらしたら、手早く冷ます。

Boil in plenty of water with salt. Quickly soak in water to cool.

巻きすでほうれん草を巻き、両手で押さえて余分な水分を絞る。

Roll the spinach in a bamboo mat. Hold the mat to squeeze out extra water from them.

日本料理の基本

Basis of Japanese food

きのこ類 Mushroom

石づきがある場合は切り落として、手でばらばらにほぐします。洗うと水分を含んでべたつくので、基本的に洗いません。

When the mushrooms are still attached to the root, separate each mushroom by hand. In general, mushrooms should not be washed as they become slimy after absorbing moisture.

えのき Enoki mushrooms

ビニール袋に入ったまま石づきを切り落とすと、ばらばらにならない。

Place the enoki mushrooms in a plastic bag to cut off the roots as they easily fall apart.

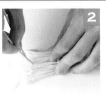

竹串を使うと早くほぐれる。

Use a bamboo stick to quickly separate each mushroom.

しめじ Shimeji mushrooms

石づきを落とし、手でほぐして小房に分ける。

Cut off the roots and separate into small bunches by hand.

マッシュルーム White or brown mushrooms

軸を落とし、かさの下の汚れをはけで取り除く。

Cut off the stems and remove dirt under the cap.

ピーマン Green pepper

ヘタ、タネ、ワタを手で取り除きます。基本的なふたつの除き方を紹介しますので、料理に合わせて使い分けてください。丸みをおびた形なので、手で押さえて平らにすると切りやすくなります。

Remove the hull, seeds and pulp by hand. There are two basic ways of removing these parts. Choose one depending on the recipe. As green pepper has a round shape, flatten it with your hand to make it easy to cut.

ヘタを落として縦半分に切り、中のタネとワタを手で取り除く。

Remove the hull and cut lengthwise. Remove seeds and pulp by hand.

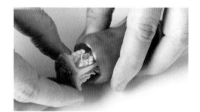

ヘタの周りに一周切り込みを入れる。ヘタをゆっくり引っ張り、タネとワタを取り除く。

Make an incision around the hull and pull the hull to remove seeds and pulp.

ブロッコリー Broccoli
カリフラワー Cauliflower

房を切るときには、バランスが悪いので根元を軽く持ち上げると切りやすくなります。房が大きい場合には、2等分するとよいでしょう。

Slightly raise the stem end for easy cutting. If the bunch is large, divide in half.

1 根元を軽く持って、茎と房が枝分かれしている部分を切り、小房に分ける。

Lightly hold the end and cut between the stem and the flowers. Separate the flowers into small bunches.

2 水にはなち、シャキッとさせる。内側の細かい汚れを落とすこともできる。

Soak the vegetable in water to make it crisp. Small particles of the dirt can also be washed out.

かぶ Turnip

取り除きづらい茎の間の汚れは、竹串を使うときれいに落ちます。筋が硬いので必ず厚めに皮をむきます。

Use a bamboo stick to remove dirt between leaf stems. As turnip has tough fibers, peel the skin thickly.

1 葉と根を切り落とし、8等分する。根元の切り口から皮をむく。

Cut off the leaves and root and cut evenly into eight pieces. Start from the bottom of the turnip to peel.

2 水につけながら、竹串を使って茎の間の汚れを取り除く。

Soak the turnip in water and remove dirt between the stems with a bamboo stick.

かぼちゃ Pumpkin

硬くて切りにくい場合は、厚みの半分ほど切ってから包丁を上下に動かし、刃先を使って少しずつ切ります。電子レンジに約30秒かけると切りやすくなります。

If the pumpkin is hard, insert a knife up to about half of the thickness of the squash. Then move the knife up and down and cut little by little using the knife edge. Cooking the pumpkin in a microwave for about 30 seconds makes cutting easier.

1 中心から包丁を入れ半分の深さまで切る。包丁の背に力を加える。

Insert a knife to the center of the pumpkin up to half of the thickness. Apply pressure on the knife.

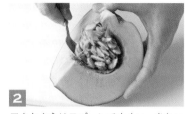

2 ワタとタネはスプーンですくい、きれいに取り除く。

Carefully remove the pulp and seeds with a spoon.

トマト Tomato

ヘタは、包丁の切っ先をさしてトマトを回すときれいに簡単に取れます。また、皮をむく場合は火であぶったり、熱湯に落とすときれいにむけます。

To remove the hull successfully and easily, stab the knife tip near the hull and turn the tomato. Roast the tomato over open flame or soak in boiling water to peel the skin easily.

1 包丁の切っ先をヘタの近くにさし、トマトを回してヘタを取り除く。

Stab the knife tip near the hull and turn the tomato to remove the hull.

2 底に少し突起した、茶色の硬い部分があるので、薄くそいで落とす。

Since the light brown protrusion on the bottom of the tomato is hard, thinly chip off this part.

トマトの皮むき Peeling a tomato

1 トマトのヘタの脇にフォークをつきさす。

Stab a fork in the end near the hull.

2 皮が少しめくれてくるぐらいまで火で全体をあぶる。

Roast the entire tomato over open flame until the skin starts peeling.

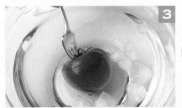

3 トマトを氷水に落とす。完全に冷めるまで、2～3分置く。

Soak the tomato in ice water and wait for 2-3 minutes until the tomato cools down completely.

4 ふきんなどで水気をふき、皮がめくれたところからていねいにむく。

Dry the tomato using a cloth and peel the skin carefully starting from the already peeling part.

さやいんげん String beans
絹さや Snow peas

ガクを引っ張って筋を取り除きます。より鮮やかな緑にするため塩ゆでし、盆ざるにあげて冷やします。

Shell by pulling the sepal. In order to make beans fresh green, boil in salt water. Cool them on a round bamboo strainer.

ガクを指でつまんで筋を取る。

Shell by pulling the sepal by fingers.

ごぼう Burdock

泥がついた状態で売られている土ごぼう
と、泥を洗い落とした状態で売られてい
る洗いごぼうがあります。土ごぼうのほ
うが保存がききます。

Burdocks are available in two forms:
with soil, and without (pre-washed).
Burdocks with soil last longer.

泥は、たわしでよくこすってきれいに洗
い落とす。

Wash off soil carefully using a scrub
brush.

切り口の変色を防ぐため、酢水に10分
ほどつける。

In order to prevent the cut surface
from discoloring, soak in vinegar and
water for about 10 minutes.

なす Eggplant

なすはガクを外し、切ったあと水にさら
します。ガクは手にささりやすいので注
意しましょう。また、皮に隠し包丁を入
れて火が通りやすいようにします。

After removing the hull and slicing the
eggplant, soak the pieces in water.
Be careful with the sharp hull. Make
some incisions on the skin so that the
eggplant can be cooked quickly.

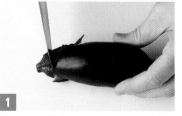

包丁の切っ先をガクに当てて、なすを手
前に回して切り込みを入れる。

Place the knife tip against the hull
and make an incision by rolling the
eggplant towards you.

ガクを取り除く。

Remove the hull.

切ったあとはアクを抜くため、10分ほど
冷水にさらす。調理前に必ず水気をきる

Soak cut pieces in cold water
for about 10 minutes to remove
harshness. Drain well before cooking.

大きなまま使う場合は、皮に浅い格子状
の切り込みを入れる。

If you use the eggplant without
cutting into pieces, make shallow
lattice-pattern incisions on the skin.

オクラ Okra

包丁の刃元で、皮をむくようにガクを取
り除きます。塩でこすると、産毛が取れ
るうえ色も鮮やかになります。

Remove the hull using the heel of
the blade in the same way as peeling
skin. Rub the okra with salt to remove
fuzzy hair and enhance the color.

ガクを取ったオクラに
塩をまぶして、指先で
こすり、産毛を取る。
水洗いして塩を落とす。

After removing the
hull, coat salt on the
okra and rub with
finger tips to remove
fuzzy hair. Wash salt
away.

きゅうり Cucumber

表面のイボは口当たりが悪いので包丁の背（みね）でこそげ取ること。また、板ずりすることで色が鮮やかになります。

Remove warts from the surface with the spine of a knife as they are harsh in the mouth. Rub the cucumber with salt on the cutting board to enhance the color.

包丁の背（みね）をきゅうりに当て、包丁を横に軽く動かして表面のイボを取る。

Lightly scrape with the spine of a knife to remove warts on the surface.

両端を落とし、切り落とした部分と切り口をこすり合わせてアクを出す。

Cut off both ends and rub the cut surface with the cut off part to remove harshness.

白いアクごと切り口の周りをむくように切る。

When a white excretion appears, peel the skin around the cut surface.

塩をふり、まな板の上で前後に転がす。水で洗って塩を落とす。

Sprinkle salt and roll the cucumber back and forth on the cutting board using both hands. Wash salt away.

アスパラガス Asparagus

アスパラガスは根元を持って軽くしならせ、ポキッと折れるところより上の部分だけを使います。やわらかい穂先をつぶさないよう気をつけましょう。

Hold the bottom of each spear and bend to snap it off. Only the upper part of the spear should be used. Be careful not to crush the soft spear point.

根元近くの硬いはかまを取り除く。ピーラーで薄く皮をむき、根元の硬い部分を折って除く。

Trim the asparagus. Use a peeler to peel thinly and remove the woody part at the bottom by snapping the spear with your hands.

さといも Taro

皮をむく前に一度洗って乾かすと、切るときにすべりにくくなります。ぬれているとぬめりが出てすべるので注意します。

As taro is slippery, wash and dry before peeling. When taro is wet, it is slimy and slippery so be careful.

表面の泥をたわしでごしごし洗って落とし、盆ざるにあげて乾かす。

Remove soil from the surface with a scrub brush and dry on a round bamboo strainer.

完全に乾いたら、天地を落とし、皮をむく。

When they dried completely, cut off the top and bottom ends. Peel the skin.

水につけて、指で表面を軽くこすりながら、ぬめりを洗い落とす。

Soak in water and rub the surface with your fingers in order to remove sliminess.

湯に落として、8分通り火が通ったら盆ざるにあげて水気をきり、ぬめりを完全に取り除く。

Boil in hot water. Be careful overdone. Drain well with a round bamboo strainer to remove sliminess.

魚の簡単なおろし方を
覚えるととても便利です

IT IS HELPFUL TO LEARN
SIMPLE WAYS OF FILLET FISH

魚をおろすのは一見難しそうですが、コツを覚えてしまえば大丈夫。ここでは、比較的簡単な、いわしやいかのおろし方を紹介します。

Fillet fish looks difficult, but once you learn how, you can do it. Here, we will introduce comparatively simple methods of fillet sardines and squids among others.

魚の部位
Fish parts

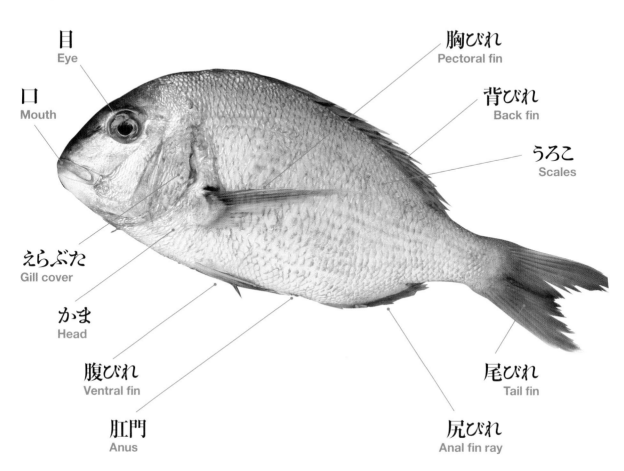

目
Eye

口
Mouth

えらぶた
Gill cover

かま
Head

腹びれ
Ventral fin

肛門
Anus

胸びれ
Pectoral fin

背びれ
Back fin

うろこ
Scales

尾びれ
Tail fin

尻びれ
Anal fin ray

魚をおろすために必要な道具
Utensils needed for filleting fishes

料理をする人なら誰でも持っている、包丁、まな板、ふきんがあれば、魚はおろせます。魚をおろすのにもっとも向いているのは出刃包丁ですが、なければ万能包丁などでもかまいません。

General utensils, a knife, cutting board and cloth, are sufficient to fillet fish. The ideal knife is a pointed carving knife, but a general purpose knife is fine, too.

必要な道具は、包丁、まな板、ふきん、すべり止めの4点。すべり止めはぬれぶきんなどで代用できます。

Four essential tools include a knife, cutting board, cloth and slip stopper, for which a wet cloth can be used.

日本料理の基本

Basis of Japanese food

あじの三枚おろし
Three piece filleting of horse mackerel

1

包丁を使い、尾から頭に向かって表面の鋭いうろこ（ぜいご）を取る。

Remove sharp scales on the surface using a knife in the direction from tail to head.

2

胸びれの後ろにななめに包丁を入れる。裏側も同様にし、頭を落とす。

Stab a knife at an angle behind the pectoral fin. Repeat the same on the other side of the fish and cut the head off.

3

腹を割いて包丁で内臓をすべてかき出す。腹の中を水で洗う。

Using a knife open the belly to remove the viscera. Wash the belly cavity in running water.

4

腹側を手前にし、腹側から尾まで中骨に沿って切り込みを入れる。

Place the fish with the belly side facing you and slice from the open belly end to the tail along the backbone.

5

背を手前にし、中骨に沿って尾から頭に向かって切り込みを入れる。

Turn over the fish so that the back is facing you and slice from tail to head end along the backbone.

6

尾と身を切り離す。裏側の身も同様にして外す。

Divide the top fillet from the tail and backbone. Turn over the fish and do the same for the other fillet.

7

中骨と2枚の身の3枚おろしにした状態。

The above picture shows the fish sliced into three fillets: the backbone part, and two side fillets.

8

身の腹骨を包丁ですくうように取る。指で取り残しがないか確認する。

Pick up the bones remaining in the side fillets with the knife. Check for remaining bones with your fingers.

いわしの手開き

Filleting sardine with fingers

1

頭と内臓を取ったら、中骨に沿って親指を使って開く。

After removing the head and viscera, open the fish by sliding your thumb along the backbone.

2

中骨に指をひっかけ、上に引き上げて取る。

Grasp the backbone and lift to remove it.

3

手開きで開いた状態。身と骨に分ける。

The above picture shows the opened fish. The body and the backbone are divided.

4

身を半分に切り、背びれを取る。骨抜きで小骨を取り除く。

Cut the body in half lengthwise and remove the back fin. Use tweezers to remove small bones.

いかをおろす

Filleting squid

1

胴の中に指を入れ、親指と人差し指で胴と内臓のつなぎ目を外す。

Insert your fingers in the body and remove the connection part between the body and the viscera using thumb and index finger.

2

足のつけ根部分をしっかり持ち、内臓ごと引き抜いて足と胴に分ける。

Firmly hold the arm joints and pull the body together with the viscera, dividing the arms and the body.

3

胴の中にある透明のなんこつを指で引き抜く。

With your fingers pull out the transparent cartilage in the body.

4

つなぎ目を外し、エンペラを引っ張って胴からはがす。胴の薄皮をむく。

Remove the joint. Pull the fin to remove it from the body. Peel the thin skin from the body.

5

エンペラの先端のなんこつを取り除く。先端に切り込みを入れる。

Remove the cartilage from the edge of the fin. Make an incision on the edge of the fin.

6

切り込み部分を持ち、身と皮の間に指を差し込み、エンペラの薄皮をむく。

Hold the incised part and insert your fingers between the body and skin to peel the thin skin off the fin.

7

胴の中を水で軽く洗い、水気をふく。なんこつがついていた部分から切り開く。

Lightly wash inside the body with running water and dry. Open the body from the part where the cartilage was attached.

8

端の部分を切り落とす。表面をこすって薄皮をむき、硬い部分があれば、取り除く。

Cut off the bottom part. Rub the surface to peel the thin skin and remove any hard part.

日本料理の基本は
だしをきちんとひくことです

THE BASIS OF JAPANESE COOKING IS PROPER SOUP STOCK

和食の基本となるだしには、昆布だし、煮干しだしなどさまざまな種類があります。料理に合わせて使い分けることが料理上手への近道です。

There are various Japanese soup stocks such as kelp stock and dried anchovy stock. The shortcut to successful cooking is choosing the appropriate soup stock for the dish.

和風だしに使われる材料　INGREDIENTS USED FOR JAPANESE SOUP STOCK

煮干し
Dried anchovy

いわしなどを煮て干した乾物。しっかりと乾燥していて、皮がはがれておらず、姿が整ったものを選ぶ。

Small fishes such as boiled or dried baby sardines are used. Choose those that are completely dried, have held their shape, and are without peeling skin.

削り節
Shavings of dried bonito

かつおの身をゆでていぶし、乾燥させて使いやすいように削ったもの。

Shavings of boiled, smoked and dried bonito are easy to use for making stock.

昆布
Kelp

厚みがあり、表面に白い粉があるものを選ぶ。使うときには表面を軽くふきんでふく。水で洗ってはダメ。

Choose a thick piece with white powder on the surface. Before using the kelp, lightly wipe with a cloth. Do not wash it in water.

かつお節（削り節）と昆布を使ったもっとも基本的なだし。吸い物やうどんのかけ汁などにぴったり。

The most basic soup stock is made from shavings of dried bonito and kelp. Ideal for clear soup and broth for hot noodles.

材料 Ingredients

水…1L
昆布…（5×10cm）1枚
かつお節…約15g

1 L   water
1 sheet (5 x 10 cm)   kelp
15 g   shavings of dried bonito

1
昆布の表面をふきんなどでふき、ほこりなどを取る。分量の水に昆布を入れ、約3時間おく。

Wipe the surface of the kelp with a cloth to remove powder. Place the kelp in water and soak for about 3 hours.

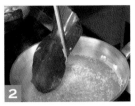

2
鍋に戻し汁ごと入れ、沸騰する直前まで中火にかける。煮たってきたら昆布を取り出す。

Pour the water with the kelp into a saucepan and heat at medium heat. When the water starts boiling, remove the kelp.

3
すぐにかつお節を加える。酸味が出たり、だし汁がにごってしまうので沸騰直前に火を弱める。

Add the shavings of dried bonito immediately. Turn down the heat just as the water starts boiling as boiling may result in an acidic taste or turbid soup.

4
アクが出てきたら取り除き、火を止める。お玉ですくったら息を吹きかけてアクだけを捨て、残りの液体は鍋に戻す。

Remove scum and turn off the heat. Take up the scum with some stock in a ladle and blow on the scum.

5
かつお節が沈んだらさらしでこす。静かにこさないと、だしがにごるので注意する。

When the shavings of dried bonito sink, filter the stock through a cotton cloth. As the stock may become turbid easily, filter it gently.

6
2で取り出した昆布、鍋に残ったかつお節は二番だしに使えるので、捨てずに取っておくこと。

The kelp removed the step No. 2 above and the remaining shavings of dried bonito can be used for a second soup stock. Keep them.

だし汁作りで覚えておくこと Tips for Making Soup Stock

水質がポイント
Water quality is Important

だしに使う水は硬水よりも軟水が向いています。ミネラルウォーターを使う場合は、軟水を選びます。また、水道水を使う場合は、ひと晩くみおきするとよいでしょう。

For making soup stock, soft water is preferable to hard water. Choose soft water if you use mineral water. If you use tap water, it is preferable to leave the water in a container overnight.

作りおきはダメ
Use soup stock immediately

だしは、風味が落ちやすいので使うときに使う分だけ作るのがベストです。ただし、冷蔵庫で2～3日までは保存が可能です。

As soup stock loses flavor quickly, make only as much as needed each time. However, soup stock can be refrigerated for a few days.

保存方法
Storing

必ず冷まし、密封してほかのにおいがつかないように冷蔵庫で保管します。だしの材料である昆布、煮干し、かつお節は、缶などで密閉して冷暗所で保管しましょう。

Cool soup stock and seal off so that it does not absorb odors from other foods in the fridge. Soup stock ingredients, kelp, dried anchovy and dried bonito should be sealed in a container and stored in a dark cool place.

二番だしのひき方　HOW TO MAKE SECOND SOUP STOCK

一番だしで使った昆布とかつお節を使うだし。色も味も濃厚になります。

Kelp and shavings of dried bonito, used for the first soup stock, can be used for the second soup stock with dark and stronger flavor.

材料 Ingredients

水…1L　　かつお節…7.5g
一番だしで使った昆布とかつお節…適量

1 L　water
7.5 g　dried bonito shavings
some kelp and shavings of dried bonito used for the first soup stock.

一番だしと二番だし

First Soup Stock and Second Soup Stock

一番だしをひいた昆布と削り節を使う二番だしは、一番だしよりも雑味が出る分濃厚になるので、丼や煮物に向いています。

Since the second soup stock is made from kelp and shavings of dried bonito used for the first soup stock, it has a bitter and astringent taste but richer. For this reason, it is suitable for rice bowl dishes and stew.

日本料理の基本

Basis of Japanese food

材料すべてを鍋に入れ強火にかける。沸騰したら弱火にし、5〜6分煮出す。

Put all the ingredients in the and cook over high heat. Once boiling, reduce heat to low and simmer for 5 - 6 minutes.

水が一割ほど減ったら新しい削り節を加え、中火にする。再沸騰したらアクを取り除く。

When the amount of water is reduced to 10%, add new shavings of dried bonito and turn the heat to medium. When the water boils again, remove scum.

火を止めて3分ほどおき、さらしでこす。削り節と昆布をさらしに出し、箸などで押してしっかりと汁を絞り出す。

Turn off the heat and let stand for 3 minutes. Place them on a cotton cloth and press using chopsticks to squeeze out.

煮干しだしのひき方　HOW TO MAKE SOUP STOCK USING DRIED ANCHOVIES

煮干しが湿っていると、だしが生臭くなってしまいます。湿気に気をつけて保管しておきましょう。

If anchovies are not completely dried, the soup stock becomes fishy. Store anchovies in a dry place.

材料 Ingredients

水…1L
煮干し…25g
酒…大さじ1

1 L　water
25g dried anchovies
1 Tbsp sake

煮干しの頭と内臓部分を指で取り除く。さっと軽く洗って水につけ、ひと晩おく。夏場は冷蔵庫に入れる。

Remove heads and viscera from anchovies with fingers. Lightly wash and soak in water overnight. Refrigerate in summer.

1 を戻し汁ごと鍋に移し、中火にかける。酒を加え、軽く沸騰する火加減でアクを取る。

Pour the water with anchovies into a saucepan and heat at medium heat. Add sake and keep heat not boiling. Remove scum.

さらに10分火にかける。火を止め、さらしで静かにこす。

Continue for 10 minutes. Turn off heat and gently filter the stock through a cotton cloth.

日本料理に欠かせない
ごはんの炊き方をマスターしましょう

LEARNING HOW TO COOK RICE,
THE STAPLE OF JAPANESE CUISINE

ごはんは、炊飯器がなくても意外と簡単に鍋で炊くことができます。米のとぎ方、炊くときの水加減や火加減などを正しく覚えておきましょう。

Even if you don't have a rice cooker, you can cook rice in a pot more easily than you might think. Learn the correct way of washing rice, the amount of water and the right heat for cooking rice.

まずは米をといでみましょう
How to wash rice

たっぷり水を入れたボウルに米を入れ、水が白くにごるまで、手早く混ぜる。

Place rice in plenty of water in a bowl and mix with fingers. Immediately drain the water.

水がにごってきたら、米がとぎ汁を吸わないうちに手早く水を捨てる。白く濃いとぎ汁を米が吸うとぬか臭くなる。

When the water becomes cloudy, immediately drain the water before the rice can absorb it. White and cloudy water gives the cooked rice a bran smell.

水を入れずに手に米をはさみ、こすり合わせるように洗う。量が多い場合は、片手でボウルに押しつけるように洗う。

After draining water, pinch and rub rice with your fingers. If you are preparing a large amount of rice, press it to the bottom of the bowl with your hand.

水を入れて軽く混ぜ、にごったら水を捨てる。水がきれいに透き通るまで、3、4の工程を3〜4回繰り返す。

Add water and lightly mix with rice. Cloudy water should be drained. Repeat steps 3 and 4 three or four times until the water becomes almost clear.

ざるに上げて水分をきる。米についた水分だけを吸わせ、表面が乾燥しないようぬれぶきんをかぶせて約30分おく。

Drain the water in a strainer. Let the rice absorbs the surface moisture and cover it with a wet cloth so that it does not dry out. Leave it for about 30 minutes.

無洗米や雑穀米などのとぎ方は？
How to treat wash-free rice or rice mixed with millet

ぬかがあらかじめ取り除かれた無洗米は、さっと洗い、少し多めの水に30分〜1時間さらします。雑穀米もさっと洗う程度。米の量の1割増しの水で2〜3時間吸水させ、その水で炊きます。

For wash-free rice, which has had the bran already removed, lightly wash and soak in a generous amount of water for 30 minutes to 1 hour. For rice mixed with millet, lightly wash and soak in water (equivalent to rice amount +10%) for 2-3 hours. Use the same water to cook rice.

鍋でごはんを炊きましょう
How to cook rice in a pot

1 洗って30分おいた米と、同量の水を入れる。例えば、洗い米1カップの場合は水は1カップ（200ml）を入れる。

Place rice left for 30minutes after washing, and pour an equal amount of water in a pot. For example, pour one cup (200ml) of water for one cup of washed rice.

2 ふたをし、強火にかける。沸騰したら弱火にし、10分炊く。火を止め、ふたをしたまま5〜10分蒸らす。

Cover the pot. Cook over high heat and bring to a boil. Once boiling, reduce the heat to low and cook for 10 minutes. Remove from heat and let stand for 5-10 minutes with the lid on to steam rice.

ごはんの炊き方と水加減
Tips for cooking rice and amount of water

米をとぐときには、必ず冷水で、割れないように力加減に注意します。乾燥した米は、ぬかが溶け出したとぎ汁を吸いやすいので、手早くとぐこと。洗った米は30分ほど吸水させます。また水加減も重要です。米は吸水すると約1.2倍に増えます。洗い米と水は1対1が基本。蒸したごはんは、底から切るように混ぜます。

洗い米 ： 水

washed rice ： water

1 ： 1

When you wash rice, use cold water and wash gently so that rice grain does not break. Dried rice easily absorbs water in which bran is suspended, so wash rice quickly. Leave it for 30 minutes. The rice volume increases 1.2 times after soaking. In general, the ratio of washed rice and water is 1:1. After rice is steamed, cut in rice from bottom of the pot and stir.

材料の量り方を
マスターしましょう

HOW TO MEASURE INGREDIENTS

同じ計量スプーンを使っても液体と粉ものでは、量り方が少し違います。「分量どおりに作ってもおいしくない」という人は、大さじ・小さじの量り方が間違っているのかも。

The measuring method for liquid and dry ingredients is slightly different even though you can use the same measuring spoons. If you think your meal does not taste good even though you followed the recipe, check the measuring methods with tablespoons and teaspoons once more.

大さじ
Tablespoon

ほとんどのものが、15ccの容量。3本か2本セットの場合、もっとも大きいさじが大さじ。

In general, a tablespoon is 15 cc. In a set of two or three spoons, the largest one is the tablespoon.

小さじ
Teaspoon

容量が5ccのものが小さじ。小さじ3で大さじ1の量を量ることができる。

A teaspoon is 5 cc. Three spoonfuls are equal to one tablespoon.

小さじ1/2
1/2 teaspoon

3本セットの場合、大さじ、小さじのほかに小さじ1/2がついている場合が多い。

In a set of three spoons, they are one tablespoon with a teaspoon and a 1/2 teaspoon.

分量対比早見表
Comparison with quantities

約1/2カップ＝大さじ7	7 tablespoons = about 1/2 cup
約1/4カップ＝大さじ3	3 tablespoons = about 1/4 cup
大さじ3＝小さじ9	3 tablespoons = 9 teaspoons
大さじ1＝小さじ3	1 tablespoon = 3 teaspoons

粉ものの計量　　MEASURING DRY INGREDIENTS

一度こんもりとさじに粉を盛り、ナイフの背などで表面を平らにします。1/2はそのあと中央に線を入れ、半分を落とします。

Scoop dry ingredient with a spoon and level it using such as the back of a knife. For a half measure, draw a line through the center and remove half.

大さじ1 1 tablespoon
小さじ1 1 teaspoon

1/2 spoon

1/4 spoon

ナイフの背や箸などで余分な粉をすりきった状態が大さじ1、小さじ1。減らすときは、等分して除いていく。

Level dry ingredient in a tablespoon or a teaspoon by removing excess ingredient with the back of a knife or a chopstick. For measuring 1/2 or 1/4, remove extra powder by halving it.

液体の計量　　MEASURING LIQUID

スプーンは底になるほど面積が狭くなるので、1/3は半分くらい、1/2は半分の深さより少し上くらいまで入れます。

The area of a spoon decreases towards the bottom of the spoon. For measuring 1/3 of a spoonful of liquid, pour the liquid approximately up to half of the spoon. For a half spoonful, pour slightly more than half of a spoonful.

大さじ1 1 tablespoon
小さじ1 1 teaspoon

1/2 spoon

1/3 spoon

スプーンから少し盛り上がるぐらいが大さじ1、小さじ1。濃度のあるものはすりきる。

When measuring liquid for 1 tablespoon or 1 teaspoon, the liquid should be poured until it rises slightly above the edge of the spoon.

計量カップ、計量スプーンは 国によって違います

MEASURING CUPS AND SPOONS VARY FROM A COUNTRY TO COUNTRY

計量カップ、計量スプーンの1杯の量が国によって違うのは、重さや液体の量の単位が違うためです。料理を作るときには分量の量り方に注意しましょう。

Measuring cups and spoons vary from a country to country. This is because units for weight and volume are different. This point should be noted when cooking.

計量スプーン	MEASURING SPOON

日本では、ccの単位を使って調味料を量ります。日本の大さじ1は15cc、アメリカでは大さじ1が14.8ccと同じくらいの量に感じますが、杯を重ねると味つけに差が出るので換算には気をつけましょう。

In Japan, seasoning is measured using the unit of cc. 1 tablespoon is 15 cc in Japan, but 14.8 cc in the U.S. The difference is small, but when several spoonfuls of seasoning arc used, the taste will be different. Be careful when calculating.

日本では In Japan

大さじ1 = 15cc   1 tablespoon =15 cc
小さじ1 = 5cc   1 teaspoon = 5 cc

アメリカでは In U.S.A.

大さじ1 = 約1/2オンス = 14.8cc   1 tablespoon = 1/2 oz = 14.8 cc
小さじ1 = 約1/6オンス = 4.9cc   1 teaspoon = 1/6 oz = 4.9 cc

オーストラリア、イギリスでは In Australia and the U.K.

大さじ1 = 約20cc   1 tablespoon = 20 cc

計量カップ

日本の1カップは200ccです。計量するときには、真横から見て目盛りが水平になるようにします。また、日本では、米を量るときに"合"という単位を使います。1合は180ccで、お米を量るときは専用の180ccのカップを使いましょう。

1 cup is 200 cc in Japan. When measuring, read the scale at eye level. "Gou" is a unit used for measuring rice in Japan. 1 gou is 180 cc. When you measure, (your eyes should be level with the scale) rice, use a designated 180 cc-cup.

日本では In Japan

1カップ＝200cc
1合＝180cc

1 cup = 200 cc
1 gou = 180 cc

アメリカでは In U.S.A.

1カップ＝0.5パイント＝8オンス＝237cc

1 cup = 0.5 pint = 8 oz = 237 cc

イギリスでは In U.K.

1カップ＝285cc

1 cup = 285 cc

オーストラリア、カナダでは In Australia and Canada

1カップ＝250cc

1 cup = 250 cc

カップ対応表 Comparative Table with Cups

日本 Japan	アメリカ U.S.A.	イギリス U.K.	オーストラリア、カナダ Australia & Canada
1合 1 gou	3/4カップ 3/4 cup	3/5カップ 3/5 cup	7/10カップ 7/10 cup
1/2カップ 1/2 cup	3/7カップ 3/7 cup	1/3カップ 1/3 cup	2/5カップ 2/5 cup
1カップ 1 cup	5/6カップ 5/6 cup	7/10カップ 7/10 cup	4/5カップ 4/5 cup

日本料理の基本

Basis of Japanese food

日本料理の調理方法を知りましょう

LEARNING ABOUT JAPANESE COOKING METHODS

日本料理は、食材本来の味を大切にし、素朴かつ繊細に仕上げたいものです。基本の調理方法は8種類あります。それぞれのコツを覚えておきましょう。

When cooking Japanese cuisine, take advantage of the original flavor of ingredients and finish simply and delicately. The followings are tips for eight basic Japanese cooking methods.

煮る	SIMMERED

食材が引き立つ味つけ
How to give a flavor to Ingredients

醤油、砂糖、みりん、酒などの調味料をバランスよく配合して食材を浸し、ゆっくり火にかけます。四季のある日本では、季節の野菜や魚を煮込みます。また落としぶたを使って食材に味を均一に含ませるのも特徴です。

Soak ingredients in sauce, which contains seasonings such as soy sauce, sugar, mirin, sake mixed in a wel-balanced way, and cook slowly over heat. In Japan, seasonal vegetables and fishes are used for this kind of cooking. A drop-lid is used to uniformly blend seasonings with ingredients.

魚 Fish

かれいの煮つけやぶり大根などが一般的。煮汁は少なめにし、落としぶたをして短時間で仕上げる。

Simmered flounder and simmered yellowtail with Japanese radish are popular dishes. Use a little less broth than usual when cooking with a drop-lid.

野菜 Vegetable

野菜がかぶる量の煮汁を入れて、ことこと煮込む。だしを使って煮ると素朴な味わいに。「筑前煮」などが有名。

Pour water to cover vegetables and simmer. Add soup stock for simple touch. "Chikuzen-ni" is a well-known dish.

焼く　　GRILLED

ひと手間加えた焼き方
Taking a little extra time for grilling

甘めのたれを食材にぬりながら焼く「照り焼き」や、塩をつけて焼く「塩焼き」などがあります。網を使って直火で焼いたり、炭火を使って焼いたりする方法もあります。

Typical dishes are "Teriyaki," grilled with a salty-sweet sauce, and "Shioyaki," grilled with salt. Grilling in direct flame on a wire mesh or using charcoal is popular.

魚 Fish

魚は網を使って焼けば、両面を均等に焼くことができるうえ、余分な脂を落とすことができる。
Grilling fish on a wire mesh evenly cooks both sides of the fish and removes extra fat from the fish.

肉 Meat

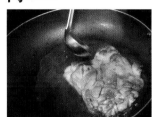

「照り焼き」は、醤油、砂糖、酒で作った甘めのたれを食材にからめながら焼く。
"Teriyaki" is a way of grilling ingredients while coating them with a salty-sweet sauce made of soy sauce, sugar and sake.

蒸す　　STEAMED

食材の持ち味を大切に
Taking advantage of ingredients

蒸気で食材の芯まで熱を通す調理方法。魚介に酒をたっぷりかけて蒸す「酒蒸し」、卵、調味料、だしを器に入れてふんわりと蒸す「茶碗蒸し」などがあります。

This is a cooking method to cook ingredients through to their center using steam. "Sakamushi," is seafood steamed with a liberal amount of sake. "Chawanmushi" is a fluffy steamed tea cup custard containing eggs, seasoning and soup stock.

魚 Fish

ねぎ、しょうがなどの薬味を一緒に入れて蒸すと風味が増す。
Steaming with spices such as scallion and ginger gives a flavor.

炒める　STIR-FRIED

手軽にサッとできる
Easy cooking

サラダ油やごま油をフライパンに熱して食材を加熱する調理方法です。代表的な家庭料理には、「きんぴら」があります。食材を油で炒め、砂糖、醤油、みりんで調味します。

Stir-frying is a cooking method whereby ingredients are cooked by heating salad oil or sesame oil in a frying pan. A typical homemade dish is "Kinpira," stir-fried ingredients with oil and flavored with sugar, soy sauce and mirin.

野菜 Vegetable

熱したフライパンで、野菜を炒め、味噌や醤油など調味料を加えて味つけする。

Stir-fry vegetables in a heated frying pan and flavor with seasonings such as miso (soybean paste) and soy sauce.

肉 Meat

肉を炒めるときは、火の通りがよくなるように薄く切る。肉と野菜を一緒に調理するときは、まず肉を炒める。

In order to cook meat quickly, slice thinly. When cooking meat with vegetables, cook the meat first.

揚げる　DEEP-FRIED

外はサクッと内はやわらかく
Outside is crisp and inside is tender

代表的な揚げ物といえば「天ぷら」です。魚介や野菜などの食材に溶き卵と薄力粉、水を混ぜた衣をつけて高温で揚げます。また、肉を調味料につけてから揚げる「唐揚げ」もよく作られます。

A typical deep-fried dish is "Tempura". Seafood and vegetables in batter made of beaten egg, flour and water are cooked in boiling oil. "Karaage," marinated meat deep-fried in boiling oil, is also popular.

魚 Fish

天ぷらは、食材に衣をつけてすぐに揚げる。食材に合わせた油の温度に調節する。

For making "Tempura", immediately fry ingredients after coating in batter. Adjust oil temperature depending on ingredients.

炊く　COOK RICE

ごはん作りはこれ!
How to cook rice

日本の主食のごはんを作るときの調理方法を指します。米と水を一緒に加熱するという、シンプルな調理方法です。ちなみに、関西地方では煮物を作ることを炊くとも言います。

Rice, a principal food in Japan, is cooked in a simple way by heating rice and water together. In the Kansai region, the same word that is used for boiling rice is used for simmering other foods.

ゆでる　BOILED

食材をやわらかく食べやすく
Making ingredients tender

硬い野菜や肉を湯に通してやわらかくするほか、パスタやうどんなどの麺類をゆでます。また、煮る、炒めるなどの調理前に食材をゆでる下ごしらえのことを「下ゆで」といいます。

Tough vegetables and meat can be softened by boiling. This method is also used for cooking pasta and udon noodles. "Shitayude" is pre-cooking by boiling ingredients before stir-frying or simmering.

和える　MARINATED

混ぜるのが基本の手軽な方法
Simple method to marinate Ingredients

食材に調味料などを加えて混ぜるだけという簡単な調理方法。箸休めの一品として出されることが多いです。昔から食べられている「ほうれん草のごま和え」は、ゆでたほうれん草に砂糖、醤油、ごまなどを混ぜた家庭料理の定番です。

Simple method to combine ingredients with seasonings. Usually served as a refreshing side dish. A typical homemade dish is "Horenso no Gomaae", which contains boiled spinach mixed with sugar, soy sauce and sesame.

日本料理でよく使う
食材について知りましょう

LEARNING ABOUT COMMONLY USED INGREDIENTS FOR JAPANESE CUISINE

日本料理の味つけによく合い、使われている食材を紹介します。これらは日本の風土や文化に培われつつ発達してきました。

The following are commonly used ingredients suited to the taste of Japanese cuisine. These ingredients are often used because they suit Japanese climate and culture.

穀物系 | GRAIN

日本の穀物といえば米です。最近では白米のほかに、きびやひえなどを加えた雑穀米や、玄米（精白されていない状態の米）も人気です。また、小麦粉が原料のうどんや、そばの実が原料のそばも日本伝統の麺類として好まれています。

The most important grain in Japan is rice. In addition to polished white rice, rice mixed with millet and brown rice (unpolished rice) are popular. Udon made of flour and soba made of buckwheat are also popular Japanese traditional noodles.

薬味系　SPICES

薬味とは、料理の味を引き締めて香りを加える効果がある香味野菜やスパイスのことです。ねぎ、しょうが、青じそ、みょうがなどは、刺身のつまやうどんの薬味としてよく使われます。

Herbs and spices are used to provide accent and add flavor. Scallions, ginger, green perillas and myoga ginger are often used in relish for sashimi and as spices for udon.

発酵食品系　FERMENTED FOODS

ヨーグルトやチーズのように微生物と一緒に長期間ねかせ、成分を変化させた食品のことです。日本では調味に使う醤油や味噌、みりんや、だしに使うかつお節などの発酵食品があります。

Fermented foods, such as yogurt and cheese, are processed with microbes for an extended time. Japanese fermented foods include seasonings like soy sauce, miso, mirin, and dried bonito used for soup stock.

練り製品系　　FISH CAKE

主に魚のすり身に調味料を加えて練ったもので、かまぼこやちくわなどがそうです。弾力のある食感と歯ごたえが特徴です。ちくわやがんもどきなどはおでんの定番具材です。

Fish cake is made with minced fish and seasoning. Examples are kamaboko and chikuwa, characterized by their resilient and chewy texture. Chikuwa and ganmodoki are often used for oden.

海藻系　　SEAWEEDS

欧米ではあまり食べられない海藻ですが、だしをひくのに使う昆布やおにぎりを巻くのに使うのりなど、日本料理には海藻がかかせません。海藻はミネラルが豊富な健康食品です。

Seaweeds are not popular in Western countries, but in Japan they are essential ingredients. Kelp is used for soup stock and laver is used for wrapping rice balls. As seaweeds are rich in minerals, they are healthy foods.

大豆&大豆加工品系 SOYBEANS AND SOYBEAN PRODUCTS

豆腐や納豆などの大豆加工品は昔から日本で食べられてきた伝統食です。たんぱく質を多く含む大豆は、畑の肉と呼ばれるほど。もともと日本料理は野菜や穀物中心なので貴重な栄養源でした。

Soybean products such as tofu and natto are traditional Japanese foods. Being rich in protein, soybeans are called "meat grown in vegetable gardens" and are considered an important source of nutrition in the traditional Japanese diet which mainly takes vegetables and grains.

日本で昔から使われる野菜

Japanese Traditional Vegetables

明治以前から食べられている野菜としては、
・「日本書紀」にも登場するねぎやにら、かぶ
・春の七草のひとつ、大根
・奈良時代以前に伝わったとされるなす
・食用習慣が日本と朝鮮半島のみといわれる
　ごぼう
・江戸時代中期には食べられていた春菊、タケノコなどが挙げられます。

Vegetables eaten before the Meiji era:
・Chinese chive and turnip: They were introduced in "Nihon Shoki" (The Chronicles of Japan, completed in 720).
・Japanese radish: One of seven wild spring herbs.
・Eggplant: It is believed that eggplants were brought to Japan before the Nara era.
・Burdock: It is said that burdocks are traditionally eaten only in Japan and the Korean Peninsula.
・Garland chrysanthemum and bamboo shoot: They were already popular in the middle of the Edo era.

こんなものも和の食材です

OTHER INGREDIENTS FOR JAPANESE CUISINE

日本料理でよく使われる食材のなかにも、意外と洋食に合う食材があるかもしれません。

Some typical Japanese ingredients may be used for cooking western foods.

こんにゃく Konnyaku

こんにゃくいもから作られる。ぷるぷるの食感が特徴で、煮物や味噌田楽などに使う。
This is made from konnyaku plant. The texture is chewy and it is used for simmered dishes and Misodengaku.

しらたき Shirataki noodles

こんにゃくと同様、こんにゃくいもから作られ、煮物や鍋料理などに使う。
Like konnyaku above, it is made from konnyaku plant. Used for simmered dishes and hot pot dishes.

梅干し Umeboshi (Pickled plum)

梅を塩漬けして干したもの。はちみつ漬けなど甘いものもあるが、基本は酸味がある。
Salted and dried Japanese apricots. Some contain honey for a sweeter taste, but usually they are sour.

かんぴょう Kanpyo

夕顔の実を紐状にむいて乾燥させたもの。水で戻して煮物や巻き寿司に使う。
Kanpyo is dried shavings of calabash. Used for simmered dishes and rolled sushi by rehydrating.

しらす Shirasu (Yaung sardines)

白い稚魚のこと。ごはんや大根おろしと食べる。
Young white fish. Sprinkled on cooked rice or with grated Japanese radish.

寒天 Agar

海藻のてんぐさから作られる。水で戻して使い、ゼリーのような見た目と食感がある。
Made of agar-ager, a family of red algae. Used for cooking by rehydrating. Has a jelly-like appearance and texture.

ぎんなん Gingko nuts

いちょうの種子のこと。殻を割り、薄皮をむいて茶碗蒸しなどに使う。
Seeds of the gingko tree. Used in chawanmushi by breaking the shell and peeling the thin skin.

するめ Dried squid

するめいかを干したもので、とても硬い。あぶって酒のおつまみとしてよく食べられる。
Quite tough to chew. Roasted and used as an appetizer served with sake.

切り干し大根 Dried shredded Japanese radish

大根を細切りにして干したもの。水で戻して煮物などに使う。

Thinly shredded and dried Japanese radish. Used for simmered dishes by rehydrating.

煮干し Dried anchovy

いわしなどを塩水で煮て干したもの。そのまま食べるほか、だしにも使う。

Small fishes such as sardine boiled in salt water and dried. Can be eaten as it is or used for soup stock.

山菜 Mountain vegetables

うどやわらびなど、山野に自生する食用の植物のこと。苦みがあるものが多い。

Edible wild plants such as udo and warabi. Often have a bitter taste.

干物 Dried fish

魚を干したもの。みりんや醤油などで味つけされたものもある。

Some are flavored with mirin or soy sauce.

めざし Mezashi

小魚を塩漬けした後に、数尾ずつ目から下あごへわらなどをさして束ねて干したもの。

Salted and dried fish tied together by a straw piercing the eye socket and exiting through the mouth.

いくら Ikura (Salmon roe)

さけの卵で、塩漬けや醤油漬けにする。ごはんにかけたり、寿司の具材に使う。

Salmon roe marinated with salt or soy sauce. Sprinkled on cooked rice or used for sushi.

たらこ Tarako (Cod roe)

たらの卵巣を塩漬けにしたもの。ごはんによく合い、おにぎりやお茶漬にもよい。

Salted cod ovary. Good for cooked rice and rice balls or Ochazuke.

数の子 Kazunoko (herring roe)

にしんの卵を干して塩漬けしたもので、黄金色をしている。歯ごたえがある。

Dried and salted herring roe. Has a gold color and crisp texture.

らっきょう Rakkyo (Pickled shallot)

強いにおいと辛みを持つ。塩や醤油、酢に漬けて作る。

Has a strong odor and sharp taste. Pickled with salt or soy sauce.

日本茶 Japanese tea

せん茶や番茶、ほうじ茶などの種類があり、ほのかな苦みがある。

Many varieties such as sencha, bancha (the second flush of sencha) and hojicha are available. Has a slightly bitter taste.

食材の旬を知りましょう

LEARNING ABOUT BEST THE SEASON FOR INGREDIENTS

四季のある日本では、料理に季節感を出すというのが、献立を考えるうえでとても大切なことです。

As Japan has four seasons, it is very important to create a sense of the season in dishes when deciding a menu.

春の野菜
Spring vegetables

夏の野菜
Summer vegetables

山菜
Mountain vegetables

素材の味を生かしたシンプルな調理法がオススメ。天ぷらや和え物に。
Simple cooking is recommended in order to take advantage of the taste Suitable for Tempura and marinated food.

そら豆
Broad beans

独特の風味がある。塩ゆでや揚げ物、豆ごはんに。
Have a unique flavor. Suitable for cooking in salt water, deep-fried, and cooking with rice.

トマト
Tomato

太陽の恵みをたっぷり浴びたトマトは、サラダや焼きトマトまたは彩りに。
Tomatoes, which grow in sunshine, are suitable for salads, roasting and as garnish.

たけのこ
Bamboo shoots

生は鮮度が命なので、買ったらすぐに下ゆでし、吸い物や炊き込みごはんに。
Since uncooked bamboo shoots do not last long, boil immediately. Good for clear soup and seasoned cooked rice.

絹さや
Snow peas

筋を取って塩ゆでする。煮物や肉じゃがの飾りに。
Remove strings and boil pods in salt water. Used for simmered dishes and as garnish for Nikujaga (simmered meat and potatoes).

えだ豆
Edamame (Green soybeans)

大豆の未熟豆。塩ゆでしてさやから出し、そのまま食べる。
Green soybeans cooked in salt water can be eaten by removing beans from their pods.

旬の野菜はアク抜きがポイント
Skimming Scum Is Essential When Using Seasonal Vegetables

旬の野菜は、味とともに香りや歯ごたえなども抜群です。アクが強い時期でもあるので、下ごしらえをきちんとするのが調理のポイントです。

Seasonal vegetables have excellent taste, flavor and texture but produce a pungent scum, so it is important to conduct proper pre-cooking treatment.

秋の野菜
Autmn vegetables

冬の野菜
Winter vegetables

みょうが
Myoga ginger

食欲を増進させる効果がある。刻んで削り節をかけたり、天ぷらに。
It increases appetite. Chopped and served with shavings of dried bonito or suitable for tempura.

松茸
Matsutake (Pine mushroom)

風味豊かな香りが生かせる、土瓶蒸しや松茸ごはんに。
Suitable for dobinmushi (steamed in a tea pot) and matsutake rice, both of which maintain the rich flavor of matsutake.

根菜類
Root vegetables

繊維が多いので、時間をかけて味をしみこませる煮物などに。
Since they are fibrous, they are suitable for simmered dishes which allow time for flavor to blend with the vegetables.

ゴーヤ
Bitter melon

わたが残っていると苦みが強いので取り除く。炒め物やおひたしに。
Remove bitter pulp. Suitable for stir-frying or boiled and flavored with seasoning.

いも類
Potatoes

さつまいもは秋から冬が旬。じゃがいもは9〜10月が旬。
Sweet potatoes are best in autumn and winter. Potatoes are best in September and October.

かぶ
Turnip

冬のかぶは甘味があり、身がしまっておいしい。煮物や汁ものに。
Turnip, available in winter, is sweet and firm. Suitable for simmered dishes or soup.

周りを海に囲まれている日本では1年を通してさまざまな魚介を食べます。脂肪をたくわえる産卵前が旬です。

Japan is surrounded by oceans, so a variety of seafood are available year round. The best season for any fish is just before they spawn, as that is when they gain fat.

あさり
Asari (Littleneck clam)

味噌汁や酒蒸しなど、貝類の中でもっとも食べられているもののひとつ。塩水につけ、砂抜きして調理する。

Asari are popular in dishes such as miso soup and sakamushi. Soak in salt water to remove sand before cooking.

あじ
Horse aji (Mackerel)

まあじやむろあじなど種類が多い。ぜいごという鋭いうろこがある。刺身や干物に。

There are many kinds of horse mackerel, such as maaji and muroaji. These fish have hard scales, called zeigo. Suitable for sashimi or as dried fish.

はまぐり
Hamaguri (Clam)

日本で昔から親しまれている貝。そのまま焼き中の汁ごと食べたり、酒蒸しや汁ものに。

Hamaguri has been popular in Japan since early times. Can be grilled and eaten used for sakamushi or soup.

うに
Sea uni (Urchin)

適度な水分があり、ひとつずつがしっかりしているものがよい。塩漬けや練りうになどもある。

Choose a firm one with a certain moisture. Can be preserved with salt or cooked and seasoned.

春 Spring

夏 Summer

秋 Autumn

冬 Winter

さんま
Pacific sanma (Saury)

秋の代表的な魚。丸ごと塩焼きにすることが多く、内臓の苦みも好まれる。

Representative fish in autumn. The entire fish can be grilled with salt. Some like the bitter taste of the viscera.

さば
Saba (Mackerel)

家庭でよく食べられる魚。身がやわらかく、傷みが早いので、早めに調理する。

Commonly eaten at home. Since its flesh is soft and perishable, cook as soon as possible.

かつお
Katsuo (Bonito)

春には「初がつお」、秋には「戻りがつお」の2回の旬があり、脂ののった身が好まれる。たたきや刺身に。

Bonito is good in spring, and autmn. Fat bonito are preferable. Good for tataki and sashimi.

かに
Kani (Crab)

ずわいがにや毛がに、たらばがにamong。味噌を食べたり殻からはだしが取れます。

The crab family includes snow crab, horsehair crab and red king crab. Crab innards are edible and shells make good soup stock.

旬の果物　　SEASONAL FRUIT

食後のデザートにする果物は、夏にはみずみずしく酸味があるもの、冬には甘みが強いものが好まれます。

For desert, juicy and sour fruits in summer and sweet fruits in winter are preferable.

さくらんぼ
Cherry

産地は山形県が有名。小粒で色鮮やかなので飾りとしても重宝される。

Yamagata prefecture is well known for producing cherries. Since they are small and bright in color, they are sometimes are used as garnish.

すいか
Watermelon

ウリ科の果菜類で夏を代表する果物。果芯近くの種がある部分がもっとも甘みがある。

Watermelon is a gourd family fruit/vegetable and a representative fruit in summer. The part near the center with seeds is the sweetest.

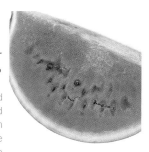

いちご
Strawberry

本来の旬は初夏だが、ハウス栽培により、11〜5月に多く出荷される。

Strawberry season was traditionally early summer, but now many are delivered from greenhouses between November and May.

春
Spring

もも
Peach

皮をむき、中央の種に沿って果肉を切る。変色しやすいので、盛りつける直前に切る。

Peel skin and cut flesh along the center seed. As the flesh changes color quickly, serve immediately after cutting.

夏
Summer

ぶどう
Grapes

日本では、大粒で皮が紫黒色の巨峰や甘みのある甲州という種類が有名。

In Japan, large dark purple Kyoho grapes and sweet Koshu grapes are well known.

秋
Autumn

冬
Winter

みかん
Mandarin orange

みかんをはじめ、柑橘類には多くの種類がある。表面につやがあり、ヘタの小さいものがよい。

Besides mandarin oranges, many kinds of citrus fruit are available. Choose those with a shiny surface and small hull.

かき
Persimmon

日本および中国原産。渋がきの皮をむき、干しがきとして食べるなど、なじみの深い果物。

Produced in Japan and China, persimmons are familiar to Japanese. Sour persimmons can be eaten by peeling the skin and drying.

りんご
Apple

産地は青森県や長野県が有名。変色しやすいので、盛る直前に皮をむいて切る。

Aomori and Nagano prefectures are well known for producing apples. Since apple flesh changes color quickly, serve immediately after cutting.

日本料理の基本

Basis of Japanese food

日本料理でよく使う
調味料を知りましょう

LEARNING ABOUT COMMON
JAPANESE SEASONINGS

和食の味つけ順の基本といえば "さしすせそ"

日本では、味つけの順番を「さしすせそ」と覚えます。さは砂糖、しは塩、すは酢、せは醤油、そは味噌を意味し、この順番に加えます。

　砂糖と塩は最初のほうで加えて味を含ませます。塩は砂糖よりも分子が小さく浸透性が高いため、先に入れると砂糖がなじみにくくなります。必ず砂糖を先に加えましょう。

　酢には酸味を与え、味をまろやかにする働き

があり、醤油、味噌は味つけのほかに香りづけという大切な役割もあります。長く火を通すと、酢は酸味が、醤油と味噌は風味が飛んでしまいます。また、醤油や味噌を最初から加えると料理の味や色が濃くなる原因にもなります。素材の色を生かしたいときは色の薄い薄口醤油を使います。酢、醤油、味噌は、仕上げに加えて風味を損なわないようにするのが鉄則です。

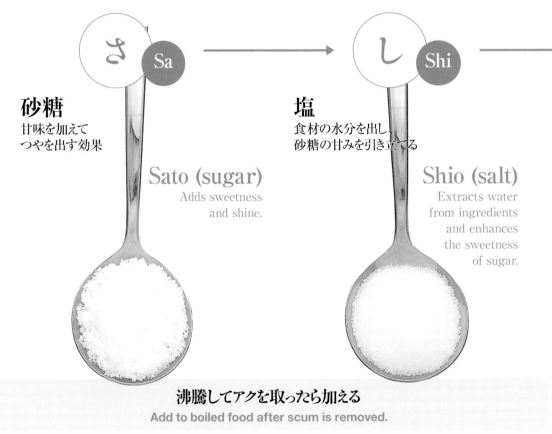

砂糖
甘味を加えて
つやを出す効果

Sato (sugar)
Adds sweetness
and shine.

塩
食材の水分を出し、
砂糖の甘みを引き立てる

Shio (salt)
Extracts water
from ingredients
and enhances
the sweetness
of sugar.

沸騰してアクを取ったら加える
Add to boiled food after scum is removed.

The General Order for Adding Japanese Seasonings is Called "Sa-Shi-Su-Se-So"

In Japan, the order for introducing seasonings in cooking is called "Sa-Shi-Su-Se-So". Sa: Sato (sugar), Shi: Shio (salt), Su: Su (vinegar), Se: Shoyu (soy sauce) and So: Miso (soybean paste). In general, use the seasonings in this order.

Sugar and salt should be added at the beginning of cooking so that they blend well with ingredients. As salt has a smaller molecule than sugar and penetrates ingredients easily, adding salt first will impede the ability of sugar to blend with ingredients. Make sure to add sugar first.

Vinegar adds a sour taste and mellowness to ingredients. Soy sauce and miso have important roles in flavoring ingredients in addition to their role as seasonings. If cooked for too long, the sour taste of vinegar and the flavor of soy sauce or miso will disappear. Also, if soy sauce and miso are added at the beginning of cooking, ingredients will become too salty and too dark. In order to take advantage of the original color of the ingredients, use usukuchi shoyu , a variety of soy sauce which is saltier and lighter in color than usual soy sauce. The cardinal rule is to add vinegar, soy sauce and miso later in order to get flavor.

日本料理の基本

Basis of Japanese food

す Su

酢
酸味づけのほか
腐敗や変色を防止

Su (vinegar)
In addition to imparting a sour taste, it prevents ingredients from going bad and changing color.

せ Se

醤油
風味や色づけ
長く熱すると香りが飛ぶ

Shoyu (soy sauce)
Adds flavor and color. Flavor will disappear if overheated.

そ So

味噌
香りと味をつける
臭みを消す性質も

Miso (soybean paste)
Adds flavor and taste. Also gets rid of odor.

火からおろす直前に加える
Add immediately before ingredients are removed from heat.

味噌にもいろいろあります

VARIETIES OF MISO

味噌は大豆、塩、麹から作られ、麹の種類、塩分の量、配合比率、熟成期間によって味や色に違いが出ます。米どころは米味噌、関西は白味噌などと、食文化や風土に根ざした味噌が各地にあるのも特徴です。

Miso is made with soybeans, salt and rice malt. Taste and color vary depending on the type of rice malt, the amount of salt, the combining ratio and aging period. Miso varieties are found across Japan depending on the food culture and climate. For example, rice miso is often made in areas with abundant rice production and white miso is well known in the Kansai region.

信州味噌
Shinshu Miso

米味噌、もしくは、麦味噌。色が淡く、辛口なのが特徴。
Made of rice or barley. Has a light color and salty taste.

越後味噌
Echigo Miso

米味噌。淡色に近く、味噌の中に米の粒が見える。
Made of rice. Has a relatively light color and contains rice grains.

仙台味噌
Sendai Miso

米味噌。赤色が濃く、塩分が12〜13%と辛口。
Made of rice. Dark red color and salty with 12-13% salt content.

九州麦味噌
Kyushu Mugimiso

麦の芳香が豊かで、甘口。淡色のものがほとんど。
Made of barley. Has the rich flavor of barley and is sweeter than usual miso. Has a light color.

関西白味噌
Kansai Shiromiso

米味噌。甘口で、魚や肉の漬け床としても活躍。
Made of rice. Has a sweeter taste and is also used for marinating fish and meat.

八丁味噌
Hatcho Miso

豆味噌。愛知県岡崎市の名物。辛みが強くて硬さがある。
Made of soybeans. A specialty in Okazaki city, Aichi prefecture. Salty and firm.

江戸甘味噌
Edo Amamiso

米味噌。塩分が比較的低く、上品な甘みがある。
Made of rice. Relatively low salt content with a delicate sweetness.

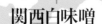

醤油のいろいろ　　VARIETIES OF SOY SAUCE

濃口醤油
Koikuchi Shoyu

一般に醤油といえば、濃口醤油を指す。色が濃く、香りがよい。塩分が約18％と、薄口醤油よりも低い。

General soy sauce. Has dark color and a good flavor. Salt content is about 18 % , lower than usukuchi shoyu.

薄口醤油
Usukuchi Shoyu

塩分は約20％。薄い色を出すため、鉄分の少ない水を使用。素材の味や色を生かしたいときに。

Salt content is 20%. In order to make the color lighter, water containing less iron is used. Used for maintaining the color and flavor of ingredients.

たまり醤油
Tamari Shoyu

味が濃厚で、独特の香りがある。風味や照りを出すために少量使うとよい。たれや刺身醤油に。

Has a rich taste and unique aroma. Use of small amounts is recommended for adding flavor or enhancing luster. Also used for sauce and sashimi.

酢のいろいろ　　VARIETIES OF VINEGAR

穀物酢
Grain Vinegar

とうもろこしや小麦などの穀物が主原料。食品添加物を加えた合成酢に比べ、加熱しても香りが飛ばない。

Main raw material is grain such as sweet corn or wheat. Unlike compound vinegars with food additives, grain vinegar keeps its aroma even when heated.

米酢
Rice Vinegar

米を主原料にして作られた酢。米のみで作られたものは純米酢という。まろやかな酸味とコクがある。

Made from rice as the main raw material. Pure rice vinegar is made of rice alone. Has a mellow, rich sour taste.

酒　　SAKE

清酒
Seishu (Clear sake)

米、米麹、水だけを使い、発酵させたもの。これに添加物を加え、人工的に作った合成清酒は味が落ちる。

Made only with rice, rice malt and water and then fermented. Synthetic sake, which has additives, loses flavor.

本みりん　　MIRIN

本みりん
Hon Mirin (sweet sake)

焼酎と米麹などを混ぜ、熟成させたもの。みりん風調味料はアルコール分をほとんど含まない。

Rice malt mixed with shochu (a distilled beverage) and fermented. Mirin-fu chomiryo (mirin-like seasoning) contains almost no alcohol.

日本料理の基本

Basis of Japanese food

砂糖のい・ろ・い・ろ　　VARIETIES OF SUGAR

上白糖
Johakuto (White sugar)

一般に砂糖といえば上白糖のことを指す。糖度が高く、甘みを強く感じる。しっとりとして溶けやすい。

Commonly used sugar. Has high sugar content and pronounced sweetness. Moist and easily dissolved.

三温糖
San-onto (Soft brown sugar)

褐色で、甘みや旨みが強いのが特徴。煮物や佃煮、豆を煮るときなどに使うと、料理にコクが出る。

Dark in color with pronounced sweetness and flavor. Used to add rich flavor to simmered dishes, tsukudani (small pieces of seafood, meat or seaweed simmered in soy sauce) or cooked beans.

黒砂糖
Kurozato (Brown sugar)

砂糖きびのしぼり汁を煮つめて作られる。ミネラルが豊富で香りが強い。煮物に向く。

Made by boiling sugarcane juice. It is rich in minerals and has a strong flavor. Suitable for simmered dishes.

塩のいろいろ　　VARIETIES OF SALT

食塩
Table Salt

主に味つけに使う。乾燥しているので、さらさらしており、塩分を感じやすい。

Mainly used for seasoning. Dry and imparts a salty flavor.

並塩
Refined Salt

水分が少し含まれた、湿った塩。やや甘みがある。下ごしらえにはそのまま使い、料理の仕上げには煎ってから使う。

Contains a little moisture and has a slight sweetness. Used as is for pre-treatment or roasted for finishing cooking.

粗塩
Coarse Salt

ミネラル分が豊富なので、野菜をゆでるときや、長時間の煮込み料理などに使うと、風味がよくなる。

Since it is rich in minerals, it is used for boiling vegetables or slow simmering to improve flavor.

日本でよく使われるそのほかの調味料
Other Seasonings in Japan

山椒
Sansho (Sichuan Pepper)

ミカン科の植物の実。粉末にしたものはうなぎの蒲焼きの臭み消しに使う。若葉は「木の芽」と呼ばれ、彩りに使う。

Seeds of a citrus family plant. Powdered seeds are used to get rid of the fishy smell of grilled eel fillets. Young buds, called "Kinome" in Japanese, are used as garnish.

七味唐辛子
Shichimi Togarashi (Seven Flavor Chili Pepper)

赤唐辛子を主原料として、辛みと香りのスパイスで作られる。うどんやそば、焼き鳥などの薬味に使う。

Made of spices for adding spicy taste and flavor. Red chili pepper is a main ingredient. Used as a condiment for udon noodles, soba noodles and yakitori (grilled chicken).

ゆず胡椒
Yuzu Kosho

胡椒と名がついているが、胡椒は使われておらず、青唐辛子・ゆずの果皮・塩で作られている。焼き鳥やしゃぶしゃぶにつけると美味。

Although it is called "kosho" (black pepper), no black pepper is used. It is made of green chili pepper, yuzu peel and salt. Excellent with yakitori (grilled chicken) and shabu-shabu hot pot.

手軽なチューブ入りスパイス
Convenient spices in tubes

家庭でよく使うスパイスは、あらかじめすりおろされたチューブ入りのものが市販されています。わさびやしょうが、にんにく、辛子などが一般的。少量をさっと使いたいときに便利です。

Common spices, such as wasabi, ginger, garlic and mustard are available, already ground, in tubes at stores. They are convenient for quick use.

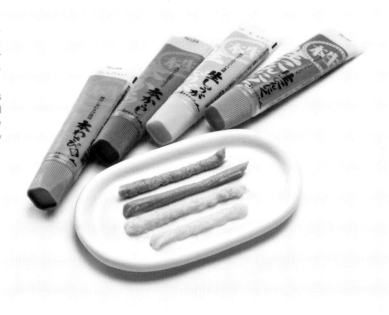

日本料理の基本

Basis of Japanese food

61

日本料理では
彩りのよい盛りつけが大事です

Color Is an Important Consideration in the Presentation of Japanese Cuisine

器の大きさや色、材質などの違いでそれに合う料理も変わってきます。料理と器の色合いや、盛りつける量、形状など、全体のバランスを考えながら、器を選びましょう。

Selecting tableware of suitable size, color and material is important in Japanese cuisine. Choose the right tableware by considering overall balance, including color coordination between food and plate, the amount and the shape of food.

主菜を盛るなら… — PLATES FOR MAIN DISHES

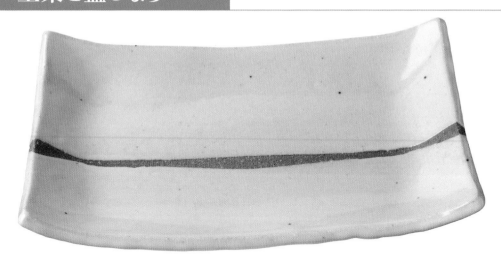

材質
Material

陶器は吸水しやすく、香りがつきやすいので、料理の下に葉や懐紙をしいて盛る。磁器は軽くて吸水しにくい。

Since pottery easily absorbs moisture and odor, place leaves or Japanese paper under food. Porcelain china is lightweight and does not absorb moisture readily.

色・柄
Color and Design

食材と同系色の器は、なるべく避ける。また、もみじや桜などの柄が入っているものは季節感が出る。

Try to avoid tableware that is similar in color to food. Tableware with patterns of autumn leaves or cherry blossoms provides a sense of the season.

形
Shape

深い器の場合は、立体的に盛って高さを出す。平皿の場合は、間隔をあけてバランスよく盛るとよい。

For a deep plate, create height by stacking food. For a flat plate, leave some space between the food items to create a sense of balance.

大きさ
Size

器ばかりが大きく、料理が少ないと寂しいので、盛りつける料理の量を考えて選ぶ。

Consider the amount of food when selecting a plate, so that the plate will not be too large for the serving.

材質
Material

煮汁などを飲む場合は、口当たりがよいものを選ぶ。表面がざらざらした器は避ける。夏はガラスや木、竹製の器を使うと涼しさを演出できる。

For soup, choose material soft to the mouth. Avoid plates with rough surfaces. Glass, wooden or bamboo plates are good in summer as they give a cool feeling.

色・柄
Color and Design

白い食材を使った料理は濃い色の器に盛るなど、料理全体の色に合わせて選ぶ。また、冬に色の濃い器を使うなど季節感を取り入れる。

Choose tableware by considering the color of the servings. For example, white food should be served on dark colored plates. In winter, dark colored plates are recommended to give a sense of the season.

形
Shape

華やかな料理にはシンプルな器、地味めなものには変形の器を選ぶ。蒸し料理にはふたつきの皿など、料理に適した器を使うとよい。

Choose a simple plate for colorful food and an odd-shaped plate for somber food. Choose a plate suited to the dish. For example, a plate with a lid is suitable for steamed dishes.

大きさ
Size

食材の量に合う器を使う。量が多い場合は、高さをつけて盛ると美しいので、深い器を選ぶ。食卓に並べたときのバランスも考える。

Choose a plate by considering the amount of food. For a large amount of food, stacked food looks beautiful in a deep dish. Think about the balance of the arrangement on the table.

日本料理の基本

Basis of Japanese food

和食器の取り扱い方法
Handling Japanese Tableware

器を保管するときには、割れたり、傷がついたりするのを防ぐため、器と器の間にペーパータオルを挟みます。また、焼き物や漆器を長期間使わないときは、布で包んで箱に入れ、冷暗所で保管するのがベスト。

When storing Japanese tableware, insert paper towels between plates in order to prevent breaking or scratching. When pottery and lacquerware are not used for a long time, place them in a box after wrapping with cloth and store in a dark cool place.

器選びの基本とポイント

HOW TO CHOOSE TABLEWARE

もっとも大切なのは、料理が映える器であること。また、使い勝手がよいものを選びましょう。大きさや材質なども重要です。

The most important thing is that a plate makes the food look good. Choose easy-to-use tableware. Also choose appropriate size and material.

淡い色や無地の器は、比較的どんな料理にも合いやすく、季節を問わずに年間を通して使うことができるので、そろえておくとよいでしょう。

A set of subtly colored plates or plain plates is recommended. They are convenient as they are relatively easy to match with any kind of food and can be used regardless of season.

器の持つ季節感を大切に

和食器には、材質や形、色や模様など、四季を表すのにふさわしい器がたくさんあります。春には桜の花をかたどった器、夏にはガラス製の涼しげな器など、季節に合った器を選ぶことが大切です。

There are many kinds of Japanese tableware suitable for expressing a sense of the season by their material, shape, color and design. It is important to choose tableware suited to each season, such as a cherry blossom shaped plate in spring or a cool glass plate in summer.

春 Spring

桜の色を思わせる淡いピンクや若草色、桜の花をかたどったかわいらしい器を使うとよい。
Choose light pink or bright green, or a pretty plate shaped to resemble a cherry blossom.

淡い色合いの器
Light color plate

桜型の器
Plate with the shape of a cherry blossom

夏 Summer

涼しげなイメージの薄い水色や濃い青、清涼感のあるガラス製の器がオススメ。
Cool light water colors and dark blue, or plates made of glass are recommended.

青磁器
Celadon

ガラスの器
Glass plate

秋 Autumn

月見の月やもみじなどの秋の絵柄の器や、もみじや菊をかたどった器がよい。
An autumn motif such as the harvest moon or autumn leaves, or the shape of Japanese maple or chrysanthemum is recommended.

もみじの形の器
Plate with the shape of a Japanese maple leaf

秋の絵柄の器
Plate with an autumn motif

冬 Winter

厚みのある陶器が向いている。色は黒や茶の濃い色のものを。
Thick pottery is suitable. Choose dark colors such as black or brown.

陶器
Pottery

重箱
Jubako Box

日本料理の基本

Basis of Japanese food

飾り切りに
チャレンジしてみましょう

LET'S TRY DECORATIVE CUTTING

いつもの料理をランクアップさせたいというときには飾り切りがオススメです。おもてなしや見た目を華やかにしたい時に挑戦してみてはいかがでしょうか。

Decorative cutting is recommended to give an accent to your usual dishes. You can entertain guests and adorn dishes.

梅花むき
Japanese Apricot Blossom

円形の野菜を梅の花に見立てます。にんじんなど、赤い野菜を使うとより梅のように見え、かわいらしく仕上がります。型を使うと簡単です。

Cut round vegetables into Japanese apricot blossom shapes. Reddish vegetables such as carrot serve well and will look like red blossoms. Blossom shaped cutters are available.

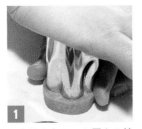

1 にんじんを1cmの厚さの輪切りにし、花形の型で抜く。

Cut a carrot into 1cm thick cross sections and cut out the shape using a blossom shaped cutter.

2 3枚分の花びらの部分を薄くそぎ、残り2枚の花びらと段差をつける。

Thinly cut three of the petals to make them shorter than the remaining two petals.

3 2で薄くそいだ部分に2本の切りこみを入れ、写真のようにねじれ模様をつける。

Make two incisions on the above three petals to give a twisted effect as shown in the photo.

大根ばら
Rose from Japanese Radish

野菜や包丁を少し湿らせておくときれいに切れるうえ、乾燥も防げます。野菜の輪切りの大きさを調節すれば、好みのサイズが作れます。

Slightly wet Japanese radish and a knife in order to cut easily and prevent radish from drying out. Cut the radish into slices of a suitable thickness.

1 輪切りにした大根の3/4の長さを薄くむく。上部を波立たせるとよい。

Peel a ribbon or strip off 3/4 of the length of radish slice, leaving a wavy edge on the top.

2 最後までむき終わったらくるくると巻き、バラの花のように形を整える。

When you come to the end of the ribbon, roll it to make a rose shape.

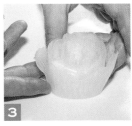

3 巻き終わり部分に水をつけてくっつけると、簡単にはりつく。

Wet the end of the ribbon to easily attach it to the roll.

66

筆しょうが

Ink Brush Shaped Ginger

甘酢漬けにしたはじかみしょうがの先端を、筆に見立てて切ります。細かい作業なので、ペティナイフなどを使うとよいでしょう。

Cutting the tip of a sweet pickled ginger into an ink brush shape. A petit knife is suitable for this detailed work.

1　しょうがの先端の白い部分の3/4ほどの長さまで1～2mmに薄く切り込みを入れる。
Make 1-2mm thick incisions up to 3/4 of the white part of the ginger tip.

2　全部で4～5等分にする。厚さを均等にすると、より美しくなる。
Evenly divide the tip into 4 or 5 parts. It will be more beautiful if these parts are of even thickness.

3　別バージョン。**2**に縦の切り込みを入れ、筆の毛ように細かくする。
Another way to cut the ginger is to make fine incisions lengthwise like the bristles of a brush.

ゆず松葉切り

Pine Needle Shaped Yuzu

ゆずの皮を松の葉に見立て、互い違いに切って絡ませたもの。折れ松葉切りともいいます。鮮やかな黄色なので、どんな料理にも映えます。

Cut yuzu skin into pine needle shapes and combine each piece. Also called bent pine needle cut. Yuzu skin's vivid yellow look good on any dishes.

1　ゆずの皮を薄くむき、2×1cmの長方形に切る。
Thinly peel yuzu skin and cut it into 2 x 1cm rectangles.

2　縦に2本、5mm程度の幅を残して左右から交互に切りこみを入れる。
Make incisions alternately from both sides by leaving two lengthwise uncut parts (about 5mm).

3　切り込みを入れた両端を持ち上げ、交差させる。
Lift both cut ends to cross them.

ラディッシュちょうちん

Radish Lantern

ラディッシュは皮の赤と中の白がきれいな色合いなので、ちょうちんや花に見立てたり、輪切りを料理の彩りに使います。

The vivid contrast of radish's red skin and white flesh is excellent for making a lantern shape or flower. Round slices can be used as garnish.

1　ラディッシュは軽く洗い、包丁でVの字に切り込みを入れる。
Wash the radish lightly and make a V-shaped incision on it with a knife.

2　**1**を等間隔にぐるりと一周包丁で切り込みを入れる。
Repeat step No. 1 at regular spaces to a circuit of the radish.

3　できあがり。葉や茎は少し残したままにする。
Finished radish. Leave some leaves and stems.

日本料理の基本

Basis of Japanese food

料理をひきたてる
あしらいについて知りましょう

GARNISHING DISHES

和食には、料理を目で楽しむという概念があり、料理の内容だけでなく、器や料理の盛り方、あしらいにも重点がおかれます。

One of the principles of Japanese cuisine is the visual enjoyment of dishes. Not only the food itself, but tableware, the way of serving, and garnish are also important.

かいしきを自由に使って盛りつけを楽しもう

よく使われるのが「かいしき」で、旬の葉を使って季節感を表現したり、シンプルな器に立体感や彩りを添えたりします。身近で採れる葉を使うのが一般的でしたが、最近では庭のある家庭も少なくなり、店で購入することが多くなりました。本物の葉の代わりに手軽なビニール製の「葉らん」を使うこともあります。

また、揚げ物には懐紙（かいし）を使うと、余分な油を吸い取ってくれるのでべたつきません。ほかにも、器を持ち上げる代わりに受け皿として使ったり、食べ残しを隠したりと、懐紙の使い方はさまざま。和紙や色つきのものなど、種類も豊富です。料理に合わせて活用しましょう。

MAKE FREE USE OF KAISHIKI
TO PLACE FOOD

"Kaishiki" is a thin sheet placed between a plate and food. Seasonal leaves are often used to express a seasonal feeling. Kaishiki also gives a stereoscopic effect and color to a simple plate. Traditionally leaves available in the neighborhood were used, but recently many people without gardens buy the leaves at stores. Plastic leaves "Baran" can also be used.

Kaishi (Japanese mini paper napkin) is useful for placing fried food since it absorbs extra oil. Kaishi can be used in many other ways as well, for example, as a tray to remove food instead of moving a plate, or for hiding leftovers. Varieties such as Japanese paper or with colors are also available. Choose one suited to the dishes.

懐紙の折り方

How to Fold Kaishi

天ぷらの下に敷いて油を吸い取る役目があります。折り方にも決まりがあるので、正しい折り方を知りましょう。

Kaishi can be used to place tempura on in order to absorb oil. Correct etiquette for folding kaishi is as follows:

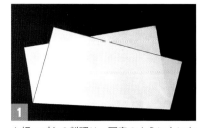

お祝いごとの料理は、写真のように上になる方が右下がりに、仏事や葬式は右上がりに。

At an auspicious occasion, fold the paper as shown. At Buddhist services or a funeral, fold the paper should be feld right is higher.

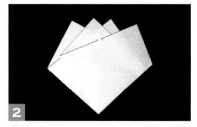

食卓で使う場合は、料理や器の大きさに合わせて、さらに半分に折るなど美しく見えるように形作る。

For the dinner table, beautifully adjust kaishi size, for example, by folding twice, depending on the dish and plate size.

かいしきのいろいろ　　VARIETIES OF KAISHIKI

なんてんは、殺菌・防腐効果がある。表面がつるつるしており、器に置く、料理にさすなどして使う。

Branches of nandin have bactericidal and antiseptic qualities. The leaf surface is smooth. Used by directly placing on a plate or inserting into food.

笹の葉には防腐作用があり、食品を長持ちさせるために使われる。くま笹、小笹などの種類がある。

Since a bamboo leaf has an antiseptic quality, it is used for keeping food for a long time. Varieties include low bamboo and short bamboo.

赤いもみじは秋の代表的なかいしき。春から夏に出る、緑色の青もみじもよく使用される。

Red maple leaf represents fall. Green maple leaf, available from spring to summer, is also commonly used.

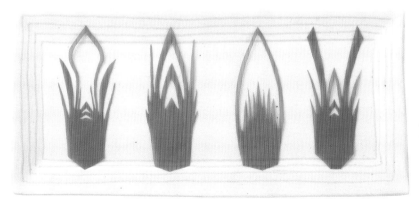

本物の葉に見立てたビニール製のかいしき（葉らんともいう）。左の写真のように飾り切りすることもある。

Plastic kaishiki (called baran) resembling a real leaf is also available. As shown in left photos, decorative cuts can be made.

日本の食卓の
四季を知りましょう

SEASONS IN JAPANESE DINING

日本には、季節の行事に合わせた行事食があります。料理と一緒に、健康や繁栄を願って季節の酒を飲むことも古くからの習慣です。

In Japan, special food is made for each seasonal event. Drinking seasonal sake with dishes in the hope of health and welfare is also a traditional custom.

1月 January

おせちや雑煮には、今年も健康に幸せに過ごせるようにという願いが込められている。
Osechi (New Year dishes) and zoni (soup containing mochi rice cakes) are prepared in the hope of a healthy new year.

2月 February

節分に、その年の恵方を向いて恵方巻きを丸かぶりすると、縁起がよいとされている。
On Setsubun (February 3rd), eating uncut sushi roll (Eho-maki) in silence while facing the yearly lucky compass direction will bring good fortune.

3月 March

女の子の健やかな成長を祈る桃の節句では、お祝いとしてちらし寿司がよく食べられる。
For the Dolls' Festival (March 3rd), which is held to pray for the healthy growth of girls, chirashi zushi (a bowl of sushi rice with other ingredients mixed in) is often eaten.

4月 April

桜色の見た目の愛らしい桜もちや桜酒などがある。
Pretty sakuramochi and sake with salted cherry blossom are common.

5月 May

端午の節句ではお供え物の柏もちのほか、ちまきを食べる。
On the Boys' Festival (May 5th), kashiwamochi and chimaki, glutinous rice dish wrapped in a bamboo leaf, are common.

あんの入った桜色の生地を、塩漬けした桜葉で包んだ桜もち。
A sweet pink rice cake covering red bean paste and wrapped with a salted cherry blossom leaf.

あんの入った生地を柏葉で包んだ柏もち。
The photo shows kashiwamochi, a sweet rice cake and red bean paste wrapped with a kashiwa (oak) leaf.

6月 June

6月の別名は「水無月」。その名前を持つ和菓子などもあります。

Another name for June in Japanese is "Minaduki". You can find a Japanese sweet with the same name.

7月 July

土用の丑の日に、うなぎの蒲焼きを食べて栄養をつけ、暑い夏を乗りきる。

Nutritious grilled eel fillets are eaten on a day falling within the Doyo period (between mid July and early August) for surviving the heat of the summertime.

8月 August

暑い夏には、見た目から涼しくなれるわらびもちや水ようかんが好まれる。

On hot summer days, warabimochi, a confection made from bracken starch and covered with sweet toasted soybean flour, and mizuyokan, sweet jellied bean paste, are favored for their cooling sensation.

9月 September

十五夜に食べる月見だんごや、彼岸のお供えもののおはぎがある。

Dumplings for the Moon Festival and ohagi, glutinous rice cake offered to ancestors, are common.

10月 October

秋に収穫されたそばの実で作られる新そばや、旬である松茸の土瓶蒸しがある。

New soba noodles made from newly harvested buckwheat and dobinmushi with seasonal matsutake mushroom are available.

11月 November

子どもの成長を祝う七五三の千歳飴は、子どもが細く長く生きられるようにとの願いが込められている。

Chitoseame, a long, thin, red and white candy, is eaten at the festival for children aged seven, five and three, in the hope that their life will be long and frugal.

12月 December

ふぐのひれを焼いて熱燗を注いだひれ酒を飲んだり、大晦日には年越しそばを食べる。

Hire zake, broiled blowfish fins served in hot sake, and toshikoshi soba, year-end soba noodles, are common.

お箸のマナー、できていますか？

CHOPSTICKS ETIQUETTE

ナイフやフォークを使った食事に慣れていると、初めは難しいかもしれません。正しい箸遣いで、おいしく和食をいただきましょう。

If you have always used knives and forks, chopsticks might seem a bit tricky until you become accustomed to them. Learn the correct way of using chopsticks to enjoy Japanese dishes.

基本の持ち方　BASIC WAY OF HOLDING CHOPSTICKS

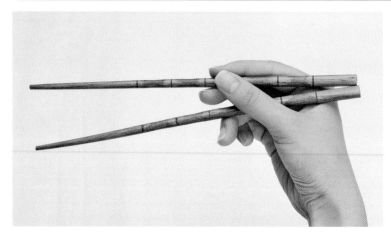

上の箸を親指・人差し指・中指の3本で持ち、使うときは上の箸だけを動かす。持つ位置は箸の頭から1～2cmほど下がったところがよい。中央より上を持つと見た目が美しい。

Hold the upper chopstick with thumb, index and middle finger. When you use chopsticks move only this top chopstick. Holding chopsticks 1-2cm away from the top end is recommended as it looks better.

割り箸の使い方
How to Use Disposable Chopsticks

1

右手で割り箸を取る。

Pick up disposable chopsticks with right hand.

2

左手で下側を、右手で上側の箸を取る。

Hold the bottom and top chopsticks with left hand and right hand, respectively.

3

手首を90度にひねり、扇を開くようにひざの上で割る。

To split the chopsticks, hold them close above your laps and twist the wrists at an angle of 90°.

箸の取り方　HOW TO PICK UP CHOPSTICKS

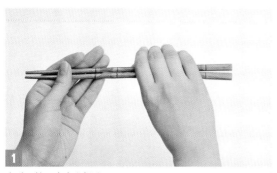

1 右手で箸の中央を軽く握るように持ち、左手は下で受けるように添える。

Lightly hold the middle of chopsticks with right hand and place left hand underneath to support chopsticks.

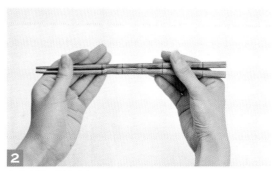

2 右手を折り返すように下に入れて持ち返す。

Move right hand underneath to hold chopsticks.

箸の置き方　HOW TO PLACE CHOPSTICKS

1 右手に持った箸のやや中央を左手で支えるように持つ。

Hold chopsticks with right hand and support it by slightly below the center with left hand.

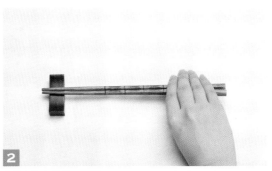

2 右手に持ち替え、箸置きに置く。箸置きがない場合は、箸袋を折って代用する。

Remove left hand and use only right hand to place it on a chopstick rest. If no chopstick rest is available, use the paper wrapping for chopsticks by folding it.

これはNG
Things Not To Do

割り箸を縦に割るのはマナー違反です。箸をねかせ、なるべく音が鳴らないように静かに割りましょう。また、箸を持ちながらどの料理を食べようかと料理の上をあちこち動かすのは、「迷い箸」といわれ嫌われます。

Never hold disposable chopsticks vertically when splitting. Hold it horizontally and try not to make noise when it. Do not wave chopsticks over dishes, wondering which food to eat. This is not good and is called "Mayoibashi" indecisive chopsticks.

日本料理の基本　Basis of Japanese food

食事の友、
日本茶を知りましょう

LEARNING ABOUT JAPANESE TEA,
THE INDISPENSABLE DRINK FOR JAPANESE DISHES

日本の茶葉にはせん茶やほうじ茶、玉露など多くの種類があります。日本茶のおいしさをひき出すための最大のポイントは湯の温度です。お茶ごとに適切な温度があり、それを守らないと、味が変わってしまいます。

There are many varieties of Japanese tea, such as sencha, hojicha and gyokuro. Water temperature is the most important for making good Japanese tea. Depending on the kind of tea, the water temperature varies; otherwise, the taste will be disappointing.

日本茶をおいしく飲むコツ
TIPS FOR MAKING GOOD JAPANESE TEA

お茶は、1煎目がもっとも風味があっておいしいのですが、2煎目以降も違った味わいを楽しむことができます。そのためには、1煎目に入れた湯をきちんときることです。湯が急須に残っていると茶葉の成分が抽出され、渋みが出てしまいます。

First served tea is the most flavorful. You can enjoy a different taste even after the second serving, provided the liquid is completely drained from a tea pot after the first serving. If water remains in the pot, ingredients from the tea leaves are extracted, leaving a bitter taste.

食事前、後に…
せん茶
Before and After Meals Sencha

せん茶は70～80℃の湯を使います。玉露なら50～60℃でゆっくり抽出します。

Use 70-80℃ water. For gyokuro, use 50-60℃ water to steep the tea slowly.

1 急須に茶葉を人数分入れる。茶さじまたはティースプーン1杯が1人分。
Place tea leaves into tea pot according to the number of people. One teaspoon for each person.

2 湯飲みに熱湯を入れ、温めておく。茶葉が湯を吸うので、湯飲みいっぱいに入れる。
Pour boiled water into tea cups to warm them up. Because tea leaves absorb water, completely fill the cups with water.

3 湯飲みの湯が70～80℃まで冷めたら、急須に湯を入れ、30秒待つ。
When the water in the tea cups cools down to 70-80℃ , pour the water into the tea pot. Leave for 30 seconds.

4 味と量が均等になるように、少しずつ交互に注ぐ。茶葉が出る場合は、茶こしを使う。
Pour into each cup little by little to make the taste and the amount of tea uniform. If tea leaves come out, use a tea strainer.

日本茶を飲むときのマナー
Manners for Japanese Tea

お茶を出されたら、片手を湯のみの下に添えて持ち、そのまま口元に運んで飲みます。このとき、熱いからといって息を吹いたり、音を立てて飲むのはNGです。

Once tea is served, place one hand under the tea cup to support it and move the cup to your mouth. Even if it is hot, do not breathe on the tea and do not make noise a when drinking.

食事中に…
ほうじ茶
During Meals Hojicha

古くなったり、乾燥してしまったりした茶葉は「ほうじ茶」にします。

Old or dried tea leaves can be roasted to make "hojicha."

1　ほうろくまたは鍋で、茶葉を濃い茶色になるまで煎る。鍋の場合は、底に和紙を敷く。
Roast tea leaves in a horoku or a pot until they become dark brown. Put a piece of Japanese paper under the leaves for a pot.

2　湯飲みに沸騰した湯を注ぐ。ほうじ茶の場合は、ここで冷ます必要はない。
Pour boiling water into cups. You don't have to cool down hot water for hojicha.

3　急須に茶葉を入れ、湯飲みに入れた湯を戻す。茶葉が湯を吸うまで1～2分待つ。
Place tea leaves in a tea pot and pour boiled water from cups into the pot. Leave for 1-2 minutes until the tea leaves absorb the water.

4　味と量が均等になるように、少しずつ交互に注ぐ。
Pour little by little into each cup so that the flavor and the amount of tea are uniform.

暑い季節なら…
冷茶
For Hot Season Cold Tea

アイスの場合は、茶葉を1人3gずつ入れます。**3**で水を注ぐことで味を調節します。

Place tea leaves (3 g per person) into a tea pot. The taste can be adjusted by adding water at step 3.

1　急須に茶葉を入れ、沸騰した湯を急須の半分まで注ぐ。熱い湯でないと味が出ない。
Place tea leaves in a tea pot and pour boiling water up to half of the tea pot. You must use boiling water to extract flavor.

2　氷をいっぱいになるまで入れる。氷で急冷することで渋みを抑えることができる。
Place ice cubes up to the top of the pot. By quickly cooling tea with ice cubes, a bitter taste is prevented.

3　氷の上から水をゆっくりと注ぐ。冷たくなるまで3分待つ。途中で急須をゆするとよい。
Gently pour water over the ice cubes. Let stand for 3 minutes shaking the pot occasionally, until it becomes cold.

4　十分に冷めたら、グラスに注ぐ。味と量が均等になるように、少しずつ交互に注ぐ。
Once it tea becomes cold enough, pour into each glass little by little. In order to make the flavor and the amount of tea uniform.

日本料理の献立
JAPANESE FOOD MENU

料理の味、色、調理方法をバランスよく組み合わせることが日本料理の献立を考えるときのコツです。基本的に5つの要素がもとになっていますので、上手に組み合わせましょう。

These are the tips for making a Japanese food menu that you balance taste, color and cooking method well. These stuffs basically consist of five elements. Let's coordinate them well.

味 TASTE

酸 SOURNESS
酢で味つけされたものなど酸みのあるもの。
Tasted acid, seasoned by such as vinegar.

苦 BITTERNESS
春の山菜など、少し苦みがきいているもの。
Tasted slightly bitter; edible wild plants in spring.

甘 SWEETNESS
新鮮野菜や砂糖など甘みを感じるもの。
Tasted sweet; flesh vegetables and sugar.

辛 SPICINESS
ねぎやわさびなど独特の辛さをもつもの。
Tasted spicy; scallion and Japanese horse radish.

かん SALTINESS
醤油や塩などの塩辛さを感じるもの。
Tasted salty; soy source and salt.

色 COLOR

   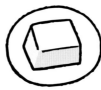 

緑 GREEN
葉もの野菜など、緑色の食材。
Green colored food, such as leafy vegetables.

赤 RED
にんじんなどの野菜や肉などの赤色の食材。
Red colored food, such as meat and vegetables like carrots.

黄 YELLOW
とうもろこしなどの野菜や、果物、卵など。
Yellow colored food, such as eggs, fruit and vegetables like corns.

白 WHITE
米や豆腐、大根やかぶなどの野菜。
White colored food, such as rice, tofu and vegetables like Japanese radish and turnips.

黒 BLACK
海藻類や黒ごま、黒豆など、色の濃いもの。
Dark-colored food, such as seaweed, black sesame and black beans.

調理法 COOKING METHOD

煮 BOILING
煮物や煮つけなど、食材にやわらかく火を通す。
Cook food in boiling water to make it soft.

焼 GRILLING
焼き魚など高温で加熱し、香ばしく仕上げる。
Cook food such as fish with dry heat to make it crisp.

生 RAW DIET
刺身やたたきなど、火を加えずに調理する。
Slice raw fish or meat and serve it without any heat like "Sashimi".

揚 FRYING
天ぷらや唐揚げなど、油で揚げる。
Cook food in hot oil like "Tempura" or "Karaage".

蒸 STEAMING
茶碗蒸しやおこわなど、蒸して甘みを凝縮する。
Steam food to condense its sweetness like "Chawan-Mushi" or "Okowa".

第2章
Part 2

メインになるおかず
Main dishes

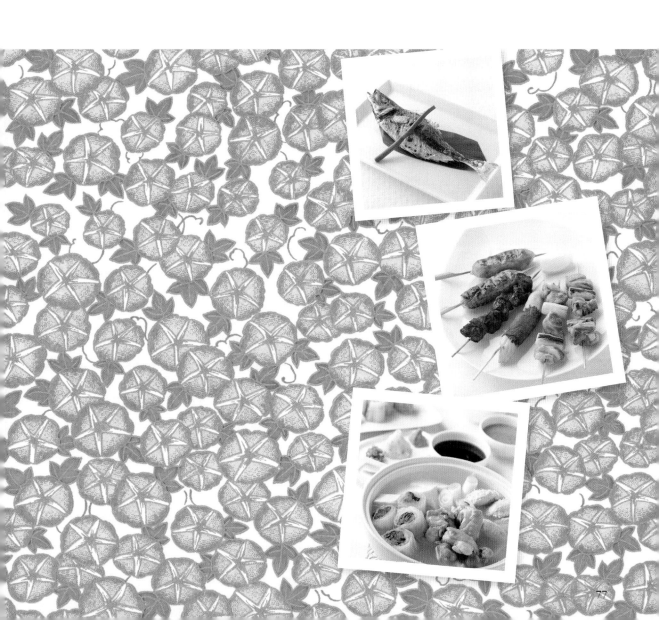

If batter is crisp,
it's successful.

Tempura & Kakiage

天ぷら＆かき揚げ

サクッと
歯ごたえのよい衣が
できたら大成功

料理のポイント
Tips for cooking

1 衣はざっくりと混ぜる。
Do not overmix the batter. Lightly beat.

2 粉をまぶしてから衣をつける。
Sprinkle flour, before dipping in batter.

3 材料により揚げ時間と温度を変える。
Change the time and oil temperature,
depending on what is being fried.

かき揚げ
Kakiage

メインになるおかず

Main dishes

Time required
所要時間
30分
30 minutes

材料（2人分）

ごぼう、にんじん	各40g
かぼちゃ	40g
桜えび	大さじ1/2
みつ葉	6本 (7g)
ほたて	2個 (80g)
ねぎ	1/2本 (50g)
ベーキングパウダー	小さじ1
冷水	50cc
卵	1/2個
薄力粉	大さじ6
揚げ油	適量

※濃口醤油、みりん、だし汁を1対1対4の割合で合わせた天つゆでいただく。

Ingredients (for 2 people)

40g each burdock and carrot
40g pumpkin
1/2 Tbsp dried cherry shrimps
6 stems honewart (7g)
2 scallops (80g)
1/2 scallion (50g)
1 tsp baking powder
cold water 50cc
1/2 egg
6 Tbsp flour
some frying oil

※Enjoy with the dipping soup made from dark soy sauce, mirin, and soup stock in a ratio of 1 : 1 : 4.

ごぼう、かぼちゃ、にんじんは4～5cmの棒状に切り、ボウルに入れる。

Cut burdock, pumpkin and carrot into sticks of 4-5cm, and put them in a bowl.

1

薄力粉大さじ1をまぶす。

Sprinkle 1 Tbsp of flour.

2

といた卵と冷水を合わせ、ふるった薄力粉大さじ4とベーキングパウダーを混ぜる。半量を2と合わせる。

Put the beaten egg and cold water together, mix them with 4 Tbsp of sifted flour and baking powder. Use half of the mixture for 2.

3

具の間にすき間を空けながら木べらにのせ、180℃の油に落とし、約5分揚げる。

Place vegetables on a wooden spatula, allowing space between, and drop in 180℃ oil for about 5 minutes.

4

ねぎは1cmの長さ、みつ葉は3～4cmの長さ、ほたては8mm角に切る。

Cut scallion into 1cm length, honewart into 3-4cm length and scallops into 8mm squares.

5

桜えびと薄力粉大さじ1をまぶし、3の衣の残りを合わせる。180℃の油で1～2分揚げる。

Sprinkle dried cherry shrimps and 1 Tbsp of flour, and mix with the remaining batter from 3. Fry in 180℃ oil for 1-2 minutes.

6

天ぷら
Tempura

Time required
所要時間
50分
50 minutes

材料（2人分）

きす	2尾 (140g)
えび	大2尾 (80g)
なす	35g
さつまいも	80g
ししとう	4本 (16g)
春菊	8g
薄力粉、揚げ油	各適量
冷水	150cc
卵	1個

※濃口醤油、みりん、だし汁を1対1対4の割合で合わせた天つゆでいただく。

Ingredients (for 2 people)

2 sillagos (140g)
2 large shrimps (80g)
35g eggplant
80g sweet potato
4 sweet green peppers (16g)
8g garland chrysanthemum
some flour, frying oil
150cc cold water
1 egg
※Enjoy with the dipping soup made from dark soy sauce, mirin, and soup stock in a ratio of 1:1:4.

2

ししとうは、ヘタを落とす。破裂するのを防ぐため、竹串で数か所をさし、小さな穴を布ける。

Cut off the tip of sweet green peppers. Make small holes using a wooden spit to avoid bursting.

3

春菊は食べやすいよう、葉を手で5cmほどにちぎる。

Tear garland chrysanthemum into bite sized 5cm length.

4

えびは背わたを取り、頭を外す。尾を残して殻をむき、尾をななめに切る。

Devein unshelled shrimps and remove heads. Remove shell leaving tails. Cut the tails diagonaly.

5

えびは腹に5～6か所ほどななめに切りこみを入れ、胴体を指でつまんで、筋をのばす。

Make 5 or 6 diagonal incisions in the stomach sides of the shrimps and lightly press the back of shrimps to straighten.

さつまいもは2等分し、なすは2等分して細かい切り目を入れ、どちらも水にさらす。

1

Cut sweet potato and eggplant in half, cut fine notches on the eggplant's surface. Immerse both in water.

6

きすのえらに手をかけながら、包丁を立て、尾から頭に向かって包丁を動かし、うろこを取る。

Place the knife and slide from the tail to head holding the sillago's gill and remove scales.

きすを背開きにする。

Split sillago open along the back.

衣を作る。
冷やしたボウルに冷水、といた卵を入れて混ぜる。

Make batter.
Mix cold water with beaten egg in a bowl.

薄力粉約1/2カップをふるい、大きく混ぜる。㊋粉気が残る状態でいい。

Sift 1/2 cup of flour and mix roughly. ⓟBatter can be lumpy.

さつまいもに衣をつけ、150℃の低温で約10分揚げる。

Dip sweet potato in batter and fry in oil at low temperature of 150℃ for about 10 minutes.

同様になすとししとうに薄力粉をまぶして衣をつけ、180℃の中温で約2分揚げる。

Likewise sprinkle flour on sweet green pepper and eggplant, dip in batter and fry at mid temperature of 180℃ for about 2 minutes.

春菊に薄力粉をまぶしてから衣をつけ、180℃の中温で衣がカリッとするまで揚げる。

Sprinkle flour on garland chrysanthemum, dip in batter and fry at mid temperature of 180℃ till batter is crisp.

きすとえびに薄力粉をまぶす。粉が多いと衣がつきにくいので、はたいて余分な粉を落とす。

Sprinkle flour on sillagos and shrimps. Shed excess flour, as batter will not stick well with too much flour.

きすとえびに、衣をしっかりとつける。㊋衣のボウルは氷水で冷やしながら使う。

Put enough batter on sillagos and shrimps. ⓟ Use the batter bowl cooled in iced water.

きすは180℃の中温で1～2分揚げる。皮目は長めに揚げる。

Fry sillagos at mid temperature of 180℃ for 1-2 minutes. Leave longer for skin sides.

えびは190～200℃の高温で約1分揚げる。尾を持ち、手前から奥へねかせるように入れると、まっすぐ揚がる。

Fry shrimps at high temperature of 190-200℃ for about a minute. Hold tails and place in oil by laying from near to far side to fry straight.

Saba no misoni

A dish to smooth meals
with a zestful miso flavor.

さばの味噌煮

風味豊かな
味噌の香りで
ご飯がすすむ一品

料理のポイント
Cooking tips

1 さばに塩をふって臭みを出させる。
Sprinkle salt on mackerel to deodorize.

2 皮目に十字の切りこみを入れる。
Make a cross incision on skin side.

3 火が通ってから煮すぎない。
Do not continue to cook after it's cooked.

Time required
所要時間
45分
45 minutes

材料（2人分）

さば	半身（200g）
しょうが	厚切り2枚（5g）
みぶな	2株（60g）
Ⓐ ┌ だし汁	160cc
薄口醤油	小さじ4
└ みりん	小さじ4
ねぎ	1/2本（50g）
酒	大さじ2
水	200cc
砂糖	大さじ1
みりん	大さじ1
味噌	大さじ2
薄口醤油	小さじ2

Ingredients (for 2 people)

half mackerel (200g)
2 pieces thick sliced ginger (5g)
2 stocks mibuna (60g)
Ⓐ ┌ 160cc soup stock
      4 tsp light soy sauce
   └ 4 tsp mirin
1/2 scallion (50g)
2 Tbsp sake
200cc water
1 Tbsp sugar
1 Tbsp mirin
2 Tbsp miso paste
2 tsp light soy sauce

2 みぶなを熱湯に根元から入れ、しんなりしたら全体を入れる。

Put mibuna in boiling water from the root When softened, put the whole mibuna in.

3

1〜2分たったら、盆ざるにあげて手早く冷ます。

After 1-2 minutes, put on a strainer and cool them down.

4

みぶなが十分に冷めたら水気をきり、Ⓐを合わせたものに浸す。

When mibuna are completely cooled down, squeeze excess liquid and soak in a sauce made with Ⓐ ingredients.

5

みぶなは巻きすで軽く水気をきる。端を落として3〜4cmの長さに切る。

Drain excess liquid with bamboo mat lightly. Cut the roots and chop them into 3-4cm length.

半量のしょうがをせん切りにし、水にさらす。残りは半分に切る。

Cut half of the ginger into thin strips and soak these in water. Cut the remainder into halves.

1

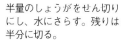

6

ねぎは火が通りやすいよう表面にななめに切りこみを入れてから、4cmほどの長さに切る。

Make a diagonal incision into the surface of scallion for easy cooking, then cut into 4cm length.

魚焼きグリルで焼き、軽く
火が通ったら、表面に半量
の薄口醤油をぬりこんがり
焼く。

7

Roast with a fish grill.
When it is lightly
cooked, apply half of
the light soy sauce until
golden.

筋っぽい尾の先を切り落と
し、2等分する。

10

Cut off the stringy tip of
the tail and cut into two.

塩をふったバットにさばの
身を置き、30cmの高さか
ら塩（分量外）をふる。

8

Place the mackerel on
the salted tray and
sprinkle with salt (ex-
tra) from 30cm above.

皮目に十字に切りこみを入
れる。味がしみやすく、火
が通りやすくなり、皮が縮
まない。

11

Cut a cross notch on
the skin side. This
makes it easier for flavor
to soak in, cook well
and skin does not
shrink.

バットをななめにし、約
10分おき、余分な水分と
臭みを出す。

9

Drain excess liquid and
odor by tipping the tray
for about 10 minutes.

盆ざるにのせて皮目を上に
してふきんをかぶせる。上
から80℃の熱湯をかける。

12

Place them on a strainer
skin sides up and cover
with a cloth. Pour 80℃
hot water on top.

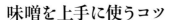

味噌を上手に使うコツ
Tips for using Miso

和食には、味噌汁や魚の味噌漬けなど味噌を使う料理
がたくさんあります。味噌を調理するときは、火を入
れすぎないこと。長く火を通すと香りが飛び、風味が
なくなります。また、空気にふれないように密閉して
保管しましょう。

There are lots of Japanese dishes that use miso
such as Miso soup and Miso marinated fish.
When you use miso, do not overcook. Overcook-
ing results in lost flavor and taste. Seal miso to
preserve it completely.

フライパンに酒、水、しょ
うがを入れて火にかける。
煮たったら、砂糖、みりん
を入れる。

13

Put sake, water and gin-
ger in a frying pan, and
heat. When it comes to
boil, add sugar and
mirin.

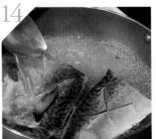

さばは皮目を上にしてフラ
イパンに並べ、煮汁をかけ
ながら火を通す。

14

Put the mackerel in a
frying pan skin sides up
and cook pouring sauce
on them.

皮目が乾燥しないように、落としぶたをする。

Cover with a drop-lid (Japanese style under-sized wooden lid designed to float on top of the liquid in a pan while simmering food) to prevent the skin sides from getting dry.

15

味噌をこし器でこしながら、さばに回しかける。

Pour miso onto the mackerels, while filtering with a strainer.

20

煮汁が少なくなってきたら、フライパンのまわりにはりついたアクをふき取る。

When the sauce has boiled down, wipe off scum clinging around the pan.

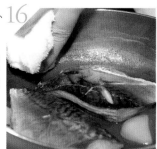

16

煮汁にとろみがつくまで軽く煮る。器に盛り、みぶなと焼きねぎ、針しょうがを添える。

Cook till sauce has thickened. Serve in a dish, with mibuna, grilled scallion and stick cut ginger.

21

煮汁に残りの薄口醤油を加え、煮汁をかけながら煮る。

Add light soy sauce to the remaining cooking sauce and scoop the sauce over the fish to baste.

17

失敗しないために To avoid a failure

味噌をざるでこしてもダマが取れない

Lumps remain even when it's filtered with a strainer.

粒の粗い味噌を使うとき、目の粗いざるではこしてもダマが残ります。目の細かいこし器を使いましょう。

When rough miso is used, lumps will remain if a coarse mesh strainer is used. Use a fine filter.

17の煮汁を少し取り出し、味噌に加える。

Take some 17's sauce out and add to miso.

18

水分が少なくさばに火が通らない

Not much liquid and mackerels are not well cooked.

魚に対して大きいフライパンを使うときは、煮汁をよく回しかけましょう。

When larger frying pan is used compared to the size of fish, ensure to tip it and pour cooking sauce over them.

泡立て器で混ぜながら、味噌を煮汁でときのばす。

Dilute miso with sauce by mixing with a whisk.

19

If it's precooked well,
it will be beautifully browned.

Aji no shioyaki

あじの塩焼き

下ごしらえを
ていねいに行えば
美しい焼き上がりに

材料（2人分）

あじ	2尾（360g）
塩、サラダ油	各適量
筆しょうが	2本
Ⓐ 酢	大さじ6
砂糖	大さじ3
塩	小さじ1/2

Ingredients (for 2 people)

2 horse mackerels (360g)
some salt and cooking oil
2 brush ginger
Ⓐ 6 Tbsp vinegar
3 Tbsp sugar
1/2 tsp salt

料理のポイント
Cooking tips

1 ひれに塩をまぶして焦げを防ぐ。
Sprinkle salt on fins to avoid burning.

2 おどり串を打つ。
Weave the skewer.

Ⓐを強火で沸騰させ、葉を落とした筆しょうがを入れ、煮たったら火を止めてそのまま冷ます。

Boil Ⓐ with high heat, put brush ginger without leaves in, when cooked, turn off the heat and allow to cool.

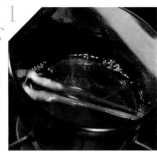

あじはうろこを取り、尾の近くの硬い部分（ぜいご）を取り除く。

Remove scales and the hard part near the tail (scute) from the horse mackerels.

えらぶたを開いて包丁の先端を差しこみ、えらを取り除く。

Open gill cover, insert the tip of knife and remove the gill.

盛りつける面の裏側の腹に切れ目を入れ、内臓を取り除く。水洗いして水気をふく。

Make an incision in the stomach on the opposite side from that to be served and remove the guts. Wash and remove the excess water.

おどり串を打つ。左手で魚を押さえながら、盛りつける面の裏側に金串を当て、目のすぐ下にさす。

Weave a skewer. Place a steel skewer in the back of the serving side, holding fish with left hand, and pierce right under the eye.

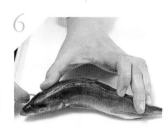

金串は、表面のえらの下を通して身をよじらせながら差しこみ、尾びれ付近に金串の先端を出す。

Insert a steel skewer under the gill, bending the body in a wave shape to pierce through, leaving just the tip near the tail.

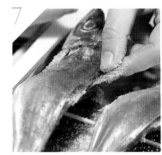

化粧塩をする。まずすべてのひれにぎゅっと塩をつけてから全体にまぶす。

Dress with salt. First squeeze salt on all the fins, then sprinkle whole.

竹串で2尾を固定する。魚焼きグリルの網にサラダ油をぬり、あじをのせる。

Fix 2 fishes with bamboo skewers. Oil grill net and place horse mackerels.

約5分焼いて裏返し、さらに約5分焼く。金串を回しながら抜き取って器に盛り、1を添える。

Grill for about 5 minutes, turn over and grill for another 5 minutes. Remove a steel skewer by rotating it and serve on a plate. Add 1.

メインになるおかず　Main dishes

Sanma no watayaki

さんまのわた焼き

秋の味覚
さんまを
よりおいしく

Make mackerel pike,
the dish that represents autumn,
even better.

材料（2人分）

さんま	2尾（300g）
卵黄	1個分
濃口醤油	大さじ2
酒、みりん	各大さじ2

※かぶの甘酢漬けを添えてもよい。

Ingredients （for 2people）

2 mackerel pike's (300g)
1 egg yolk
2 Tbsp dark soy sauce
2 Tbsp per sake and mirin
※ Turnips pickled in sweet vinegar can
be added.

料理のポイント
Cooking tips

1 うろこを取る。
   Remove scales.

2 わたをこしてなめらかに。
   Smooth guts by straining.

さんまのうろこを包丁で取り、冷水で洗う。

Remove scales with a knife and wash with cold water.

頭と尾を切り落としてさんまの体内からわたを出し、包丁でたたく。

Chop off heads and tails, remove guts and beat them chopping with a knife.

たたいたわたをこし器でこす。

Filter beaten guts.

さんまを2等分し、わたを抜いた部分に箸を入れて、中をきれいに洗う。

Cut mackerel pike into two, insert a chopstick in where the guts were and wash the inside thoroughly.

3のわたに卵黄、濃口醤油を少しずつ加えて混ぜ、酒とみりんを加える。

Gradually add egg yolk and dark soy sauce in 3, and mix. Add sake and mirin.

さんまを漬けて落としラップをする。約15分たったら裏返してさらに15分漬ける。

Soak mackerel pikes and put clinging wrap on top like a lid. After about 15 minutes, turn them over and soak for a further 15 minutes.

表面に切りこみを入れ、魚焼きグリルで両面を5分ずつ焼く。焼き色がついたらはけで6のたれをぬり、皮がパリッとするまで焼く。

Make incision on the surface. Cook each side for 5 minutes on fish grill. Once browned, brush baste from 6, and cook till the skin is crispy.

魚の盛りつけ
Displaying fish

日本料理に限ったことではありませんが、魚を丸ごと1尾で盛りつけるときは、正面に向かって頭が左に、手前が腹になります。日本料理の場合、頭がない魚は、背中が奥で手前がわたになります。

Not only in Japanese cuisine but when a whole fish is served, the head is to the left with the stomach to the near side. A headless fish in a Japanese dish is served with the back to the far side and the stomach to the near side.

Basting that soaks
into tender fish meat
is excellent.

Kinne no nitsuke

金目の煮つけ

やわらかな身に
しっとりしみこむ
たれが絶品

Time required
所要時間
50分
50 minutes

材料（2人分）

金目だい ……………………… 2切れ（240g）
Ⓐ 酒……………………………… 大さじ4
　 みりん ………………………… 大さじ3・1/3
　 濃口醤油………………………… 大さじ1・2/3
※魚焼きグリルで焼き目をつけたねぎや、
木の芽を添えてもよい。

Ingredients（for 2 people）

2 alfonsino fillets (240g)
Ⓐ 4 Tbsp sake
　 3・1/3 Tbsp mirin
　 1・2/3 Tbsp dark soy sauce
※Can be served with skin browned
scallion roasted with a fish grill or baby
leaves of Japanese pepper.

料理のポイント
Cooking tips

1 たっぷりの湯で臭みを取る。
Deodorize with plenty of hot water.

2 調味料が煮たってから魚を入れる。
Put fish in boiled sauce.

金目だいの切り身をまな板の上に置き、上からキッチンペーパーをかぶせる。

Place alfonsino fillet on cutting board and cover with a kitchen roll.

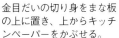

その上から80℃くらいの湯をたっぷりとかけて臭みを取る。●熱湯をかけると身が反るので注意。

Pour plenty of 80℃ hot water over it to remove smell. **P** Be careful as pouring on, boiling water will make the fish bend.

氷水に2を入れる。

Put 2 in iced water.

氷水の中で、指先をこすりつけるように動かし、うろこを取る。

Remove scales by rubbing finger tips on it in iced water.

水分をしっかりふき取ったら、味がしみやすいように十字の切れ目を入れる。

After completely wiping off excess water from the fishes, make a cross incision, so that it absorbs flavor better.

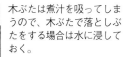

木ぶたは煮汁を吸ってしまうので、木ぶたで落としぶたをする場合は水に浸しておく。

To prevent the wooden drop-lid from absorbing cooking sauce, soak the lid in water beforehand.

フライパンに Ⓐ を沸騰させる。

Boil Ⓐ in a frying pan.

切れ目を入れた面を上にして金目だいを入れ、スプーンで煮汁をすくってかける。

Put alfonsinos in the pan with incision side up and pour on cooking sauce with a spoon.

落としぶたをし、弱火にする。約5分たったらふたを取り、煮汁をかけながら、とろみがつくまで煮る。

Put on the drop-lid and reduce heat to low. Remove the lid after about 5 minutes, and cook basting with sauce until thickened.

Sake no kasudukeyaki

Thoroughly absorbed
and sophisticated flavor.

さけの粕漬け焼き

味がしっかりと
しみこんだ
上品な味わい

材料（2人分）

さけ	2切れ（240g）
酒粕	300g
みりん	150cc
煮きり酒	大さじ3
砂糖	大さじ1
塩	小さじ2

※れんこんの酢漬けを添えてもよい。

Ingredients (for 2 people)

2 salmon fillets (240g)
300g sake lees
150cc mirin
3 Tbsp boiled sake
1 Tbsp sugar
2 tsp salt

※ Can be served with pickled lotus roots.

92

料理のポイント
Cooking tips

1 **粕床はしっかり混ぜる。**
Mix sake lees well.

2 **焦げやすいので弱火で焼く。**
Grill fishes over a low flame to avoid burning.

フードプロセッサーを使う場合は、みりん、煮きり酒を数回に分けて加える。

When you use a food processor, gradually add in mirin and boiled sake a few times.

30cmの高さからさけの切り身に両面塩（分量外）をふり、バットをななめにして約30分おく。

Sprinkle salt (extra) on salmon fillets from 30cm above, tilt the tray and leave it for about 30 minutes.

水で洗って臭みを取り除き、水気をふく。

Wash with water, remove the smell and wipe off excess water.

すり鉢に酒粕を入れ、みりん、煮きり酒を加えながらすり混ぜる。砂糖と塩を加え、さらに混ぜる。

Put sake lees in mortar, add mirin and boiled sake, grinding and mixing. Then add sugar and salt, and continue to mix.

すくうとどろりとするぐらいの硬さの粕床にする。

Make the consistency of the kasudoko (lees bed) sloppy when scooped.

密閉容器に1/3量の粕床を平らにのばす。

Spread 1/3 kasudoko flat in a container.

さけを並べ、上からガーゼをかぶせる。

Line salmon and cover with gauze.

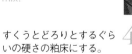

残りの粕床を平らにかぶせ、ラップで覆い冷蔵庫で1日ねかせる。粕床は水気を取れば2〜3回使える。

Spread rest of kasudoko flat, cover with clinging wrap and let it stand for a day in the fridge. If the excess liquid is removed, it can be used 2 or 3 more times.

粕床からさけを取り出し、表面をさっとふく。魚焼きグリルで皮目に焦げ色がつくまで両面を約5分ずつ焼く。

Remove salmon from kasudoko and give a quick wipe. Grill on a fish grill for about 5 minutes on each side until browned.

Tara no saikyo yaki

たらの西京焼き

Appetizing miso flavor
with a savory grilled aroma.

味噌の香りと
香ばしい焼き目が
食欲をそそります

Time required
所要時間
60分
60 minutes

材料（2人分）

銀だら ·················	2切れ（200g）
白味噌 ····················	300g
甘酒 ·······················	大さじ2
みりん ·····················	大さじ1
煮きり酒 ···················	大さじ2

※うどの甘酢漬けを添えてもよい。

Ingredients (for 2 people)

2 codfish fillets (200g)
300g white miso
2 Tbsp sweet alcoholic drink
1 Tbsp mirin
2 Tbsp boiled sake
※Can be served with sweet pickled
Japanese udo.

料理のポイント
Cooking tips

1 味噌の味をみて魚の塩加減を変える。
Change the amount of salt depending on the taste of miso.

2 ガーゼを使うと魚の出し入れが楽。
Using gauze makes it easier to get the fish in and out.

銀だらに塩（分量外）をふる。皮目を上にしてバットをななめにし、約30分おく。

Sprinkle salt (extra) on codfish and place them skin side up on the tray. Tilt the tray and leave it for about 30 minutes.

ボウルに味噌を入れ、ゴムべらで練り混ぜながら甘酒、みりん、煮きり酒を加えて、味噌床を作る。

Put miso in a bowl and add sweet alcoholic drink, mirin, and boiled sake, mix with a rubber spatula to make misodoko.

密閉容器に2の1/3量を広げてガーゼをしく。水気を取った銀だらを並べる。

Spread 1/3 of 2 in the container and place gauze on top. Then place fish wiped off excess water.

銀だらの上にさらにガーゼをかぶせる。

Put another gauze over fish.

残りの2をまんべんなくぬり、平らにならす。ラップをして冷蔵庫に1日おく。

Spread rest of 2 evenly. Put on cling wrap and let it stand for a day in the fridge.

残った味噌は、味噌床の水分を取れば何回も使える。

If the excess liquid is removed, misodoko can be used a few times.

魚焼きグリルで焦げないように弱火で、両面を5〜6分ずつ焼く。

Grill each side over a low flame on a fish grill for 5-6 minutes to avoid burning.

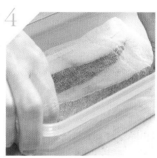

メインになるおかず

Main dishes

西京焼き
Saikyo yaki

西京とは文字どおり西の都という意味です。西京焼きは京都で白味噌を西京味噌ということから、その名がつきました。赤味噌に比べて白味噌は塩分量が少なく、甘みが強いことが大きな特徴です。

Saikyo literally means west capital.The name saikyo yaki comes from white miso that is known as saikyo miso in Kyoto. White miso is lower in sodium and sweeter compared to red miso.

焼き鳥

Yakitori

Enjoy to the fullest
by eating aromatic chicken
fresh from the grill.

香ばしい焼きたてを
いただくのが
醍醐味

料理のポイント
Cooking tips

1 串は下のほうに小さい身をさす。
Place smaller pieces on the lower part of the skewer.

2 鶏は身から皮の方向にさす。
Pierce from meat to skin side.

3 たれはつけながら焼く。
Grill while brushing sauce.

材料（2人分）

レバー串の材料

鶏レバー	100g
塩、粉山椒	各適量
レモン	1/4個

鶏ささみ梅しそ串の材料

鶏ささみ	2本
梅肉	小さじ2
青じそ	2枚
濃口醤油、おろしわさび	各適量

ねぎま串の材料

鶏もも肉	160g
ねぎ	1本

つくね串の材料

鶏ひき肉	200g
ねぎ	3cm
しょうがの絞り汁	小さじ1/2
やまいも	10g
とき卵	1/2個分
薄口醤油、酒、片栗粉	各小さじ1

たれの材料

濃口醤油、みりん	各大さじ6
酒	大さじ2

Ingredients (for 2 people)

Ingredients for liver skewer
100g chicken liver
some salt and Japanese pepper powder
1/4 lemon

Ingredients for chicken breast with Japanese plum and perilla skewer
2 tender chicken breast
2 tsp plum meat
2 leaves green perilla
some dark soy sauce, and green horseradish paste

Ingredients for negima skewer
160g chicken thigh
1 scallion

Ingredients for tsukune skewer
200g minccd chicken
3cm scallion
1/2 tsp ginger juice
10g yam
1/2 beaten egg
1 tsp per light soy sauce, sake and starch

Ingredients for sauce
6 Tbsp per dark soy sauce and mirin
2 Tbsp sake

1

レバー串を作る。レバーは血管や筋の掃除をしてひと口大に切る。

Make liver skewers. Remove blood vessels and sinews, and cut into bite sized pieces.

2

氷水にさらして血抜きをする。

Bleed liver by soaking in iced water.

3

バットにタオルをしき、レバーをのせて水分を取る。

Place a towel on a tray before putting livers on it to absorb excess liquid.

4

串にさす。串の下のほうを小さい身にする。

Pierce with skewers putting the smaller pieces on the lower part of the skewer.

5

鶏ささみ梅しそ串を作る。鶏ささみは筋を取り、中心に縦に1本切りこみを入れる。

Make chicken breast with Japanese plum and perilla skewer. Remove gristle from chicken breast and make vertical line incision in the center.

梅肉はたたき、しそは縦半分に切る。

Beat Japanese plum meat and cut perilla in a vertical half.

鶏もも肉は余分な筋や脂肪を取り、2〜3cm角に切る。

Remove excess vessels and fat, and cut into 2-3cm cubes.

たたいた梅肉をささみの切りこみに入れこむ。

Insert beaten plum meat into incision in the chicken breast.

串に鶏もも肉、ねぎを交互にさす。鶏は身から皮の方向に串をさす。

Skewer the chicken thigh from the meat to the skin side and alternate with scallion.

塩（分量外）を適量ふり、しそを巻く。

Sprinkle some salt (extra) on and wrap with green perilla.

つくね串を作る。ねぎを粗みじん切りにする。

Make tsukune skewer. Chop scallion.

串にさす。中心部にさすようにする。

Pierce with skewers. Try to place in the center.

ボウルに鶏ひき肉、しょうがの絞り汁、醤油、酒、やまいものすりおろしを加え練り合わせる。

Mix minced chicken, ginger juice, soy sauce, sake and grated yam.

ねぎま串を作る。ねぎを3cm長さに切る。一番最初に切ったものと長さを合わせながら切るとよい。

Make negima skewer. Cut scallion in 3cm length. Use the first cut one to measure the length.

写真のように、なめらかになるまで手で練る。

Mix them by hand as smooth as shown in the photo.

よく練ったら、とき卵を入れてさらに混ぜる。

After the ingredients have been well kneaded, add and mix beaten egg.

16

ねぎ串、つくね串を焼く。🅿魚焼きグリルで焼く場合は、串の先端をアルミホイルで巻くと焦げない。

Grill negima skewer and tsukune skewer. 🅿 Wrap the skewer top with foil to avoid burning on a fish grill.

21

ねぎと片栗粉を入れて混ぜ合わせる。

Add and mix chopped scallion and starch.

17

ねぎま串に焼き色がついてきたら、はけでたれをぬり、さらに焼く。

Brush sauce on negima once it's browned, and grill some more.

22

手に油（分量外）をつけて1/4量を取り、形を整える。

Put some oil (extra) on hands. Take 1/4 of the mixed ingredients and shape.

18

つくね串も焼き色がついてきたら、たれをたっぷりぬりながら焼く。

Brush sauce also on tsukune once it's browned, and grill with plenty of sauce.

23

平たい串に棒状につける。

Put it on flat skewer like a stick.

19

レバー串と鶏ささみ梅しそ串は両面を焼く。

Grill both sides of the liver skewer and chicken breast with Japanese plum and perilla skewer.

24

たれを作る。たれの材料をすべて混ぜ、半量になるまで煮つめる。

Make sauce. Mix all the sauce ingredients and boil until reduced by half.

20

レバー串は塩と粉山椒を合わせたものとレモンで、鶏ささみ梅しそ串はわさび醤油をつけていただく。

Serve with a mix of salt and Japanese pepper powder, together with lemon for liver skewer, and soy sauce for chicken breast with green horseradish paste skewer.

25

メインになるおかず　Main dishes

照り焼き2種

Teriyaki

A cooking style that makes ingredients look good with gloss and glaze.

つやと照りで
食材が映える
料理方法

料理のポイント
Cooking tips

1 ぶりの薄力粉はしっかりはたく。
   Brush off flour on yellowtails well.

2 素材と煮汁をよくからめる。
   Thoroughly dress the ingredients with sauce.

3 フライパンに出た余分な脂を取る。
   Remove excess oil from the frying pan.

ぶりの照り焼き
Teriyaki yellowtail

Time required
所要時間
30分
30 minutes

材料（2人分）

れんこん	・・・・・・・	50g
Ⓐ 酢	・・・・・・・	100cc
水	・・・・・・・	100cc
砂糖	・・・・・・・	30g
唐辛子	・・・・・・・	2本
かぶ	・・・・・・・	1個（100g）
ゆず	・・・・・・・	1/4個分
ぶり	・・・・・・・	2切れ（180g）
薄力粉	・・・・・・・	大さじ3
酒	・・・・・・・	大さじ2
みりん	・・・・・・・	大さじ2
濃口醤油	・・・・・・・	大さじ2
しょうが（スライス）	・・・・・・・	1かけ分
サラダ油	・・・・・・・	小さじ1

Ingredients (for 2 people)

50g lotus root
Ⓐ 100cc vinegar
　 100cc water
　 30g sugar
2 red peppers
1 turnip (100g)
1/4 yuzu citron
2 yellowtail fillets (180g)
3 Tbsp flour
2 Tbsp sake
2 Tbsp mirin
2 Tbsp dark soy sauce
1 piece ginger (sliced)
1 tsp cooking oil

れんこんを沸騰した湯に入れてゆで、冷まして皮をむき、輪切りにする。唐辛子は種を取る。

Put lotus root in boiling water to cook, once it has cooled, peel the skin and cut it into round slices. Seed red peppers.

鍋にⒶを入れて中火にかけ、砂糖がとけたら火を止める。1を漬けて冷ます。

Put Ⓐ in a saucepan at medium heat, and turn off the heat when the sugar has dissolved. Add 1 to pan, soak and allow it to cool down.

すりおろして水気をきったかぶと、すりおろしたゆずの皮を混ぜ合わせる。

Mix grated and drained turnip and grated yuzu citron skin.

塩をふったぶりをボウルに入れ、落としぶたをする。80℃の熱湯をかけ約1分おく。

Put salted yellowtails in a bowl and cover with a drop-lid. Pour over 80℃ hot water and leave it for about 1 minute.

ぶりを氷水に取り、冷めたら手でうろこや血を取る。

Put yellowtails in iced water. Remove scales and blood with hands, once it's cooled.

乾いたふきんで水気をしっかりふく。

Absorb liquid well with a dry cloth.

薄力粉をまぶす。余分につ
いた粉ははたいて落とす。

Sprinkle with flour.
Brush off excess flour.

サラダ油を熱したフライパ
ンにぶりを並べ、全体に焼
き色がつくまで、強火で焼
く。

Place yellowtails in a
frying pan with heated
oil, and cook at high
heat until browned.

焼き色がつき、八分通り火
が通ったら、魚から出た脂
をキッチンペーパーでふき
取る。

Once it's brown and
80% cooked, wipe off
the oil from the fish with
kitchen roll.

酒、みりん、濃口醤油、しょ
うがを加え、ぶりに火を通
す。

Add sake, mirin, dark
soy sauce and ginger,
and thoroughly cook yel-
lowtails.

ぶりにたれがからまったら、
れんこん、3と一緒に器に
盛る。

Once yellowtails have
been marinated with
sauce, serve with lotus
root and 3.

鶏の照り焼き
Teriyaki Chicken

| Time required |
| 所要時間 |
| **30**分 |
| 30 minutes |

材料（2人分）

わさび …………………………	1本（適量使用）
鶏もも肉 ………………………	300g
酒 ……………………………	大さじ3・1/3
みりん …………………………	小さじ2
砂糖 …………………………	小さじ2
濃口醤油 ………………………	大さじ2
むかご …………………………	10個
紫スプラウト …………………	10g
塩 ……………………………	小さじ1/2

Ingredients (for 2 people)

1 green horseradish (Use a portion of it)
300g chicken thigh
3・1/3 Tbsp sake
2 tsp mirin
2 tsp sugar
2 Tbsp dark soy sauce
10 bulbils
10g purple sprouts
1/2 tsp salt

わさびはたわしで洗い、表
面の汚れを落とす。茎の先
端をななめに削る。

Wash a green horserad-
ish with a scrubber and
clean the surface.
Scrape the tip of stem
diagonally.

おろし金などでわさびをす
りおろす。円を描くように
動かすと風味が出る。

Grate a green horserad-
ish as drawing circle to
bring out flavor.

鶏肉の脂や肉からはみ出た余分な皮を取り除き、筋に切りこみを入れる。

Remove fat and excess skin from chicken thigh, and make incision in the gristle.

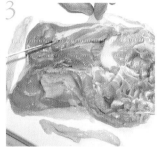

3

酒、みりん、砂糖、濃口醤油を入れ、とかしてから鶏肉にからめる。

Put sake, mirin, sugar and dark soy sauce in a pan, and dress chicken with it after sugar has dissolved.

8

味がしみやすいように、皮側にも包丁で切りこみを入れる。

Make some more incisions in the skin side to better absorb the flavor.

4

お玉などで煮汁をかける。ときどき裏返すと、均一に火が通る。

Pour cooking sauce with a ladle. Turn over occasionally to cook evenly.

9

皮目を下にしてフライパンに置き、焼き色がつくまで強火で両面を焼く。

Place on a frying pan skin sides down and cook at high heat until both sides are brown.

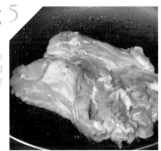

5

包丁で切りこみを入れ、火の通り具合を確かめる。中まで火が通ったらスライスする。

Make incisions with a knife to check if it is thoroughly cooked. Once cooked to the center, slice them.

10

身が縮んで反ってしまうので、ときどき上から押さえて均一に焼き色をつける。

Press the chickens occasionally to even the burnt color and to prevent the meat shrinking.

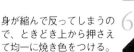

6

むかごは、160℃の低温で竹串がすっと通るまで素揚げする。

Fry bulbils at low heat of 160℃ until a bamboo skewer can pierce through smoothly.

11

フライパンを傾け、鶏肉から出た脂をきれいにふく。

Tilt the frying pan and wipe chicken extract oil thoroughly.

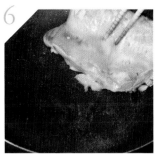
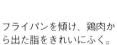

7

むかごに塩をふる。鶏肉を、紫スプラウト、わさびと盛り、鶏肉に煮汁をかける。

Sprinkle salt on bulbils. Put chicken with purple sprouts and green horse-radish paste, and pour cooking sauce over chicken.

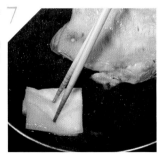

12

Tori no mizutaki

鶏の水炊き

A standard
Japanese winter menu,
that accommodates
a large number of people.

大勢集まっても安心な
日本の冬の
定番中の定番

料理のポイント
Cooking tips

1 鶏のさばき方を覚えよう。
Learn how to cut a whole chicken.

2 スープは常に沸騰した状態に。
Keep soup boiled all the time.

3 具材の大きさをそろえる。
Unify size of ingredients.

Time required
所要時間
120分
120 minutes

材料（2人分）

丸鶏	小1羽（1kg）
ねぎ	2本（200g）
春雨	20g
木綿豆腐	1丁（300g）
小松菜	2株（80g）
白菜	4枚（200g）
米	大さじ4
昆布	5cm幅15cm長さ
万能ねぎ	1束（30g）
大根、赤唐辛子	各適量

つくねの材料

鶏ひき肉	100g
鶏なんこつ	20g
ねぎ	3cm
しょうが	1/5かけ
Ⓐ 酒	小さじ1
白味噌	小さじ1

※丸鶏の代わりに、市販の鶏ガラスープ600ccと
鶏もも肉400gを使用しても可。

Ingredients (for 2 people)

1 small sized whole chicken (1kg)
2 scallion (200g)
20g vermicelli
1 tofu (300g)
2 brassica campestris (80g)
4 chinese cabbage (200g)
4 Tbsp rice
5cm width and 15cm length kelp
1 spring onion (30g)
some Japanese radish and red pepper

Ingredients for tsukune

100g minced chicken
20g chicken gristles
3cm scallion
1/5 piece ginger
Ⓐ 1 tsp sake
　 1 tsp white miso

※Store bought chicken stock soup 600cc and
400g chicken thighs can be used instead of a
whole chicken.

1

昆布は表面をふきんなどで
さっとふき、水2000cc（分
量外）にひと晩ひたしてだ
しを取る。

Wipe the surface of a
kelp with a cloth and
soak in 2000cc water
(extra) overnight to
make broth.

2

122、168ページを参考
に丸鶏をさばき、食べやす
い大きさに切る。手羽は手
羽中と先端を切り分ける。

Clean a whole chicken
referring 122 and 168
page and cut into bite
sized pieces. Carve up
chicken wings into mid-
dle joint wings and wing
tips.

3
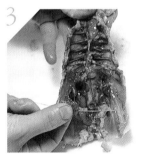

丸鶏のガラは、スープを取
る前に内側についた内臓を
きれいに取り除く。

Remove guts entirely
before making broth
from chicken bones.

4

ガラについている血や水分
をふき取る。4〜5cm角に
切る。

Wipe off blood and wa-
ter from the chicken
bones. Chop them into
4-5 cubes.

5

1の昆布と戻し汁を鍋に入
れ、火にかける。

Pour kelp soup from 1
into a pan and heat.

6

鍋がふつふつと沸いてきたら、沸騰直前に昆布を取り出し、ガラ、さばいた鶏の手羽の先端を入れる。アクを取りながら強火で約1時間火を通す。味見をして鶏の味が十分に出ていたら、別鍋にこす。

Just before it boils, remove a kelp and add chicken bones and wing tips. Skim the scum from the top and cook on high heat for about one hour. Do a taste test to check for strength of chicken flavor, then place in another pan.

7

鶏肉、米を加え、アクを取りながらさらに約25分強火で煮る。

Add chicken meat and rice. Cook at high heat for about 25 minutes while skimming off the scum.

8

つくねを作る。ねぎとしょうが、鶏なんこつをみじん切りにし、鶏ひき肉、Ⓐとともにボウルに入れる。

Make tsukune. Finely chop scallion, ginger, and chicken gristles, and place them in a bowl together with minced chicken and Ⓐ.

9

指先で練り合わせるようにこねる。

Knead with fingers like rubbing together.

10

白菜を塩ゆで（分量外）する。しんなりしたら小松菜を軸のほうから入れる。

Boil Chinese cabbage in salted water (extra). Add brassica campestris to it from the stem end.

11

約1分たったら白菜、小松菜の順に盆ざるに取り、冷ます。小松菜は軸を切り落とす。

After about a minute, remove the Chinese cabbage and brassica campestris using a drainer, and cool them down. Cut off brassica campestris's stem.

12

巻きすにゆでた白菜2枚を広げて置き、中心に小松菜を置いて巻き、ぎゅっと絞る。

Put two leaves of boiled Chinese cabbage on a bamboo mat spread, and place brassica campestris in the center. Roll it tight and squeeze.

地域色豊かな鍋料理
Local special hot pot

いわゆる「鍋料理」にはさまざまな種類があります。魚介や野菜を味噌仕立てでいただく北海道の石狩鍋、魚醤で味つけする秋田県のしょっつる鍋、千葉県のいわしのつみれ汁、広島県のかきの土手鍋など、日本各地にさまざまな味わいの鍋が存在しています。

There are a great variety of so called "Nabe-ryori (hot pot)". They originate from all over Japan, such as Ishikari-nabe from Hokkaido seafood and vegetable with miso based soup, Akita's Shottsuru-nabe seasoned with fish sauce, minced sardines soup from Chiba, Oyster Dote-nabe from Hiroshima.

形が整ったら巻きすから外
し、ひと口大に切る。同様
にもう1本作る。

Once it's shaped, re-
move it from a bamboo
mat and cut into bite
sized pieces. Make an-
other roll in the same
way.

木綿豆腐はひと口大に切り、
ねぎはななめ切りにする。

Cut tofu into bite sized
pieces and cut scallion
diagonally.

春雨は水に約5分浸し戻し、
水気をきる。

Soak vermicelli in water
for about 5 minutes, and
drain water once recon-
stituted.

もみじおろしを作る。大根
に菜箸で穴をあけ、種を
取った赤唐辛子をつめてお
ろし、水気を軽くきる。

Make momiji oroshi.
Make holes in Japanese
radish with cooking
chopsticks. Push red
peppers without seeds
into holes. Grate and
drain water lightly.

万能ねぎは小口切りにし、
もみじおろし、ゆず胡椒と
ともに薬味にする。

Cut spring onion into
pieces and serve as rel-
ish with momiji oroshi
and yuzu citrus pepper.

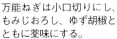

たれも手作りで！
Handmade dips!

ごまだれ
Sesame dip

白ごまペースト20gをだし汁
大さじ2でとき、なめらかに
なったら濃口醤油大さじ2、酢
小さじ2を混ぜる。

Mix 20g of white sesame
paste with 2 Tbsp of soup
stock until it's smooth, then
mix with 2 Tbsp of dark soy
sauce and 2 tsp of vinegar.

味噌だれ
Miso dip

白味噌大さじ2と砂糖大さじ1
を混ぜ合わせる。酒・みりん各
大さじ1、だし汁大さじ2を加
えてとき混ぜる。

Mix 2 Tbsp of white miso
and 1 Tbsp of sugar. Add 1
Tbsp of sake and mirin and
2 Tbsp of Tbsp soup stock
and mix.

ポン酢
Ponzu dip

ボウルに濃口醤油大さじ4とす
だちのしぼり汁大さじ1を混ぜ、
みりん・酢各大さじ1/2を加
え、混ぜ合わせる。

Mix 4 Tbsp of dark soy
sauce and 1 Tbsp of Suda-
chi citrus juice, then add
1/2 Tbsp of mirin and vinegar and mix.

鶏肉を鍋から土鍋に移し、
スープもこして注ぐ。

Move chicken meat to
an earthen pot, then
strain soup before pour-
ing it into the pot.

つくねはスプーンで成形し
鍋に落とす。ほかの具も煮
ながら、好みのたれでいた
だく。

Shape tsukune with a
spoon and drop in the
pot. Cook other ingredi-
ents too, and enjoy it
with your favorite dip.

Sukiyaki

すき焼き

Sukiyaki

牛肉と
濃厚なたれ
旨みたっぷりの鍋

A flavorful hot pot of beef
with rich sauce.

材料（2人分）

牛肉（すき焼き用）	200g
牛脂	適量
焼き豆腐	1/2丁（130g）
麩	2個
しらたき	75g
しいたけ	4枚（75g）
ねぎ	1本（60g）
春菊	1/2束（75g）
にんじん	60g
卵	2個

割り下の材料

濃口醤油	100cc
酒	50cc
水	50cc
みりん	100cc
砂糖	大さじ2

Ingredients (for 2 people)

- 200g beef (thin slice)
- some of beef fat
- 1/2 grilled tofu (130g)
- 2 dried wheat gluten
- 75g shirataki noodle
- 4 shiitake mushrooms (75g)
- 1 scallion(60g)
- 1/2 batch garland chrysanthemum (75g)
- 60g carrot
- 2 eggs

Ingredients for warishita

- 100cc dark soy sauce
- 50cc sake
- 50cc water
- 100cc mirin
- 2 Tbsp sugar

Time required
所要時間
40分
40 minutes

料理のポイント
Cooking tips

1 野菜を入れる前に牛肉を焼く。
Cook beef before adding vegetables.

2 割り下は2回に分けて入れる。
Add warishita seasoning in two portions.

麩はやわらかくなるまで水に浸し、手ではさんで水気をきる。

Reconstitute dried wheat gluten until it is softened, then squeeze water out with hands.

割り下を作る。強火でみりん、酒を煮きる。水、醤油、砂糖を入れて煮たて、しばらくねかせる。

Make warishita seasoning. Boil mirin and sake at high heat. Add water, soy sauce and sugar, and bring to boil, then let it stand for a while.

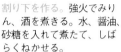

ねぎはななめ切りに、豆腐は縦1.5cm幅に、下ゆでしたしらたき、春菊はざく切りにする。

Cut scallion diagonally and tofu into 1.5cm cubes, chop cooked shirataki and garland chrysanthemum.

しいたけの石づきを切り落とし、表面に飾り切りをする。

Cut off stems from shiitake mushrooms and make decorative cut on their surface.

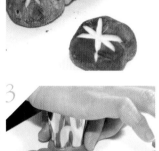

すき焼き鍋に牛脂をとかし、牛肉の1/10量を焼く。割り下の1/2量を入れて煮こむ。

Melt beef fat in Sukiyaki pot and cook 1/10 of beef. Add 1/2 of warishita seasoning and cook.

にんじんは5mm厚さに切り、型で抜く。

Slice carrot to 5mm thickness and cut out with a trimming cutter.

1割程度煮つまったら、残りの具材と割り下を加減しながら加えて煮こむ。

Once it is about 10% cooked, add the remaining ingredients and cook, adjusting warishita seasoning by adding as needed.

にんじんを下ゆでしておく。

Boil carrots beforehand.

最後に肉を入れる。具材に火が通ったら、とき卵にくぐらせていただく。

Add beef. Once cooked, enjoy it by dipping in beaten egg.

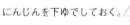

メインになるおかず

Main dishes

おでん

冬に大活躍の
あったか
鍋料理

A perfect hot pot
for winter time.

料理のポイント
Cooking tips

1 牛すじは別鍋で煮ておく。
Cook beef tendon in another
saucepan beforehand.

2 練り製品や昆布などだしの出る具を入れる。
Add fish cakes and kelp for soup stock.

3 具材の中まで味をしみこませる。
Let ingredients absorb a flavor.

材料（2人分）

大根	200g
牛すじ	100g
こんにゃく	1/4枚（60g）
昆布	5cm幅15cm長さ
じゃがいも	小2個
ゆで卵	2個
さつま揚げ	2枚
練り辛子	小さじ1/2

もちきんちゃくの材料

かんぴょう			2本
油揚げ	1枚	切りもち	1枚

えび団子の材料

むきえび	100g
白身魚のすり身	50g
やまいも	50g
銀杏	2個
ゆりね	2枚（14g）
枝豆	10粒（10g）

Ⓐ	塩	小さじ1/2	酒	大さじ2
	みりん	大さじ2	卵黄	1/2個分

煮汁の材料

Ⓑ	だし汁	1カップ	塩	ひとつまみ
	酒	小さじ1	みりん	小さじ1
	薄口醤油			大さじ2

Ingredients (for two people)

200g Japanese radish
100g beef tendon
1/4 konjac food (60g)
5cm width and 15cm length kelp
2 small potatoes
2 boiled eggs
2 satsumaage (fried fish cake)
1/2 tsp Japanese mustard paste
Ingredients for mochi-kinchaku
2 dried gourd strips
1 deep fried bean curd
1 cut rice cake
Ingredients for shrimp ball
100g shrimps (no shell)
50g minced white fish
50g yam
2 ginkgos
2 slices lily root (14g)
10 green soybeans (10g)

Ⓐ	1/2 tsp salt	2 Tbsp sake
	2 Tbsp mirin	1/2 egg yolk

Ingredients for cooking sauce

Ⓑ	1 cup soup stock	1 pinch salt
	1 tsp sake	1 tsp mirin
	2 Tbsp light soy sauce	

1

大根は1.5cm幅に切り、隠し包丁、面取りをする。米のとぎ汁（分量外）で下ゆでして水にさらす。

Slice Japanese radish into 1.5cm width and make a cross incision in one side and trim off the edges. Cook in water (extra) used to wash rice, then rinse under running water.

2

鍋にたっぷりの水と牛すじを入れ、約3時間煮こむ。

Add plenty of water and beef tendon in a pan, then simmer for about 3 hours.

3

圧力鍋を使えば、約30分でやわらかくなる。

If a pressure cooker is used, it will tenderize in about 30 minutes.

4

こんにゃくは表面に切りこみを入れ、三角に切る。

Make some incisions on the surface of konjac food and cut in triangle shape.

5

こんにゃくに塩（分量外）をふって余分な水分を出し、熱湯でゆでる。

Sprinkle salt (extra) on konjac food to extract liquid, and boil in hot water.

昆布は、ふきんで表面を軽くふく。

Lightly wipe the surface of kelp with a cloth.

Ⓑのだし汁に漬け、やわらかくなったら縦半分に切って結ぶ。

Soak in soup from Ⓑ and when softened, cut in half vertically, then make a knot.

もちきんちゃくを作る。かんぴょうを水に浸す。やわらかくなったら水を捨て、塩もみして洗う。

Make mochi-kinchaku. Soak dried gourd strips in water. When softened, discard water and massage with salt before washing off.

油揚げは熱湯に約5秒入れて油抜きする。水気を切り、半分に切る。

Add deep fried bean curd to boiling water for about 5 seconds to extract oil. Remove excess liquid and cut in half.

油揚げに半分に切ったもちを入れる。

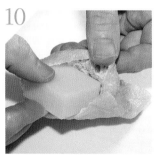

Cut a rice cake in half and put each half into a deep fried bean curd.

かんぴょうでしっかり固結びし、口を閉じる。かんぴょうの端を包丁で切る。

Tightly tie the mouth with gourd strips. Cut the ends of gourd strips with a knife.

えび団子を作る。銀杏の殻の下部を押さえ、金づちで割って中身を取り出す。

Make shrimp balls. Hold the lower part of ginkgo's shell and crush with a hammer to remove the contents.

少量の熱湯に銀杏を入れ、穴じゃくしの裏で押さえながら転がして薄皮をむき、4つ割りにする。

Put ginkgos in a small amount of boiling water, and peel the thin skin by rolling it while pressing with a slotted spoon, then cut in four pieces.

ゆりねは変色した部分を切り、やわらかくなるまでゆでる。水気をきり、5mm幅に切る。

Cut the discolored part of lily root and boil till soften. Remove liquid and cut into 5mm width.

塩ゆで（分量外）した枝豆をさやから出し薄皮をむく。

Take green soybeans boiled with salted water (extra) from their pods and remove the skin.

むきえびを1cm角に切り、半量を形がなくなるまでつぶす。

Cut shrimps (no shell) into 1cm cubes and mash half of these until there're no lumps.

じゃがいもは皮をむき、芽を取る。ゆで卵は殻をむき、さつま揚げはそのまま使う。

Peel potatoes and remove buds. Peel off boiled eggs shell and use satsumaage as it is.

白身魚のすり身を加え、さらにすり混ぜる。

Add minced white fish and grind even more.

土鍋に®を入れて煮立てる。

Put Ⓑ in an earthen pot and simmer.

やまいもをすり鉢の溝でおろす。十分に混ざったら、Ⓐを加えてさらに混ぜる。

Grind a yam using a mortar. Once it is well mixed, add Ⓐ and mix some more.

大根、じゃがいも、こんにゃく、さつま揚げ、昆布、ゆで卵を入れて約20分煮る。

Add Japanese radish, konjac food, satsumaage, kelp and boiled eggs, and cook for about 20 minutes.

残りのむきえび、ゆりね、銀杏、枝豆を入れてざっくり混ぜ合わせる。

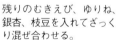

Add the rest of shrimps, lily root, ginkgos, green soybeans and mix.

弱火にし、具材を半分取り出す。19をスプーン2本を使って丸め、鍋に加える。

Turn down the heat to low and remove half of the ingredients. Add 19 using two spoons to roll in the pot.

2の牛すじを冷まし、煮ている間に外れないように、うねらせて串にさす。

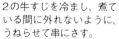

Cool beef tendon from 2, and pierce with a skewer in a wave style to prevent it coming off while cooking.

えび団子に火が通ったら残りの材料と取り出した具材を戻し、中火で火を通す。お好みで練り辛子をつける。

Once shrimp balls are cooked, add the previously removed ingredients back and cook on medium heat. Serve with Japanese mustard paste if you wish.

メインになるおかず

Main dishes

Nikujaga

肉じゃが

Steaming hot,
truly mother's cooking.

ほくほくと
おいしい
まさにおふくろの味

料理のポイント
Cooking tips

1 落としぶたで味をなじませる。
Make flavors blend with a drop-lid.

2 醤油は2回に分けて加える。
Add soy sauce in two portions.

3 混ぜすぎない。
Don't stir too much.

Time required
所要時間
50分
50 minutes

材料（2人分）

牛薄切り肉 ………………………………… 100g
じゃがいも（男爵いも） …………… 2個（200g）
玉ねぎ ……………………………… 1/2個（125g）
にんじん …………………………………… 50g
絹さや ……………………………… 7枚（14g）
しょうが ……………………………………… 1かけ
しらたき ………………………………… 100g
Ⓐ ┌ だし汁 ……………………………… 300cc
　 │ 酒 ……………………………… 大さじ1・2/3
　 │ 砂糖 ………………………………… 大さじ3
　 └ みりん ………………………………… 大さじ1
濃口醤油 ………………………… 大さじ1・2/3
サラダ油 …………………………………… 大さじ1

Ingredients （for 2 people）

100g thin sliced beef
2 potatoes (Irish cobler) (200g)
1/2 onion (125g)
50g carrot
7 snow peas (14g)
1 piece ginger
100g shirataki noodle
Ⓐ ┌ 300cc soup stock
　 │ 1・2/3 Tbsp sake
　 │ 3 Tbsp sugar
　 └ 1 Tbsp mirin
1・2/3 Tbsp dark soy sauce
1 Tbsp cooking oil

2

にんじんは皮をむき、乱切りにする。

Peel carrot and chop into chunks.

3

玉ねぎは皮をむいて芯を取り、繊維に沿って1cm幅に切る。

Peel skin of onion, remove core and cut along lines in 1cm width.

4

じゃがいもは皮をむいて8等分にし、水にさらして水気をきる。

Peel potatoes, cut into 8 even pieces, place in water, and drain.

5

しょうがは皮をむき、薄切りにする。

Peel ginger and slice.

絹さやの種がついているほうの筋を手で取る。両端を飾り切りにする。

Remove strings on seed sides of snow peas. Cut both edges decoratively.

1

6

しらたきは、さっと下ゆでしてから水気をしっかりきって、6cmの長さに切る。

Boil shirataki noodle lightly, drain liquid well and cut into 6cm length.

牛肉は3cmの長さに切る。

Cut thinly sliced beef into 3cm length.

7

沸騰した湯に塩小さじ1
（分量外）を入れ、絹さや
を入れて、約30秒で取り
出す。

Add 1 tsp salt (extra) to boiled water, add snow peas and remove them after about 30 seconds.

8

絹さやを盆ざるに広げ、す
ぐにあおいで冷ます。

Spread snow peas on a strainer and fan to cool straight away.

9

10

鍋を強火にかけ、温まった
ら弱火にし、サラダ油と薄
切りしたしょうがを入れる。

Heat a saucepan over high heat, then turn down the heat to low, and add cooking oil and sliced ginger.

11

鍋を回して油をなじませる。
火加減はしょうがのまわり
にブクブクと小さな泡が出
ているほどの弱火で。

Spread oil by moving the pan in a spiral motion. Keep the heat low enough for small bubbles to release around the ginger.

12

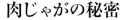

しょうがの香りが立ったら
中火にして、牛肉を鍋底に
広げて炒める。

Once ginger is aromatic, turn the heat up to medium, and spread thinly sliced beef on the bottom of the pan and saute.

13

牛肉の両面が茶色くなり、
火が通ったら、にんじんと
玉ねぎを鍋に加える。鍋底
から混ぜ、よく炒め合わせ
る。

Once both sides of beef are browned and cooked, add carrot and onion to the pan. Mix from the bottom of the pan and saute well.

14

玉ねぎが透き通ったら、
じゃがいもを加える。火加
減は、ジュージューと野菜
を炒める音がするくらいの
中火で。

Once onion turns transparent, add potatoes. Maintain the heat on medium to keep sizzling sound.

肉じゃがの秘密
Secrets of "Nikujaga"

「肉じゃが」は、明治時代に牛肉が庶民の生活に取り
入れられたころ、誕生した料理のようです。一説によ
ると、日露戦争でバルチック艦隊を破った東郷平八郎
が、日本にある材料でビーフシチューを作ろうとして
できたといわれています。

"Nikujaga" is a dish that was created in Meiji era, when beef had just begun to be accepted by common people. One theory goes that Togo Heihachiro, who defeated the Baltic fleet during the Russo-Japanese war, tried to make beef stew using ingredients available in Japan.

野菜が色づいたら、しらたきを加える。

Once vegetables begin to change color, add shirataki noodle.

Ⓐを入れてよく混ぜる。

Add Ⓐ and mix thoroughly.

強火にして、沸騰したら中火にする。鍋をななめに傾け、アクと余分な油をすくう。

Set heat as high, once boiled, turn the heat down to medium. Tilt the pan and scoop scum and excess oil.

落としぶたをし、中火のまま約15分煮る。🔘木ぶたを使う場合は水に浸してから使う。

Place a drop-lid and cook for about 15 minutes at medium heat. Ⓟ When wooden lid is used, soak it in water before use.

約15分たったら落としぶたを外し、半量の醤油を回し入れる。

Remove a drop-lid after about 15 minutes and pour in half of soy sauce in a spiral motion.

失敗しないために　To avoid a failure

牛肉を炒めたらくっついてボロボロに
When beef is sauteed, beef will stick together and crumble.

牛肉を1か所にまとめて焼くのはNG。また、肉の温度や鍋の中の温度が低すぎてもくっついてしまいます。

Do not saute all the beef in one spot. Beef will also get stuck together if the temperature of beef and a pan are too low.

醤油の風味が感じられません
Can't taste soy sauce flavor.

醤油は香りがとばないように、2回に分けて加えます。2回目を加える前に味見をすれば、味が濃くなるのを防げます。

Add soy sauce in two portions, so that the flavor is not lost. Taste it before adding the 2nd portion of soy sauce to avoid making it too rich in flavor.

さらに中火で煮続け、煮汁が1/5量くらいに煮つまったら残りの醤油を加える。

Cook further at medium heat, cooking down the sauce until it is reduced by 1/5, then add the remaining soy sauce.

煮くずれしないよう鍋をゆすって煮汁をからませる。味をみて薄い場合は塩をふり、絹さやを加えて温める。

Shake the pan to cover evenly with the sauce, take care not to break potatoes. Check the taste. Sprinkle salt if it's too light, then add snow peas and warm up.

メインになるおかず　Main dishes

Braised pork belly

豚の角煮

Buta no kakuni

豚肉の余分な脂を
抜くことが
ポイント

The point is to extract excess fat from pork.

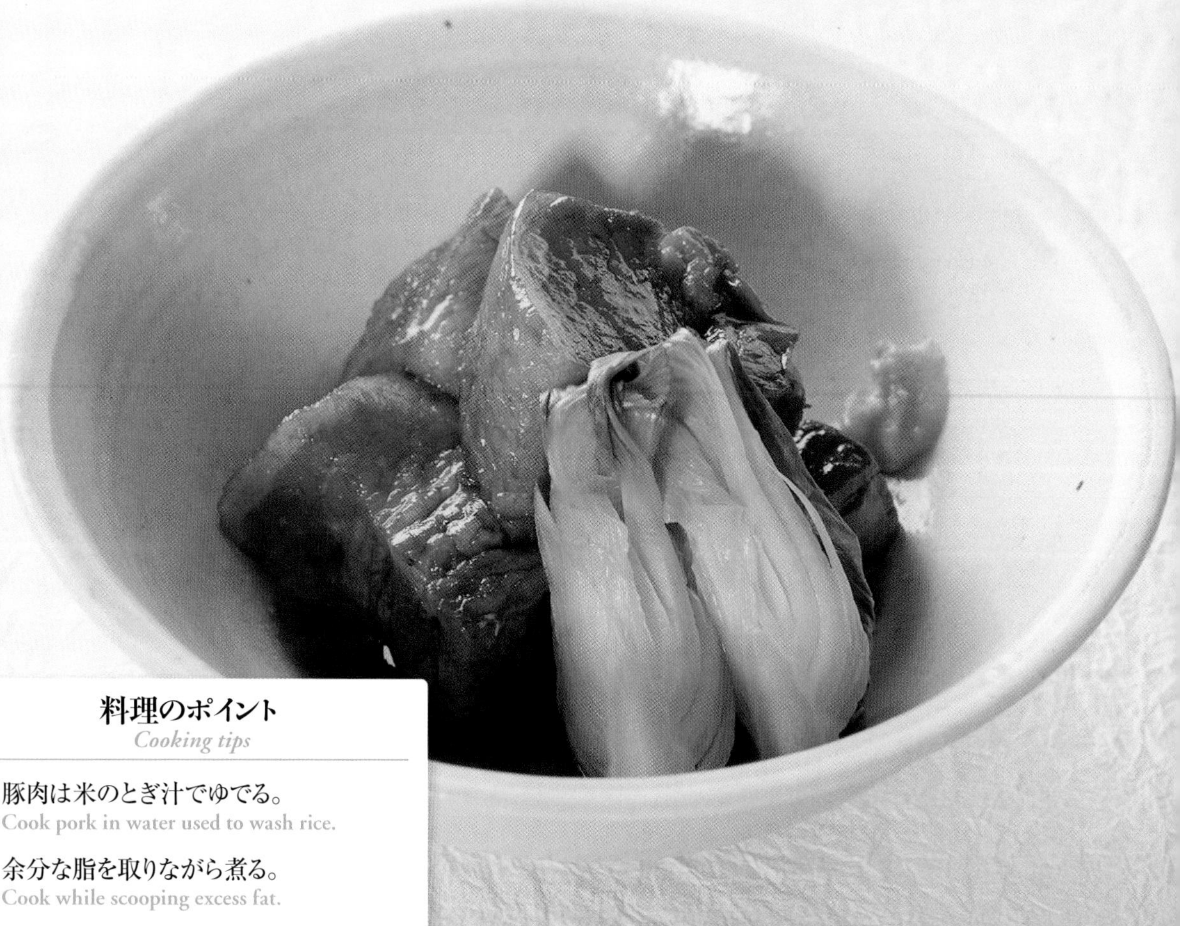

料理のポイント
Cooking tips

1 豚肉は米のとぎ汁でゆでる。
Cook pork in water used to wash rice.

2 余分な脂を取りながら煮る。
Cook while scooping excess fat.

3 落としぶたを使う。
Use a drop-lid.

材料（2人分）

ちんげん菜 ……………………………	1株（60g）
Ⓐ ┌ だし汁 …………………………	160cc
├ 薄口醤油 ………………………	小さじ4
└ みりん …………………………	小さじ4
豚ばら肉 ………………………………	400g
ねぎの青い部分 ………………	1〜2本分（50g）
しょうが ………………………………	1かけ
だし汁 …………………………………	500cc
酒 ………………………………………	大さじ5
みりん …………………………………	大さじ2
砂糖 ……………………………………	大さじ1
濃口醤油 ………………………………	大さじ3
練り辛子 ………………………………	小さじ1
サラダ油 ………………………………	大さじ1

Ingredients (for 2 people)

1 stock shanghai cabbage (60g)
Ⓐ ┌ 160cc soup stock
├ 4 tsp light soy sauce
└ 4 tsp mirin
400g pork back ribs
1-2 green part of scallion (50g)
1 piece ginger
500cc soup stock
5 Tbsp sake
2 Tbsp mirin
1 Tbsp sugar
3 Tbsp dark soy sauce
1 tsp Japanese mustard paste
1 Tbsp cooking oil

メインになるおかず

Main dishes

2

塩1%（分量外）を入れて沸騰させた湯に根元から入れ、しんなりしたら全体を入れて1〜2分ゆでる。

Put it in boiled 1% salted water (extra) from the root, and once softened, put the whole in for 1-2 minutes to boil.

3

盆ざるにあげ、うちわであおいで冷ます。

Place on a strainer and fan to cool.

4

Ⓐを混ぜたものに浸し、味をしみこませる。

Dip in mixed Ⓐ and let a flavor soak in.

5

フライパンにサラダ油を熱し、豚肉の脂身を下にして強火でこんがり焼く。

Heat cooking oil in a frying pan and cook pork till browned with fat side down.

6

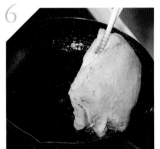

焼き色がついたら裏返し、六面とも焼き色がつくまで強火で手早く焼く。

Once browned turn it over and quickly cook all six surfaces at high heat until browned.

ちんげん菜は根元に切りこみを入れ、手で4等分にさく。

1

Make an incision on the bottom of Shanghai cabbage and cleave into four with hands.

表面全体が香ばしく焼けたら、米のとぎ汁（分量外）に豚肉を入れる。

Once all surfaces are cooked brown, put it in rice washed water (extra).

7

10

沸騰したら弱火にし、落としぶたをして約2時間ゆでる。

Once boiled, turn heat down to low and cover with a drop-lid. Cook for about 2 hours.

ねぎの青い部分を2等分にし、しょうがを皮つきのまま厚切りにする。

Cut green part of scallion in two and slice the skinned ginger thickly.

8

11

脂が浮いてくるので、途中で脂をすくい取る。

Fat will float to the surface, so scoop it out during cooking.

7の鍋にねぎ、しょうがを加え、強火にかける。

Add scallion and ginger to pot 7, and place on high heat.

9

12

落としぶたをしたまま流水にさらす。

Put under running water leaving a drop-lid on.

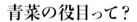

青菜の役目って？

What are greens for?

豚の角煮とほうれん草やちんげん菜を一緒に盛るように、和食では煮物に青菜を添えることがよくあります。煮汁の色で地味になりがちな煮物に彩りを加えるためです。彩りだけでなく、旬の青菜を使えば、季節感も出ます。

In Japanese dishes, greens are quite often served with simmered dishes, like braised pork belly with spinach or shanghai cabbage. It adds color to otherwise plain looking simmered food. In addition to color it can add a seasonal flair through the use of seasonal greens.

13

冷ました豚肉を4〜5cm角に切り分ける。ホ ゆでる前に切ると縮む。

Cut cooled pork in 4-5cm cubes. P It will shrink if cut prior to cooking.

14

ふきんで軽く豚肉の水気をふき取る。

Lightly wipe liquid off with a cloth.

120

煮汁を作る。鍋に酒を入れて、アルコール分がとぶまで煮きる。

Make cooking sauce. Put sake in a saucepan and boil off alcohol.

15

だし汁、みりん、砂糖を入れて強火で煮たてる。

Put soup stock, mirin and sugar in and simmer at high heat.

16

豚肉を入れ、ときどき脂を取りながら中火で煮る。

Add pork and remove fat occasionally, while cooking at medium heat.

17

竹串がすっと通り、持ち上げるとすぐに落ちるくらいやわらかくなるまで煮る。

Cook until they are soft enough for a bamboo skewer to pierce smoothly, and it drops straight away when lifted.

18

醤油大さじ2を加える。

Add 2 Tbsp of soy sauce.

19

失敗しないために

To avoid a failure

豚肉の身が硬くなる
Pork gets hard.

豚肉を入れる前の煮汁に醤油を入れると、肉の身がしまり、硬くなってしまいます。先に豚肉を入れてゆで、やわらかくなってから醤油を加えましょう。

If soy sauce is added to the cooking sauce prior to the pork, the meat will clench and harden. Add the pork first and cook until it is tender, before adding the soy sauce.

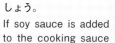

豚肉がやわらかくなるまで煮て、煮汁が減ったら落としぶたをして煮る。

Cook until pork is tender, and sauce reduced, then cover with a drop-lid.

20

味がしみこんだら落としぶたを外し、煮汁にとろみがつくまで煮つめる。

Once flavor has soaked in, remove a drop-lid and cook until sauce thickens.

21

残りの醤油で味を調える。漬け汁ごと温めた4、練り辛子と一緒に器に盛る。

Adjust seasoning with soy sauce. Serve with the warmed up cooking sauce, of 4 and Japanese mustard paste.

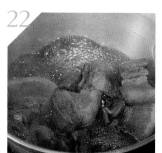

22

メインになるおかず

Main dishes

丸鶏の下ごしらえに挑戦①

LET'S TRY TO DRESS A WHOLE CHICKEN①

鶏を丸ごと使うときの下ごしらえのコツは、肉の内側の余分な脂と鎖骨にあたる小さな骨を取り除くことです。さばく場合は、この処理をした後にP168を参考に作業してください。

The tip to prepare the way for a whole chicken is getting rid of excess fat and small bones called collarbone. Please refer to page 168, when you finish the process below.

1
コンロの火にかざし、表面の毛をあぶる。
Singe its hairs and tiny feathers over a stove.

2
尻に手を入れて中の余分な脂を指でかき出す。
Remove excess fat from back end with fingers.

3
腹の中に血のかたまりがある場合は、一緒に除く。
Remove clotted blood as well when you find it.

4
腹の中をふき、血や脂が残らないようにする。
Wipe and clean inside not to leave any blood and fat

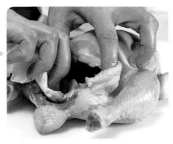

5
尻の肉の皮に切り込みを入れ、中の臭い脂を除く。
Cut in the back end skin and remove the excess fat.

6
首の皮を軽く引っぱり、首から尻に切り込みを入れる。
Make a long cut in from neck to back end, pulling the neck skin gently.

7
首の皮をめくり、内側についた白い脂を手で除く。
Turn over the neck skin and get rid of white fat from inside.

8
V字になっている鎖骨を包丁で切り、引き抜く。
Cut V-shaped collarbones with a knife and extract it.

第3章
Part 3
洋風&中華風のおかず
Western and chinese dishes

The aroma of ginger
compliments a pork flavor.

豚肉の
しょうが焼き

Butaniku no syogayaki

しょうがの香りが
豚肉の旨みを
引き立てます

料理のポイント
Cooking tips

1 豚肉の筋切りをていねいに。
  Make incisions to the tendon carefully.

2 豚肉は直前まで冷やしておく。
  Keep pork cool until right before cooking.

3 豚肉から出る余分な脂をふき取る。
  Wipe off excess fat that comes out of pork.

材料（2人分）

豚ロース肉	200g
しょうが	1/2かけ
Ⓐ 濃口醤油	大さじ2
みりん	大さじ1
酒	大さじ1
トマト	1/2個（100g）
キャベツ	130g
青じそ	2枚
きゅうり	1/2本（50g）
ねぎ	1/2本（50g）
サラダ油	小さじ1

Ingredients (for 2 people)

200g pork loin
1/2 piece ginger
Ⓐ ⌈ 2 Tbsp dark soy sauce
  │ 1 Tbsp mirin
  └ 1 Tbsp sake
1/2 tomato (100g)
130g cabbage
2 leaves green perilla
1/2 cucumber (50g)
1/2 scallion (50g)
1 tsp cooking oil

3

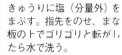

きゅうりに塩（分量外）を
まぶす。指先をのせ、まな
板の上でゴリゴリと転がし
たら水で洗う。

Sprinkle salt on cucumber (extra). Place finger tips on it and roll it around on a cutting board, then wash it with water.

4

5cm長さの薄切りにする。

Cut into 5cm length and slice thin.

5

さらに端から1〜2mm幅
のせん切りにする。

Cut into julienne of 1-2mm from the edge.

1

つけ合わせの野菜を切る。
キャベツは1mm幅のせん
切りにする。

Cut side vegetables. Cut cabbage in fine 1mm strips.

6

ねぎは2等分して、縦に切
りこみを入れ、内側の芯を
取り出す。

Cut scallion in two and make incision vertically to remove core inside.

2

包丁の背をきゅうりに当て
て左右に動かし、表面につ
いたイボを取り除く。

Press back of a knife on cucumber and move it sideways to remove lumps on the surface.

7

指で押さえながら極細のせ
ん切りにする。

Hold with fingers and cut into very fine strips.

青じそは茎を切り落として、切りやすいようにクルクルと巻く。

8

Cut off stems of green perilla and roll it for easy cutting.

トマトはヘタを落とし、放射状に包丁を入れてくし形に切る。

11

Debutton tomato and use a knife radially to make wedges.

端から1〜2mm幅のせん切りにする。

9

Cut into julienne of 1-2mm from the edge.

豚肉は繊維に直角に、5mm厚さに切る。●直前まで冷やしておくと切りやすい。

12

Cut pork into 5mm thicknesses at a right angle to the fibers. ●It is easier to cut if it has been kept cool right before.

切った野菜をすべて氷水にさらし、シャキッとしたら水気をきり、冷蔵庫に入れる。

10

Put all the cut vegetables in iced water and when they are crisp, drain (water) and keep them in the fridge.

脂身（白い部分）と赤身の間に包丁の先端をさし、下まで貫通させて筋切りをする。

13

Stick tip of a knife between fatty meat (white part) and red meat, and cut right through to fibers.

豚ばら薄切り肉を使えば、もっと早くもっと簡単！

Using thin sliced pork ribs makes it much faster and much easier!

厚切り肉の代わりに薄切り肉を使う場合は、合わせた®の調味料におろししょうがを合わせて漬けこみます。筋切りなどの手間が省けるので、簡単です。

Using thin instead of thick sliced meat, add grated ginger to seasoning from Ⓐ and marinade. It is easier as there is no need to cut the fibers.

フライパンを強火にかけ、サラダ油を熱します。うす煙が出てきたら、薄切り肉を入れて手早く強火で炒めます。肉の中まで火が通ればOKです。

Put a frying pan on high heat and heat up cooking oil. When it begins to smoke lightly, add the thin sliced meat and saute quickly on high heat. It is done once meat is cooked through to the center.

裏側も同じように切れ目を
入れる。こうすると焼いて
も肉が反らない。

Do the same on the oth-
er side. This prevents
the meat from curling.

包丁の刃元を使って、肉を
コツコツとたたいて筋を
切ってもよい。

You can also pound
meat using heel of a
knife.

焼いているうちに肉が反った
Meat curled while cooking.

肉は焼くと、筋が縮んで
身が反ってしまいます。
調理前に、赤身と脂身の
間の筋に切れ目を入れて
おけば、肉が反ることな
く、両面とも焼きやすい
です。

When meat is cooked,
the fibres shrink and
the meat will curl. Make a cut in the fiber between red meat and the fatty part to avoid meat
curling and make it easier to cook both sides.

しょうがはすりおろす。

Grate ginger.

茶色く焼き色がついたら
ひっくり返す。

Turn it over when it is
browned.

Ⓐと16を合わせる。Ⓟお
ろし金についたしょうがを
調味料で流しながら混ぜる。

Mix Ⓐ and 16. ⓅRe-
move ginger stuck on a
grater and rinse off with
seasoning, and mix.

脂が出てきたら、キッチン
ペーパーに吸わせる。

Use a kitchen roll to ab-
sorb the grease when it
comes out.

フライパンにサラダ油を熱
し、煙が出てきたら豚肉を
焼く。

Heat oil in a frying pan
and cook pork when it
begins to smoke.

17の調味料を入れ、豚肉
とからめる。トマトや、水
気をきった野菜とともに器
に盛る。

Dress 17's seasoning
with pork. Serve with to-
mato and well drained
vegetables.

洋風＆中華風のおかず

Western and chinese dishes

127

Tori no karaage

Marinating chicken
makes it even tastier.

鶏のから揚げ

鶏肉に下味を
つけておくと
一層おいしくなる

しっとりから揚げ
Moist fried chicken

カリッとから揚げ
Crispy fried chicken

料理のポイント
Cooking tips

1 鶏肉をフォークでさす。
  Pierce chicken with a fork.

2 下味をよくなじませる。
  Allow the flavors blend.

3 2度揚げすれば完璧。
  Frying twice makes perfect.

材料（2人分）

鶏もも肉	…………………………	1枚（250g）
Ⓐ 濃口醤油	…………………………	大さじ1・1/2
砂糖	…………………………	小さじ1/2
酒	…………………………	大さじ1
しょうが	…………………………	1/2かけ
にんにく	…………………………	1/3かけ
塩	…………………………	適量
コショウ	…………………………	適量
揚げ油	…………………………	適量

しっとりから揚げの衣

とき卵	…………………………	1/2個分
薄力粉	…………………………	大さじ1・1/2ほど

カリッとから揚げの衣

片栗粉	…………………………	約65g

Ingredients (for 2 people)

1 Chicken thigh (250g)
Ⓐ 1・1/2 Tbsp dark soy sauce
  1/2 tsp sugar
  1 Tbsp sake
1/2 piece ginger
1/3 piece garlic
some salt
some pepper
some frying oil
Batter for moist fried chicken
1/2 beaten egg
1・1/2 Tbsp flour
Batter for crispy fried chicken
about 65g starch

2

肉の端に足首の筋があれば、縮みを防ぐため、切れ目を入れておく。

If there are ankle fibers, make some cuts on the edges of chicken thighs to avoid shrinking.

3

鶏肉の下からはみ出している、余分な皮や脂身を切り落とす。

Cut off excess skin and fat that stick out from the meat.

4

皮を上にし、フォークで全体をさして縮みを防ぐ。味もしみやすくなる。

Prong meat all over with skin side up to avoid shrinking. This allows flavor to penetrate.

5

皮がずれないように押さえながら、鶏肉を3〜4cm角に切る。

Cut chicken in 3-4cm squares holding firmly so that skin does not move.

鶏肉の皮を下にしてまな板に置く。包丁でそぐようにしてなんこつがあれば取り除く。

Put chicken skin side down on a cutting board. If there is gristle, remove it by chipping off with a knife.

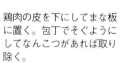

1

6

厚手のビニール袋を用意し、切り分けた鶏肉を入れる。

Have a thick plastic bag ready for the cut chicken thighs.

にんにくとしょうがをおろし金ですりおろす。

Grate garlic and ginger.

7を鶏肉を入れたビニール袋に加える。

Add 7 into the plastic bag containing the chicken.

続いてⒶを加えて下味をつける。

Add Ⓐ next to marinade.

軽く塩とコショウをビニール袋の口からふり入れる。

Sprinkle some salt and pepper from the mouth of the plastic bag.

ビニール袋の上から手全体でよくもみ、鶏肉に味をしみこませる。

Use hands to massage the chicken well through the plastic bag to allow flavors to blend.

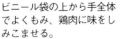

空気を抜いて口をしばり、涼しい所に約30分おく。

Let the air out of the bag and tie the mouth, let it stand for about 30 minutes in a cool place.

しっとりから揚げの場合。袋の口を開けて鶏肉にとき卵を入れる。

For moist fried chicken. Open the mouth of the bag and add beaten egg.

続いて薄力粉を加える。

Add flour.

袋の口を片方の手でつまみながら、もう一方の手で袋ごとよくもむ。

Hold the mouth of the bag closed with one hand and massage the bag with the other hand.

衣をつけた鶏肉を、180℃の中温に熱した揚げ油にひとつずつ静かに落とす。途中で返しながら4〜5分揚げる。

Drop battered chicken gently into 180℃ medium temperature frying oil. Fry them for 4-5 minutes while turning.

ひとつ割ってみるか、唐揚げに金串をさしてみて、自分の下唇の下にその金串を当てて熱ければOK。

To check either open up one of chickens, or pierce it with an iron skewer and put the skewer under your lower lip to feel hot, it is ready.

カリッとから揚げの場合。バットに片栗粉を広げ、12の鶏肉をのせる。

For crispy fried chicken. Spread starch on a tray and then place the chicken from 12 on the tray.

片栗粉をまぶし、固まりがないように余分な粉を落とす。

Sprinkle starch and shake off excess to avoid lumps.

16と同様に揚げる。

Fry them as in 16.

どちらのタイプの唐揚げも、網を重ねたバットなどで油をよくきる。

For both types of fried chicken, place on a grilling mesh in a tray to allow excess oil to drain.

鶏肉の皮のつき方がまちまち
Chicken skins are uneven.

切るときに皮と身がずれてしまうと、皮ばかりのものと皮がないものとができてしまいます。皮目を下にして皮がずれないようにして切るといいでしょう。

If the skins moved when cutting, some may have just skin and others have no skin at all. Cut the chicken skin side down and make sure the skins don't move.

衣をサクッと揚げるには
How to fry crisp

衣に片栗粉を使う場合は、鶏肉を入れたビニール袋に直接片栗粉を入れてはダメ。下味をしみこませた鶏肉をバットなどに移してから片栗粉をまぶすと、サクッと揚がります。

When you use starch for batter, do not add it to the plastic bag that contains the chicken. Sprinkle the starch after marinated chicken are placed in a tray for crispy finish.

食べる直前に、200℃の高温で約15秒ほど2度揚げして、油をしっかりきる。

Fry them a second time in oil at high temperature of 200℃ for about 15 seconds right before serving, and drain oil thoroughly.

洋風＆中華風のおかず

Western and chinese dishes

Tonkatsu

とんかつ

Pound pork well
for tender texture finish.

豚肉をよ〜くたたくと
やわらかな食感に
仕上がります

材料（2人分）

豚肩ロース肉	……………	2枚（約200g）
Ⓐ┌ 塩、コショウ	………………	各適量
│ 水	………………	大さじ1
│ サラダ油	………………	小さじ1
└ 卵	………………	1個
薄力粉、パン粉、揚げ油、		
塩、コショウ	………………	各適量
レモン	………………	1/4個
とんかつソース	………………	大さじ3
マスタード	………………	小さじ1

※つけ合わせにキャベツ、トマト、きゅうり、ポテ
　トサラダを添える。

Ingredients (for 2 people)

2 boston butt (about 200g)
Ⓐ┌ some salt and pepper
　│ 1 Tbsp water
　│ 1 tsp cooking oil
　└ 1 egg
some flour, bread crumbs, frying oil, salt and
pepper
1/4 lemon
3 Tbsp pork cutlet sauce
1 tsp mustard
※Serve with cabbage, tomato, cucumber
and potato salad.

料理のポイント
Cooking tips

1 豚肉はたたいてやわらかくする。
  Pound pork to tenderize.

2 中温でカラリと揚げる。
  Fry crispy in oil at medium heat.

豚肉の赤身と白い部分（脂身）の間の筋を切る。

Cut the fibers between the red and white parts （fat） of pork.

豚肉をラップではさみ、肉たたきで両面を真上からたたき、やわらかくする。

Wrap meat with clinging wrap and pound both sides to tenderize.

湿らせたふきんでバットをふき、塩、コショウをふる。

Wipe a tray with a wet cloth and sprinkle on salt and pepper.

ラップを外した豚肉を並べ、上から塩、コショウを均等にふる。

Unwrap the meat and lay them on a tray. Sprinkle salt and pepper evenly.

別のバットに薄力粉をふるう。肉の両面に薄力粉をまぶし、余分な粉を落とす。

Dust flour on another tray. Sprinkle flour on both sides of the meat and shake off the excess.

衣を作る。Ⓐをボウルに入れてよく混ぜ、こし器でこしながらバットに移す。

Make batter. Put Ⓐ in a bowl, mix and sift on to the tray, using a strainer.

肉全体にしっかり卵液をつけ、余分な卵液をきる。

Spread the egg mixture to cover the meat entirely, shake off the excess.

別のバットでパン粉をまぶす。軽くはたいて余分なパン粉を落とし、180℃で揚げる。

Cover the pork with bread crumbs in another tray. Lightly shake off the excess and fry it at 180℃.

4分たったら裏返し、さらに4分揚げる。好みでレモンを絞り、とんかつソースとマスタードでいただく。

Turn it over after 4 minutes and fry the other side for a further 4 minutes. Squeeze lemon if you wish. Serve it with pork cutlet sauce and mustard.

Ebifurai

えびフライ

Crispy batter stimulates your appetite.

カリッとした
衣の食感が
食欲をそそります

Time required
所要時間
30分
30 minutes

材料（2人分）

えび（ブラックタイガー）	ゆで卵 …………… 1個
………… 4本（160g）	玉ねぎ ………… 30g
薄力粉………… 適量	ピクルス ……… 15g
卵…………… 適量	パセリ ………… 適量
パン粉………… 適量	塩、コショウ … 各適量
揚げ油………… 適量	**野菜サラダの材料**
マヨネーズの材料	紫キャベツ … 2枚（3g）
卵黄…………1個分	かいわれ大根 … 10g
酢 ……… 小さじ1	にんじん ……… 50g
サラダ油 …… 150cc	
塩、コショウ … 各適量	
タルタルソースの材料	
マヨネーズ …… 100g	

Ingredients （for 2 people）

4 prawns (Black tiger) (160g)
some flour
some eggs
some bread crumbs
some frying oil
Ingredients for mayonnaise
1 egg yolk
1 tsp vinegar
150cc cooking oil
some salt and pepper
Ingredients for tartar sauce
100g mayonnaise
1 boiled egg
30g onion
15g pickles

some parsley
some salt and pepper
Ingredients for vegetable salad
2 leaves red cabbage (3g)
10g white radish sprouts
50g carrot

料理のポイント
Cooking tips

1 衣はえびの胴体のみにつける。
Batter should be put only on the body.

2 えびの腹に切りこみを入れる。
Make incision on the prawn's stomach.

マヨネーズを作る。ボウル
に塩、コショウ、卵黄、酢
を入れて混ぜ、サラダ油を
たらしながら乳化させる。

Make mayonnaise. Mix
salt, pepper, egg yolk
and vinegar in a bowl
and emulsify, drizzling
cooking oil.

タルタルソースを作る。ピ
クルス、パセリ、玉ねぎは
みじん切りに、ゆで卵の白
身は細かく切り、卵黄はつ
ぶす。

Make tartar sauce.
Chop pickles, parsley
and onion finely. Cut
white parts of a boiled
egg into small pieces,
mash the yolk.

2に1を100g分加えて混
ぜる。塩、コショウで味を
調える。

Add 100g of 1 in 2. Ad-
just seasoning with salt
and pepper.

にんじんと紫キャベツはせ
ん切りに、かいわれ大根は根
元を切り、水にさらす。

Julienne carrot and red
cabbage, and cut roots
of white radish sprouts
and immerse in water.

えびの背わたを取り、胴の
殻をむく。尾をななめに切
り、腹側に1cm間隔にな
なめに切りこみを入れ、筋
をのばす。

Remove back vein and
shells. Cut the tails di-
agonally and make diag-
onal incisions on the
stomach every 1cm to
straighten.

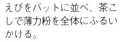

えびをバットに並べ、茶こ
しで薄力粉を全体にふるい
かける。

Lay prawns in a tray and
sprinkle all over with
flour, using a tea strainer.

余分な粉をはらい、えびの
胴体にとき卵をつける。

Shake off excess flour
and cover the body with
beaten egg.

パン粉をたっぷりまぶし、
きゅっと押さえ、余分なパ
ン粉を落とす。

Cover with bread
crumbs, then squeeze
and shake off excess
bread crumbs.

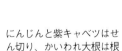

190℃で揚げる。泡が小さ
くなってきたら、転がして
全体に均等に火を通す。揚
がったら、水気をきった4
を添える。

Fry at 190℃. As soon
as the bubbles become
smaller, roll it to heat
whole prawns evenly.
Once fried, serve it with
water drained 4.

洋風＆中華風のおかず

Western and chinese dishes

135

表面はサクッ
中はジューシーな
かきを味わって

かきフライ

Enjoy the crispiness outside
and juicy inside.

材料（2人分）

かき（むき身）	………………………	12個

とき衣の材料

Ⓐ 卵……………………………………1個
　┌ 薄力粉 ……………………………40g
　└ 塩、コショウ ………………… 各適量
薄力粉、パン粉 ……………… 各適量
揚げ油 ………………………… 適量

即席ソースの材料

ケチャップ	…………………	大さじ6
チリソース	…………………	大さじ1
マスタード	…………………	大さじ1
ウスターソース	………………	大さじ1

つけ合わせの材料

サニーレタス	………………	2枚（30g）
アスパラガス	………………	2本（40g）
トマト	………………	1/2個（100g）

Ingredients (for 2 people)

12 oysters (shelled)
Ingredients for batter mix
Ⓐ ┌ 1 egg
　├ 40g flour
　└ some salt and pepper
some flour and bread crumbs
some frying oil
Ingredients for instant sauce
6 Tbsp ketchup
1 Tbsp chilli sauce
1 Tbsp mustard
1 Tbsp Worcester sauce
Ingredients for sides
2 leaves lettuce (30g)
2 asparagus (40g)
1/2 tomato (100g)

Time required
所要時間
30分
30 minutes

料理のポイント
Cooking tips

1 高温で短時間に揚げる。
Fry for a short time at high temperature.

2 水分のあるかきは濃度のある衣を。
For liquidly oysters use creamy batter.

トマトはくし形に切り、サニーレタスはちぎって洗う。
Cut tomato in wedges and tear off leaf lettuce and rinse.

アスパラガスははかまを取り、下半分の皮をむいて根元を切る。熱湯で2〜3分塩ゆで（分量外）する。
Remove asparagus spears and peel lower half of skin with a peeler and cut off the bottom. Cook with boiling salted water (extra) for a few minutes.

かきは薄力粉（分量外）で優しくもんでから、水洗いして汚れを落とす。ふきんで水気を取る。
Massage oysters with flours (extra) gently and rinse with water. Absorb the liquid with a cloth.

とき衣を作る。ボウルに④を入れて泡立て器で混ぜる。
Make batter mix. Put ④ in a bowl and mix with a whisk.

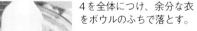

かきに薄力粉をつけて、しっかりはたく。
Cover oysters in flour and shake off thoroughly.

4を全体につけ、余分な衣をボウルのふちで落とす。
Cover it with 4 and wipe off any excess batter on the edge of the bowl.

パン粉を全体につけ、上から押さえる。
Cover in bread crumbs and press.

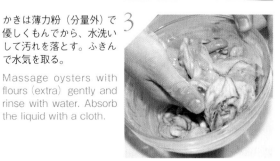

余分なパン粉を落として190℃で1〜2分揚げ、油をよくきる。
Shake off excess bread crumbs, and fry for 1-2 minutes at 190℃ and drain oil well.

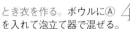

野菜を盛り、かきフライをのせ、混ぜた即席ソースを添える。
Spread vegetables on a plate and place fried oysters on top, serve with mixed instant sauce.

洋風＆中華風のおかず

Western and chinese dishes

Korokke

コロッケ2種

Closely follow the recipe for fillings and batter to ensure, they are not broken!

具も衣も
忠実に作れば
くずれません！

ポテトコロッケ
Potato croquettes

カニクリームコロッケ
Creamy cream croquettes

料理のポイント
Cooking tips

1 じゃがいもが熱いうちに作る。
Make while potatoes are hot.

2 ホワイトソースの濃度は濃く。
White sauce has to be thick.

3 油に入れて衣が固まるまでさわらない。
Do not touch until batter is solid while frying.

かにクリームコロッケ
Creamy crab croquettes

Time required
所要時間
60分
60 minutes

材料（2人分）

かにの身	75g
Ⓐ ┌ 玉ねぎ	25g
│ にんじん	10g
└ セロリ	10g
白ワイン	大さじ1・2/3
牛乳	200cc
ルウ（P.128参照）	50g
とき卵	1個分
Ⓑ ┌ サラダ油	小さじ1
└ 水	大さじ1
バター	大さじ1
薄力粉、パン粉、揚げ油、塩、コショウ	各適量

Ingredients (for 2 people)

75g crab meat
Ⓐ ┌ 25g onion
  │ 10g carrot
  └ 10g celery
1・2/3 Tbsp white wine
200cc milk
50g roux (see P.128)
1 beaten egg
Ⓑ ┌ 1 tsp cooking oil
  └ 1 Tbsp water
1 Tbsp butter
some flour, bread crumbs, frying oil, salt and pepper

2

別の鍋で牛乳を沸騰させ、ルウを加えて泡立て器でよく混ぜる。1を加え、塩、コショウして混ぜ合わせる。

Boil milk in another sauce pan, add roux and mix with a whisk. Add 1 together with salt and pepper, then mix.

3

バットに広げ、ぴったりとラップを密着させてかけ、氷水で冷やす。

Spread it in a tray and tightly cover with clinging wrap, then cool with iced water.

4

6等分にし、手に油（分量外）をつけて俵形にする。

Divide into six parts, then put oil on hands (extra) and shape each into a barrel.

5

薄力粉をまぶし、とき卵とⒷを混ぜてこした卵液にくぐらせる。

Cover with flour and plunge into mixture of beaten egg and Ⓑ.

1

鍋にバターを熱し、みじん切りにしたⒶをじっくり炒め、かにの身を加える。白ワインを加え、水分がなくなるまで煮る。

Heat butter in a pan and saute finely chopped Ⓐ thoroughly, then add crab meat. Add white wine and cook it down until no liquid is left.

6

パン粉のバットに並べ、全面にパン粉をまぶす。170℃で約5分揚げる。

Place them in a tray spread with bread crumbs and cover them with bread crumbs. Fry them in 170℃ oil for about 5 minutes.

ポテト・コロッケ
Potato croquettes

Time required
所要時間
40分
40 minutes

材料（2人分）

じゃがいも	2個（200g）
玉ねぎ	60g
牛豚合いびき肉	60g
バター	大さじ1
赤ワイン	20cc
とき卵	1個分
Ⓐ┌水	大さじ1
├サラダ油	小さじ1
└塩、コショウ	各適量
塩、コショウ	各適量
薄力粉、パン粉、揚げ油	各適量

Ingredients (for 2 people)

2 potatoes (200g)
60g onion
60g mixture of ground beef and pork
1 Tbsp butter
20cc red wine
1 beaten egg
Ⓐ ┌ 1 Tbsp water
  ├ 1 tsp cooking oil
  └ some salt and pepper
some salt and pepper
some flour, bread crumbs and frying oil

じゃがいもは皮をむいて3cm角に切る。玉ねぎはみじん切りにしておく。

1

Peel potatoes and cut into 3cm cubes. Chop onion finely.

2

じゃがいもは水にさっとくぐらせ、ラップをかけて電子レンジで約5分加熱する。

Immerse potatoes in water and wrap with clinging wrap, then place in a microwave for about 5 minutes.

3

フライパンにバターを熱し、泡がなくなり茶色く色づいたら、玉ねぎを中火で炒める。

Heat butter in a frying pan until there are no bubbles. It has turned brown, then saute onion using medium heat.

4

玉ねぎがしんなりしたらひき肉を加え、広げるようにして炒める。

Once onion softened, add minced meat and saute by spreading in the pan.

5

ひき肉がポロポロになったら赤ワインを入れ、アルコール分がとんだら火を止める。

Once the mince begin to crumble, pour on red wine, turn off the heat after the alcohol has gone away.

6

竹串が通るほどやわらかくなっていたら、じゃがいもをボウルに入れてつぶす。

If potatoes are soft enough with a bamboo skewer to pierce through, put them in a bowl and mash.

炒めた玉ねぎとひき肉を6に加え、塩、コショウ、あればナツメグを混ぜる。

Add sauteed onion and minced meat in 6. Mix salt, pepper and, if you have it, nutmeg.

バットに広げて平らにならし、4等分する。

Spread the mixture in a tray and even out, then divide into four.

タネが熱いうちにぎゅっとしっかり握りながら、小判形に形を整える。

Clasp the filling tightly while it's hot, and shape into an oval.

卵液を作る。とき卵と④を混ぜ、こす。

Make egg mixture. Mix beaten egg and ④, and sift.

茶こしを使って9に薄力粉を薄くまぶし、10にくぐらせる。

Sprinkle flour on 9 with a tea strainer and immerse in 10.

ソースの作り方
How to make sauce

カニクリームコロッケにはウスターソース大さじ1/2、ケチャップ大さじ1、マヨネーズ大さじ3を混ぜたソースを、ポテトコロッケにはとんかつソース大さじ4、マヨネーズ大さじ1、マスタード小さじ1を混ぜたソースを添えます。また、つけ合わせはレタスとトマト、それに棒状に切った野菜にコショウをふり、バターを加えて、電子レンジで3分加熱したものです。

Serve with mixture of 1/2 tablespoon of Worcester, 1 tablespoon of ketchup and 3 tablespoons of mayonnaise for creamy crab croquettes, and for potato croquettes, 4 tablespoons of pork cutlet sauce, 1 tablespoon of mayonnaise and 1 teaspoon of mustard. Side dish is made up of lettuce and tomatoes, together with vegetable sticks sprinkled with pepper, warmed for three minutes in a microwave after adding butter.

つけ合わせは、さやいんげん6本、にんじん1/6本、セロリ1/6本、長いも40g、バター3gにコショウひとふりが目安。

For another one to use 3g of butter and a sprinkle of pepper for 6 string beans, 1/6 of a carrot, 1/6 of a celery and 40g yam.

パン粉を全体にしっかりとまぶす。

Thoroughly cover with bread crumbs.

170℃の油にひとつずつ静かに入れ、途中で返しながら約5分揚げ、油をよくきる。

Gently place one at a time in 170℃ oil and fry for about 5 minutes turning it over, drain excess oil.

Spicy curry concentrated
herb flavor.

Kareraisu

カレーライス

香味野菜の旨みを
ぎゅっと凝縮した
スパイシーなカレー

料理のポイント
Cooking tips

1 香味野菜をじっくり炒める。
   Saute herbs thoroughly.

2 牛肉は焼き目をつけてから煮る。
   Simmer beef after cooking to brown.

3 スパイスの量で香りを調整する。
   Adjust flavor with the amount of spice.

材料（2人分）

牛肉（肩肉またはばら肉）‥‥‥‥‥‥‥‥‥‥500g
玉ねぎ ‥‥‥‥‥‥‥‥‥‥‥ 小2·1/2個（500g）
にんじん ‥‥‥‥‥ 50g、セロリ ‥‥‥‥ 25g
カレー粉（コリアンダー9g／ターメリック2g／クミン2.5g
／クローブ、カルダモン、シナモン、カイエンヌペッパー各1g
／ナツメグ、メース各0.5g／ガラムマサラ1.5g） 約20g
ビーフブイヨン ‥‥‥‥‥‥‥‥‥‥‥‥‥‥1000cc
しょうが、にんにく ‥‥‥‥‥‥‥‥‥‥各1/2かけ
サラダ油 ‥‥‥‥‥‥‥‥‥‥‥‥‥‥ 大さじ1·1/2
バター ‥‥‥‥‥‥‥‥‥‥‥‥‥‥‥‥ 小さじ1
塩、コショウ ‥‥‥‥ 各適量、薄力粉 ‥‥‥‥ 30g
チャツネの材料
りんご、マンゴー ‥‥‥‥‥‥‥‥ 各1個（各300g）
Ⓐ ┌ レーズン ‥‥‥‥‥‥‥‥‥‥‥‥‥‥‥ 15g
　 └ チリパウダー ‥‥‥‥‥‥‥‥‥‥ 小さじ1/4
スライスアーモンド ‥‥‥‥‥‥‥‥‥‥ 大さじ1
しょうが ‥‥‥‥‥‥‥‥‥‥‥ すりおろし小さじ1/4
にんにく ‥‥‥‥‥‥‥‥‥‥‥‥‥‥‥ 1/2かけ
水 ‥‥‥‥‥‥‥‥‥‥‥‥‥‥‥‥‥‥ 50cc
塩、コショウ ‥‥‥‥‥‥‥‥‥‥‥‥‥ 各適量

Ingredients (for 2 people)

500g beef (shoulder or short ribs)
2·1/2 small onions (500g)
50g carrot, 25g celery
20g curry powder (9g coriander/2g turmeric/2.5g
cumin/1g each clove, cardamom, cinnamon and
cayenne pepper/0.5g each nutmeg and mace/1.5g
garam masala)
1000cc beef bouillon
1/2 piece ginger and garlic
1·1/2 Tbsp cooking oil
1 tsp butter
some salt and pepper, 30g flour
Ingredients for Chutney
1 apple and mango each (300g each)
Ⓐ ┌ 15g raisins
　 └ 1/4 tsp chilli powder
1 Tbsp sliced almond
1/4 tsp grated ginger
1/2 piece garlic
50cc water
some salt and pepper

1

牛肉を3〜4cm角に切る。バットに入れて塩、コショウをふり、手でよくもみこむ。

Cut beef into 3-4cm cubes. Put them in a tray and sprinkle with salt and pepper, then massage with hands thoroughly.

2

フライパンを中火にかけ、サラダ油大さじ1/2とバターを熱する。バターが茶色くなったら牛肉を入れる。

Put a frying pan on medium heat and heat up 1/2 Tbsp of cooking oil and butter. Add beef once the butter has browned.

3

強火にして、牛肉の表面全体に焼き色をつける。Ⓟ表面を焼くと、香ばしくくずれにくくなる。

Turn the heat to high and brown all surfaces of beef. Ⓟ Cooking each surface brings out the flavor and keeps the shape of beef.

4

別の鍋でビーフブイヨンを沸騰させ、余分な脂をきりながら牛肉を入れる。

Boil beef bouillon in another saucepan, then add the beef draining excess oil.

5

強火にかけ、再沸騰したらアクを取り弱火にする。アクを取りながら、約2時間半煮こむ。

Place on high heat and skim the scum when it has boiled again, turn the heat down to low. Simmer for two and a half hours while skimming the scum.

洋風＆中華風のおかず

Western and chinese dishes

煮こんでいる間にチャツネを作る。りんごは皮をむいて芯を取り、1cm角に切る。

Make chutney while simmering the curry. Peel and core an apple, and cut into 1cm cubes.

6

マンゴーは皮と種を取り1cm角に切る。

Peel and remove a seed of a mango, and cut into 1cm cubes.

7

鍋にりんご、マンゴー、すりおろしたにんにくとしょうが、Ⓐを入れ、スライスアーモンドを砕きながら加える。

Put apple, mango, grated garlic, ginger and Ⓐ into a saucepan. Add sliced almond crushing.

8

塩、コショウをし、水を注いで鍋を強火にかける。

Add salt and pepper. Pour water into the pan on high heat.

9

ゴムべらで軽く混ぜて全体をなじませ、ふたをする。弱火で約10分煮る。

Mix with a rubber spatula to blend the ingredients and cover with a lid. Cook for about 10 minutes at low heat.

10

玉ねぎ、にんじん、筋を取ったセロリはみじん切りにする。

Finely chop onion, carrot and celery with the fiber removed.

11

フライパンにサラダ油大さじ1を熱し、玉ねぎのみじん切りを入れて、強火で炒める。

Put 1 Tbsp cooking oil in a frying pan and heat, then add finely chopped onion to saute at high heat.

12

玉ねぎが透き通ってきたら、にんじんとセロリを加え、広げて炒める。

Once onion turns transparent, add carrot and celery, and saute while spreading.

13

全体に焼き色がついたら、水少々（分量外）をときどき加えながら鍋底をこそげつつ炒める。

Once they are browned, add water (extra) occasionally and saute while scraping the bottom.

14

水分がとんであめ色になるまで約15分炒める。

Saute for about 15 minutes until water is cooked out and it turns to light brown color.

15

144

弱火にし、薄力粉を加えて粉っぽさがなくなるまで炒める。

16

Turn the heat down to low and add flour, then saute until the powdery texture disappears.

カレー粉を加えて香りが立つまで炒める。様子をみてサラダ油大さじ1/2を加える。

17

Add curry powder and saute until getting aromatic. Add 1/2 Tbsp cooking oil if needed.

5を17に少量ずつ加えてときのばし、牛肉の鍋に戻し入れる。

18

Gradually add 5 to 17 to dilute, then put it back in the saucepan containing the beef.

10のチャツネを大さじ3ほど鍋に加え、軽く混ぜる。

19

Add 3 Tbsp of chutney from 10 to the saucepan, and mix lightly.

鍋を弱火にかけ、ときどき混ぜながら約30分煮こむ。仕上げにおろしたしょうがとにんにくを加える。

20

Put the pan on low heat and mix occasionally for about 30 minutes. Add grated ginger and garlic.

野菜の水分がとびません
Vegetable liquid fails to cook out.

野菜を1か所に固めるとなかなか水分がとばないので、大きく広げて炒めます。鍋を使うと水分が蒸発しにくいので、底の広いフライパンで炒めましょう。

Spread vegetables out while cooking, if they are sauted in one spot, it is difficult to cook out the liquid. Use a wide bottom frying pan to saute, it is hard to cook out the liquid in a saucepan.

炒めているうちに野菜が焦げる
Vegetables get burned while sauteing.

香味野菜は強火で15分炒めますが、あまりにも焦げるようなら少し火を弱めます。このとき、フライパンの縁や底についた香味野菜を水で落とし混ぜながら炒めます。

Saute herbs at high heat for 15 minutes, but if it starts to burn, turn down the heat. Saute and mix herbs in a frying pan pouring water to free the herbs off the edges or bottom of the pan.

21

辛さが足りなければカイエンヌペッパーやコショウ、甘みが足りなければはちみつ（分量外）で味を調える。ライス（分量外）と共に盛る。

Season with cayenne pepper or pepper if it needs spiciness, and add honey (extra) if it needs sweetness. Serve with rice (extra).

洋風＆中華風のおかず

Western and chinese dishes

Hanbāgu

ハンバーグ

Secrets to a juicy hamburger.

ジュワ〜ッとしみ出る
肉汁の秘密を
教えます

料理のポイント
Cooking tips

1 手でこねない。
Do not knead with hands.

2 必ず試し焼きと味見をする。
Always test cook and taste.

3 空気をしっかり抜く。
Press out air completely.

146

材料（2人分）

牛豚合いびき肉	130g
玉ねぎ	30g
ドライパン粉（生パン粉の場合は大さじ3）	大さじ2
牛乳	大さじ2
とき卵	1/4個分
バター	大さじ1・2/3
塩、コショウ	各適量
ナツメグ	小さじ1/8
サラダ油	小さじ1

きのこのデミグラスソースの材料

ベーコン（ブロック）	30g
しめじ	20g
赤ワイン	大さじ1・1/3
Ⓐ ┌ デミグラスソース（缶）	80cc
└ ビーフブイヨン	50cc
バター	大さじ1/2
塩、コショウ	各適量

Ingredients (for 2 people)

130g mixture of ground beef and pork
30g onion
2 Tbsp dried bread crumbs (3 Tbsp for fresh bread crumbs)
2 Tbsp milk
1/4 beaten egg
1・2/3 Tbsp butter
some salt and pepper
1/8 tsp nutmeg
1 tsp cooking oil
Ingredients for mushroom demiglace sauce
30g bacon (block)
20g shimeji mushroom
1・1/3 Tbsp red wine
Ⓐ ┌ 80cc demiglace sauce (canned)
└ 50cc beef bouillon
1/2 Tbsp butter
some salt and pepper

1
玉ねぎは粗めのみじん切りにする。Ⓟ細かくしすぎると食感がなくなる。

Chop onion. Ⓟ If it's cut too fine, it will lose texture.

2
フライパンを強火にかけ、バター大さじ1を入れ、茶色くなるまで熱する。

Put a frying pan on high heat. Add 1 Tbsp butter and heat till browned.

3
1の玉ねぎを入れる。バターを吸って香りが立つまで、強火で約10秒炒める。

Add onion from 1. Saute onion until it absorbs butter and is aromatic for about 10 seconds at high heat.

4
ボウルに入れ、氷水で冷やす。

Place in a bowl and cool with iced water.

5
ドライパン粉を牛乳に浸しておく。生パン粉なら使う直前でよい。

Soak dried bread crumbs, in milk. For fresh bread crumbs, do not soak till immediately before using.

6
炒めた玉ねぎを入れたボウルに、ひき肉、5、とき卵、塩、コショウを加える。

Add mixture of ground beef and pork, 5, beaten egg, salt and pepper to the bowl with the sauteed onions.

洋風＆中華風のおかず

Western and chinese dishes

ナツメグを加える。材料を
全部加えてから混ぜる。

7

Add nutmeg. Mix to-
gether after adding all
the ingredients.

成形したタネの真ん中をく
ぼませる。

12

Hollow the center of the
shaped meat mixture.

ボウルの中身を味が均一に
なるまでゴムべらで混ぜる。

8

Use a rubber spatula to
mix the ingredients in
the bowl until all are
evenly blended.

裏返したバットなどにラッ
プをしきタネを置くと、フ
ライパンに入れやすい。

13

It is easier to put them
in a frying pan, if you
use a tray turned upside
down and covered with
clinging wrap to place
the shaped meat mix-
ture on.

3のフライパンを中火にか
ける。タネを少量焼いて味
をみる。味が足りなければ
タネに塩、コショウなどを
足す。

9

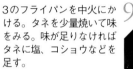

Put a frying pan from 3
on medium heat. Cook a
small amount of the
meat mixture and taste
it. If the taste is light,
add salt and pepper.

フライパンにサラダ油とバ
ター小さじ1を熱し、茶色
くなったらタネを入れて弱
火で焼く。

14

Put cooking oil and 1
tsp of butter in a heated
frying pan, once it has
turned brown, add the
shaped meat mixture
and cook it at low heat.

タネを2等分し、手にサラ
ダ油（分量外）をつけて小
判形に整える。

10

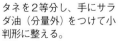

Divide the mixture into
two then put cooking oil
（extra）on hands, and
shape each into an oval.

約4分たち、ハンバーグの
底に茶色く焼き色がついた
ら裏返しどき。

15

After about 4 minutes
and once the bottom of
hamburger steaks turn
brown, turn them over.

タネをキャッチボールのよ
うに何回か投げ、しっかり
と空気を抜く。

11

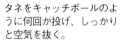

Throw meat mixture
hand to hand a few
times like catching a
ball to thoroughly re-
move air from the mix-
ture.

裏返すときは、フライパン
の側面を使い片手を添える
とよい。

16

When you turn it over,
use the side of a frying
pan and support with
your hand.

肉汁があふれ、ジュワーと
いう音が聞こえてくるまで、
さらに約4分焼く。

Cook another 4 minutes
until meat juice oozes
out with a sizzling noise.

竹串をさしてみて、透明の
肉汁が出たら、別の容器に
取り出しておく。

Pierce with a bamboo
skewer to check if clear
meat juice comes out,
then move them to an-
other container.

きのこのデミグラスソース
を作る。フライパンにバ
ターを熱し、マッチ棒大に
切ったベーコンを中火で炒
める。

Make mushroom demi-
glace sauce. Heat but-
ter in a frying pan and
saute match sized cut
bacon at medium heat.

小房に分けたしめじを入れ
る。焼き色がついたら赤ワ
インを加える。

Add small bunched
shimeji mushrooms.
Once the mushrooms
and bacon are browned,
add red wine.

アルコール分がとんだら、
Ⓐを加え、とろみがでるま
で2〜3分煮こむ。

After alcohol is cooked
away, add Ⓐ, and sim-
mer for 2-3 minutes till
thickened.

失敗しない
ために

To avoid a failure

ジューシーさが足りない
Not juicy enough.

手でタネをこねるとひ
き肉がつぶれ、手の熱
で脂がとけてしまいま
す。ボウルを氷水などで
冷やしながらゴムべら
で混ぜます。また、玉ね
ぎはさっと強火で炒め
れば水分が逃げません。

Kneading the meat mixture by hand will squash
the ground meat and the heat of hand will melt
the fat. Mix with a rubber spatula and cool a
bowl with iced water. Sauteing onion quickly at
high heat helps keep liquids content.

焼いている途中でひびが入った
It cracks while cooking.

タネの空気を抜ききれ
ていないことが原因で
す。形を整えたあとに
端を持つと、ボトッ
と落ちてしまうような
らまだダメ。両手で
キャッチボールをし、
空気をしっかり抜きま
す。

This is because air was not completely removed
from the mixture. If it drops when you held the
edges after shaping, it is not yet good enough.
Continue to throw from hand to hand like catching a ball to let the air out.

塩とコショウをふる。煮つ
まったら、器に盛ったハン
バーグにかける。クレソン
とにんじんの甘煮を添える。

Sprinkle salt and pep-
per. Once simmered
down, pour onto the
hamburger steak on a
plate. Serve with water-
cress and cooked sweet
carrot.

洋風＆中華風のおかず

Western and chinese dishes

Omuraisu

オムライス

ふんわりとした
卵が特徴の
洋食の定番メニュー

Fluffy egg is a regular specialty
on the menu of Japanese
like western dishes.

材料（2人分）

卵··4個
チャービル ································適量
バター、サラダ油················各適量
トマトケチャップの材料
完熟トマト ············ 4·1/2個（600g）
玉ねぎ··60g
にんにく································1/2かけ
Ⓐ ┌砂糖································大さじ4
　│ナツメグ························適量
　│ローリエ、クローブ ············各適量
　└粉末唐辛子····················適量
酢··小さじ1
塩、コショウ····················各適量
チキンライスの材料
鶏もも肉··································100g
玉ねぎ······································100g
ピーマン··························1個（40g）
ごはん······································300g

Ingredients（for 2 people）

4 eggs
some chervil
some butter and cooking oil
Ingredients for tomato ketchup
4·1/2 fully ripened tomatoes（600g）
60g onion
1/2 piece garlic
Ⓐ ┌4 Tbsp sugar
　│some nutmeg
　│some bay leaf and clove
　└some chilli pepper
1 tsp vinegar
some salt and pepper
Ingredients for chicken fried rice
100g chicken thigh
100g onion
1 green pepper（40g）
300g cooked rice

Required time
所要時間
40分
40 minutes

料理のポイント
Cooking tips

1 トマトは熟したものを使う。
Use fully ripened tomatoes.

2 卵は半熟に仕上げる。
Make an omelet runny.

バター小さじ1を熱したフライパンで4を炒め、塩、コショウをふる。ごはんを加え、具材とごはんをしっかり混ぜ合わせる。

Saute 4 in 1 tsp of butter heated in a frying pan, add salt and pepper. Add rice, mix ingredients and rice thoroughly.

トマトケチャップを作る。トマト、玉ねぎ、にんにくをざく切りし、なめらかになるまでミキサーにかける。

Make tomato ketchup. Chop tomato, onion, and garlic. Mix in a food processor until smoothed.

3のトマトケチャップ大さじ4を入れ、炒め合わせる。

Put 4 Tbsp of ketchup from 3 and saute.

1をフライパンに入れ、強火にかける。Ⓐと塩、コショウを入れ、濃度がつくまで煮る。

Put 1 in a frying pan on high heat. Add Ⓐ, salt and pepper, and cook till thickened.

フライパンにサラダ油とバターを熱し、塩、コショウを加えたとき卵（1人分2個）を入れて広げる。

Heat cooking oil and butter in a frying pan, pour beaten egg with salt and pepper (2 eggs per person), and spread.

煮つまったら、ローリエを取り出し、酢を加える。

Once it is simmered, remove a bay leaf and add vinegar.

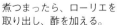

卵が半熟になったら中央に半量のチキンライスをのせ、写真のように左右をかぶせる。

Once the egg mixture is half cooked, add half of chicken fried rice to the center. Fold over the egg on left and right to cover it, as shown in the photo.

チキンライスを作る。塩、コショウした鶏肉、ピーマン、玉ねぎを8mm角に切る。

Make chicken fried rice. Cut salted and peppered chicken, green pepper and onion into 8mm cubes.

フライパンを逆さにし、ごはんが見える面を下にして器に出す。器の上で軽く形を整え、残りの3をかける。チャービルを添える。

Turn the frying pan upside down to put the rice side on a plate. Shape it and top with the remains of sauce 3. Serve with chervil.

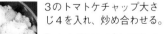

151

Hayashiraisu

ハヤシライス

Enjoy the rich taste
of demiglace sauce.

デミグラス
ソースの
深い味わいを楽しむ

材料（2人分）

牛薄切り肉（ロースまたはもも肉）	……	150g
玉ねぎ	………………………………	150g
マッシュルーム	………………	4個（40g）
にんにく	……………………………	1/2かけ
赤ワイン	……………………………	大さじ2
Ⓐ デミグラスソース	………………	150cc
ビーフブイヨン	…………………	50cc
トマトケチャップ	…………	大さじ1/2
ウスターソース	……………	小さじ1/2
パセリ	………………………………	適量
バター	………………………………	適量
塩、コショウ	………………………	各適量
バターライスの材料		
米	…………………………………	200cc
チキンブイヨン	………………	洗い米と同量
塩、コショウ	………………………	各適量
バター	………………………………	適量

Ingredients （for 2 people）

150g thin sliced beef (sirloin or round)
150g onion
4 mushrooms (40g)
1/2 piece garlic
2 Tbsp red wine
Ⓐ ┌ 150cc demiglace sauce
　│ 50cc beef bouillon
　│ 1/2 Tbsp tomato ketchup
　└ 1/2 tsp Worcester sauce
some parsley
some butter
some salt and pepper
Ingredients for buttered rice
200cc rice
the same amount as washed rice chicken
bouillon
some salt and pepper
some butter

料理のポイント
Cooking tips

1 玉ねぎはあめ色になるまで炒める。
Saute onion till lightly browned.

2 牛肉は焼き色がつくまで動かさない。
Do not remove beef until browned.

玉ねぎ、マッシュルームは2〜3mmの厚さに、にんにく、パセリはみじん切りにする。

Cut onion and mushrooms into 2-3mm thick slices, and finely chop garlic and parsley.

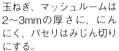

牛肉は3cm角に切る。
Cut beef into 3cm cubes.

フライパンにバターを熱してにんにくを炒め、香りが出たら玉ねぎを加えて、あめ色になるまで炒める。

Heat butter in a frying pan and saute garlic, when it is aromatic, add onion and saute until lightly browned.

Ⓐを入れ、具材とからませるように混ぜ、中火で煮る。

Add Ⓐ to the saucepan and mix with ingredients, simmer at medium heat.

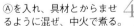

5

別のフライパンにバターを熱し、強火でマッシュルームを炒め、4に入れる。

Heat butter in another frying pan and saute mushrooms at high heat, then add them to 4.

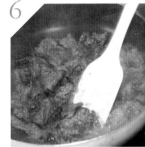

6

マッシュルームを炒めたフライパンにバターを熱し、塩、コショウをふった牛肉を強火でさっと炒め、赤ワインを加える。

Heat butter in the frying pan used for mushrooms. Saute beef seasoned with salt and pepper at high heat, then add red wine.

7

5に6を入れ、塩、コショウで味を調える。牛肉は半生状態で。

Add 6 to 5 and adjust flavor with salt and pepper. Leave beef half-cooked.

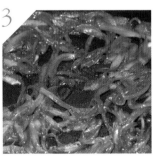

8

鍋にバターを熱し、米を炒める。チキンブイヨンを入れ、塩、コショウをしてふたをし、沸騰したら弱火で約13分炊く。

Heat butter in a saucepan and saute rice. Add chicken bouillon, salt and pepper, cover with a lid. Once boiled, cook for about 13 minutes at low heat.

9

炊けたバターライスに7を添え、パセリを散らす。

Garnish buttered rice with 7 and sprinkle with minced parsley.

和風スパゲティ2種

Wafu spaghetti

Japanese Italian dishes
that fuse seafoods
with mountain vegetables.

海と山の幸が
融合した
和風イタリアン

料理のポイント
Cooking tips

1 スパゲティは粗塩をとかしたたっぷりの湯でゆでる。
Cook spaghetti in plenty of water with sea salt.

2 ゆでたての麺をからめる。
Toss freshly boiled pasta with sauce.

3 スパゲティは余熱で火が通るので、芯が残る程度にゆでる。
Cook spaghetti leaving slightly undercooked
as the remaining heat will cook it through.

154

はまぐりときのこの酒蒸しスパゲティ
Spaghetti with sake steamed clam and mushroom

Time required
所要時間
30分
30 minutes

材料（2人分）

スパゲティ	180g
はまぐり	16個
しめじ	1/2パック (45g)
えのき	1/2パック (50g)
菜の花	6本 (45g)
にんにく	1/2かけ
オリーブオイル	適量
薄口醤油	大さじ1
酒	大さじ2
粗塩	適量
塩、コショウ	各適量

Ingredients (for 2 people)

180g spaghetti
16 clams
1/2 pack shimeji mushroom (45g)
1/2 pack enoki mushroom (50g)
6 stems canola (45g)
1/2 piece garlic
some olive oil
1 Tbsp light soy sauce
2 Tbsp sake
some sea salt
some salt and pepper

2

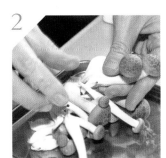

しめじの石づきを切り、手でほぐし分ける。

Cut off hard tips of shimeji mushrooms and break them into small pieces by hands.

3

えのきは根元を切ってほぐしたあと、2等分に切る。

Cut off the hard part of the stem of enoki mushrooms and break the bunch into individual pieces, then cut each into two.

4

菜の花は長さをそろえて、2等分に切る。

Align the length of stems canola and cut them into two parts.

5

フライパンでオリーブオイル、みじん切りにしたにんにくを熱し、えのき、しめじを加えて強火で炒める。

Heat olive oil and finely chopped garlic in a frying pan. Add enoki and shimeji mushrooms, saute at high heat.

1

はまぐりを塩水につけて砂抜きをする。十分に砂抜きしたら、塩で殻をこすって汚れを落とす。

Remove sand by soaking clams in salted water. Once sand is removed completely, scrub shells with salt to clean.

6

はまぐりと酒を加え軽く鍋をゆすり、全体を混ぜる。

Add clams and sake, shake the pan to mix ingredients.

洋風＆中華風のおかず

Western and chinese dishes

155

ふたをして、はまぐりの口が開いたら火を止める。

Cover with a lid. Once all the clam shells open, turn off the heat.

スパゲティは粗塩を加えたたっぷりの湯で、芯が残るくらいの硬さにゆでる。

Boil spaghetti al dente in plenty of sea salted boiling water.

ゆで上がりの約2分前に菜の花を加えてゆでる。

Add canola about 2 minutes before spaghetti is done.

スパゲティがゆで上がったら、菜の花ごとざるで水分をきって7に移す。

Once spaghetti is boiled, drain it and canola with a strainer. Move them to 7.

具材とスパゲティがからまるように混ぜ、薄口醤油、塩、コショウで味つけする。

Mix ingredients and spaghetti to blend in, and season with light soy sauce, salt and pepper.

タラコといかの香味スパゲティ
Spaghetti with cod roe and squid flavor

Required time
所要時間
30分
30 minutes

材料（2人分）

スパゲティ	160g
するめいか	1/2杯（80g）
オクラ	4本（30g）
粗塩	適量
塩、コショウ	各適量
たらこの香味だれの材料	
たらこ	1～2腹（60g）
ねぎ	1/2本（50g）
塩わかめ	15g
青じそ	3枚
濃口醤油	大さじ1
バター	15g
サラダ油	大さじ1

Ingredients (for 2 people)

160g spaghetti
1/2 squid (80g)
4 okra (30g)
some sea salt
some salt and pepper
Ingredients for cod roe flavored sauce
1-2 cod roe (60g)
1/2 scallion (50g)
15g salted wakame seaweed
3 green perilla
1 Tbsp dark soy sauce
15g butter
1 Tbsp cooking oil

オクラのガクの部分を薄くむいて塩でこすり、産毛を取ってから洗う。

Peel calyx of okra thinly and scrub with salt to remove fuzz, then wash.

8mm幅にななめ切りにする。

Cut it diagonally in 8mm width.

ねぎは開いて白い部分をせん切りにしたあと、水にさらす。

Julienne the cut opened white parts of scallion and immerse in water.

青じそは丸めてせん切りにし、水にさらす。

Julienne rolled green perilla and immerse in water.

いかは胴体にななめに細かい切りこみを入れてから、8mm幅に切る。

Make fine incisions diagonally in squid body and cut into 8mm width.

たらこは薄皮に切りこみを入れて開き、押し出すように卵を出す。

Make an incision in the membrane of the cod roe and open, then squeeze out roe.

ボウルに水で戻してざく切りにしたわかめ、ねぎ、6、バター、濃口醤油を入れる。

Add reconstituted and coarsely cut wakame seaweed, scallion, 6, butter and dark soy sauce to a bowl.

フライパンでサラダ油を煙が出るまで熱し、7にジュンと入れる。全体をざっと混ぜる。

Heat cooking oil in a frying pan until it begins to smoke, then pour it in 7 and mix together.

粗塩をとかしたたっぷりの湯でスパゲティをゆでる。

Boil spaghetti in plenty of sea salted boiling water.

ゆで上がりの約1分前にオクラ、いかを加えてゆでる。

Add okra and squid one minute before spaghetti is done.

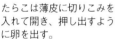

ゆで上がったら水気をきり、8と和える。塩、コショウで味つけをして盛りつけたら、青じそを散らす。

When it's boiled, drain water and dress it with 8. Season with salt and pepper, and sprinkle green parilla before serving.

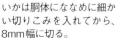

洋風＆中華風のおかず

Western and chinese dishes

餃子

Gyoza

For the best results,
try to make handmade
wrappers.

おいしく作りたいなら
手作りの皮に
挑戦しましょう

料理のポイント
Cooking tips

1 野菜の水分を絞る。
Squeeze out vegetable liquid.

2 軽く熱したフライパンに並べる。
Place in a lightly heated frying pan.

3 フライパンの底を冷やすとはがれやすい。
It is easier to remove once the base of a
frying pan has cooled.

158

材料（2人分）

豚ひき肉	················	100g
キャベツ	············	中2枚（100g）
にら	················	15g
ねぎ	················	20g
しょうが	············	1/4かけ
にんにく	············	1/4かけ
Ⓐ ┌塩	············	小さじ2/3
├ごま油	············	小さじ2/3
├酒	············	小さじ2/3
└濃口醤油	············	小さじ1
サラダ油	············	大さじ1
水	············	100cc
片栗粉	············	小さじ1/2
餃子の皮（大）	············	16枚
（手作りする場合はP.163参照）		

しょうが風味の酢醤油の材料

Ⓑ ┌酢	············	小さじ2
└濃口醤油	············	大さじ2
しょうがの薄切り	············	2枚
ねぎ（白い部分）	············	12g
サラダ油	············	小さじ2

ごまだれの材料

煎りごま	············	大さじ1
ラー油	············	小さじ1
芝麻醤、酢	············	各小さじ2
濃口醤油	············	大さじ2

Ingredients (for 2 people)

- 100g minced pork
- 2 medium leaves cabbage (100g)
- 15g chinese chive
- 20g scallion
- 1/4 piece ginger
- 1/4 piece garlic
- Ⓐ ┌ 2/3 tsp salt
- ├ 2/3 tsp sesame oil
- ├ 2/3 tsp sake
- └ 1 tsp dark soy sauce
- 1 Tbsp cooking oil
- 100cc water
- 1/2 tsp starch
- 16 dumpling wrappers (large)
- (see P.163 for handmade wrappers)

Ingredients for ginger flavored soy vinegar

- Ⓑ ┌ 2 tsp vinegar
- └ 2 Tbsp dark soy sauce
- 2 thin slices ginger
- 12g scallion (white part)
- 2 tsp cooking oil

Ingredients for sesame sauce

- 1 Tbsp toasted sesame seeds
- 1 tsp chilli oil
- 2 tsp Chinese sesame paste and vinegar
- 2 Tbsp dark soy sauce

1

キャベツ、にら、ねぎは粗みじん切りにする。

Chop cabbage, chinese chive and scallion.

2

しょうが、にんにくは細かくみじん切りする。

Finely chop ginger and garlic.

3

キャベツに塩少々（分量外）をまぶす。

Sprinkle some salt (extra) on the cabbage.

4

そのまま約15分おいて水分を出す。さらしに包み、ぎゅっと絞る。

Leave it for about 15 minutes to extract liquid. Wrap it with a bleached cloth and squeeze.

ボウルにひき肉を入れ、Ⓐを加える。

Put minced pork in a bowl and add Ⓐ.

ひき肉に調味料を吸収させるよう、手でよく練り合わせる。

Knead with hands thoroughly so that the minced pork will fully absorb seasoning.

下味がついたら、キャベツ、にら、ねぎ、しょうが、にんにくを加える。

Once it's marinated, add cabbage, chinese chive, scallion, ginger and garlic.

手で全体を混ぜ合わせる。時間があれば冷蔵庫でひと晩寝かす。

Mix with hands. If possible, let it stand overnight in the fridge.

あんをバットに広げて16等分にし、皮の数と中身の量を均一にする。

Spread filling in a tray and divide into 16, match the number of wrappers to the fillings.

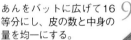

へらであんを取って皮の中央にのせ、水を周囲にぬる。

Take filling with a spatula and place it in the center of the wrapper, wet the edges with water.

手前の皮1/3をあんにかぶせる。

Cover the filling with 1/3 of the near side wrapper.

カーブを作るように右手前からひだを作り、両面をはり合わせていく。

Begin from the right front side and make pleats in a curve to form a seal.

包んだものから、打ち粉（強力粉［分量外］）をした板にのせる。

Place each dumpling on a floured (bread flour [extra]) board.

ラップを上にかぶせて並べ、乾燥を防ぐ。

To prevent them from becoming dry, cover with clinging wrap.

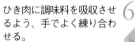
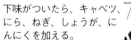
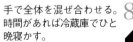

しょうが風味の酢醤油を作る。ねぎとしょうがをせん切りにする。

Make ginger flavored soy vinegar. Julienne scallion and ginger.

Ⓑに15を加え、煙が出るまで熱したサラダ油をかける。

Add 15 in Ⓑ, and pour in cooking oil heated until it begins to smoke.

ごまだれを作る。煎りごまをすり鉢ですり、芝麻醤、ラー油を加えすり合わせる。

Make sesame sauce. Grind sesame seeds with a mortar, then add Chinese sesame paste and chilli oil, and grind to mix.

17をすりこ木で混ぜながら、酢と濃口醤油を加える。

Mix 17 with a wooden pestle adding vinegar and dark soy sauce.

フライパンを軽く熱し、サラダ油を入れて餃子を並べる。

Heat a frying pan lightly, add cooking oil and place dumplings.

皮がはりついて取れない
The wrappers stick and do not come apart.

手作りした皮は、そのまま放っておくと皮同士がくっつくので、たっぷり打ち粉をしましょう。皮は乾きやすいので、固く絞ったふきんかラップを必ず上からかぶせます。

Handmade wrappers will stick together if left as they are, so cover them with plenty of bread flour. Wrappers will dry out easily, so cover them with a tightly squeezed wet cloth or clinging wrap.

餃子の皮からあんがはみ出る
Fillings come out from the wrapper.

皮に包むとき、欲ばってたくさんあんを入れるとうまく包めません。すき間があるとそこから具や肉汁が逃げてしまいます。見栄えが多少悪くても、あんを完全に包みこみましょう。

If there is too much filling, it cannot be wrapped correctly. If there is any gap, fillings and meat juice will ooze out from there. Fillings should be wrapped completely even the shape is not so good.

洋風＆中華風のおかず

Western and chinese dishes

フライパンの火加減は、置いたときに軽くジュンと音がするくらいで。

The time when the dumplings make a sizzling noise in a frying pan is good at the correct temperature.

水と片栗粉を合わせたものを回し入れる。⦅水⦆底にパリッとした薄膜ができておいしい。

21

Pour mixture of water and starch in spiral motion. **P**It creates a tasty crispy, thin skin on the bottom.

ふたをして約7分、中火で蒸し焼きする。

22

Cover with a lid for about 7 minutes, steam and roast at medium heat.

ふたを外し、約3分焼いて水分を完全にとばす。

23

Remove the lid and cook for about 3 minutes to completely cook off liquids.

餃子の焼き面がこんがりして水気がなくなったら火からおろす。

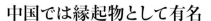

24

Remove from the heat when the dumpling's cooked surface is crispy brown and no liquid is left.

ぬれぶきんの上に、フライパンを約10秒のせると餃子がはがれやすくなる。

25

Place the frying pan on a wet cloth for about 10 seconds to ensure easy removal of dumplings.

フライ返しで餃子を逆さにして器に盛る。しょうが風味の酢醤油やごまだれでいただく。

26

Place dumplings upside down on a plate using a spatula. Serve with ginger flavored soy vinegar or sesame sauce.

水餃子にする場合は、たっぷりの湯を沸かし、沸騰したらひとつずつ餃子を落とす。

27

For boiled dumplings, heat plenty of water and drop in dumplings one by one, once it has boiled.

餃子が躍るくらいの温度を保ちながら約5分ゆでる。

28

Boil for about 5 minutes maintaining the temperature that keeps dumplings dancing.

中国では縁起物として有名

They are famously considered a lucky food in China.

日本で餃子といえば焼き餃子が主流ですが、本場である中国北方では水餃子がポピュラーです。子を授かることを意味する「交子（ヂャオヅ）」と発音が同じこと、明・清時代のお金と形が似ていることなどから、縁起物として春節に食べられています。

When it comes to gyoza dumplings, baked dumplings are the main stream in Japan, but boiled dumplings are the most popular type in the place of origin, the northern part of China. It is served during the Chinese new year as a lucky food, because the word 'dumpling' has a similar pronunciation as [交子jiaozi] meaning to have a child, also the shape resembles the money of the Ming/Qing era.

餃子の皮の作り方
How to make dumpling wrappers

材料（2人分）

強力粉	80g
薄力粉	40g
熱湯	75cc
塩	小さじ1/5

Ingredients (for 2 people)

80g bread flour
40g flour
75cc boiled water
1/5 tsp salt

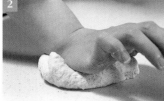

粉をボウルにふるい、塩、熱湯を加えてフォークで混ぜる。台にのせて練り、なめらかになったらラップに包み室温で約15分ねかせる。

Sift flour in a bowl, and add salt and boiling water, mix with a fork. Put the dough on a board and knead, wrap with clinging wrap once it is smooth, and let it stand at room temperature for about 15 minutes.

ラップを外して打ち粉（強力粉［分量外］）をした台にのせ、生地を両手で押さえて転がしながら棒状にのばし、16等分にカットする。

Remove the clinging wrap and put it on a board covered with flour (bread flour[extra]) and roll it into a bar shape pressing with both hands, cut it into 16 pieces.

カットした断面を上にむけ、打ち粉をした台にのせて手で押さえてつぶす。

Place on the flour covered board with cut surface up, and press it flat using your hand.

生地を左手で回転させながら、右手で麺棒を転がし、中央が厚くなるよう約8cmの円形に薄くのばす。

Roll out the dough with a rolling pin on right hand, and turn it around with left hand to make thin 8cm diameter circles with some thickness to the center.

こんな包み方もあり！
These ways of wrapping are good too !

① 半分に折って皮をはり合わせる。② 両端をつまみ、中央で合わせ、形を整える。

① Fold in half and stick skin together. ②Pinch together both side edges, bring them to meet in the middle, and shape it.

①あんを中心に指でつまんで十字に皮を立てる。②皮同士をはり合わせる。

① Stand the wrapper up in cross shape with fillings in the center, ②then stick the skin together.

Golden fried rice
with a shine of each grain.

五目チャーハン

Gomoku chāhan

ごはんひと粒ひと粒が
光り輝く
黄金チャーハン

料理のポイント
Cooking tips

1 ごはんを卵と油でコーティング。
Coat rice with eggs and oil.

2 ごはんを鍋に広げて焼く。
Saute rice spreading in a wok.

3 野菜は仕上げ直前に加える。
Add vegetables right before finishing.

Time required
所要時間
30分
30 minutes

材料（2人分）

ごはん（硬めの温かいもの）	400g
ハム	6枚（60g）
えび	2尾（30g）
レタス	大1枚（13g）
ねぎ	35g
卵	2個
Ⓐ┌ 卵白	小さじ1/2
│ 片栗粉	大さじ1/2
└ 塩	適量
塩、コショウ	各適量
酒	小さじ1
濃口醤油	小さじ1
ごま油	小さじ1
サラダ油	大さじ1

Ingredients (for 2 people)

400g cooked rice (warm hardish)
6 slices ham (60g)
2 prawns (30g)
1 large leaf lettuce (13g)
35g scallion
2 eggs
Ⓐ ┌ 1/2 tsp the white of an egg
│ 1/2 Tbsp starch
└ some salt
some salt and pepper
1 tsp sake
1 tsp dark soy sauce
1 tsp sesame oil
1 Tbsp cooking oil

レタスは5mm角に切る。

Cut lettuce into 5mm squarcs.

1

2

ねぎは5mm角に切る。はじめに縦に切れ目を入れて、端から切っていく。

Cut scallion into 5mm squares. Make the first incision vertically then cut from the edge.

3

ハムも5mm角に切る。

Cut ham into 5mm squares.

4

えびの2～3節目に竹串をさす。左右に動かしつつ上にひっぱり、背わたを抜く。

Pierce a bamboo skewer in 2nd -3rd segment of the prawns body. Pull upwards moving sideways and devein.

5

えびの殻を足のほうからむく。尾は、つけ根をつまみながらひっぱり、殻のみを取る。

Remove prawn shell from the leg side. Remove tail's shell pinching to pull base of the tail.

6

きれいにむけたら、厚みと幅を半分に切る。

Once shelled, cut them in half both in thickness and width.

切ったえびは、ほかの具材
と大きさを合わせて、さら
に5mm角に切る。

Cut the prawns into
5mm pieces adjusting to
match the size of other
ingredients.

中華鍋を強火にかけてサラ
ダ油を入れる。鍋を回して
全体になじませ、煙が出る
まで熱する。

Put a wok on high heat
and add cooking oil.
Swirl to coat the pan
and heat until it begins
to smoke.

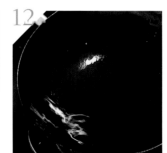

きざんだえびを器に入れ、
Ⓐを加える。

Put the cut prawns in a
bowl and add Ⓐ.

煙が上がってきたら、強め
の中火にして、10のとき
卵を一気に流し入れる。

Once it starts smoking,
turn the heat down to
medium-high and add
all the beaten egg from
10.

液体を吸わせるように混ぜ
ると、えびの歯ごたえがよ
くなる。

Mix and let it absorb the
seasoning liquid to ten-
derize.

卵が半熟のうちにごはんを
加え、卵でひと粒ひと粒を
コーティングするように炒
める。

Add rice while egg is
undercooked, and stir
fry to coat each grain of
rice with the beaten
egg.

卵をボウルに割り入れ、菜
箸でときほぐす。

Break eggs in a bowl
and beat with cooking
chopsticks.

ざっと炒めたら中華鍋の上
で大きく広げ、じっくり焼
きつける。

Once it's sauteed,
spread it in the wok to
cook thoroughly.

硬めに炊いた温かいごはん
を用意する。冷めていたら
電子レンジで約1分温める。

Prepare warm, hard
cooked rice. If it is cold,
warm it up in a micro-
wave for about 1 min-
ute.

水分がとんできたら、塩と
コショウをふりかけ、ざっ
くり炒めて広げる。

Cook down the liquid,
sprinkle salt and pepper
and stir fry it.

続いて、きざんだハムとえびをごはんに加え、大きく混ぜて広げ、水分をさらに蒸発させる。

Add chopped ham and prawns to rice, and mix roughly to spread and cook down any liquid.

中華鍋を前後に動かし、中身を大きく回転させながら、へらで切るように混ぜる。

Move the wok to and fro and toss the ingredients, mix by cutting in with a spatula.

えびが赤く色づいたら、ねぎとレタスを入れる。●歯ごたえが残るよう、野菜は仕上げ直前に加える。

Once the prawns have turned red, add scallion and lettuce. ●Add vegetables just before finishing so that they maintain texture.

鍋肌から酒をすべらすように回し入れる。

Smoothly pour the sake onto the surface of the wok.

醤油を鍋肌から回し入れる。●鍋の縁から流すと全体から香りが立ちのぼる。

Pour soy sauce around the surface of the wok. ●Pouring on the edge of the wok will help to fully bring out the aroma.

失敗しないために **To avoid a failure**

できあがりがべちゃっとした

It ends up too gooey.

ごはんをやわらかく炊いたのが原因。チャーハンに使うごはんは硬めに炊きます。また広げて水分を蒸発させると、あとから液体や水分の多い野菜を入れてもべたっとなりません。

This is a result of cooking rice with too much water. Rice should be cooked hard for fried rice. If rice is spread in a wok to let the water dry off, it will not be sticky even when liquid or watery vegetables are added later on.

ごはんがくっついてしまう

The rice sticks together.

大量のごはんを一度に中華鍋で炒めると、水分がなかなかとばないうちに焦げてしまいます。1回に2人分が限度です。たくさん作る場合は分けて作ってください。

When a large amount of rice is stir fried in a wok at one time, it gets burnt before the water is cooked off. Cook a serving for two at a time max. When you need to cook for more, cook in several batches.

鍋を前後にゆすって大きく混ぜ、香りづけのごま油を鍋肌からたらして、さっと混ぜたら火を止める。

Rock the wok to and fro and mix roughly, drip sesame oil in from the surface of the wok and stir quickly, turn off the heat.

洋風＆中華風のおかず

Western and chinese dishes

丸鶏の下ごしらえに挑戦②
LET'S TRY TO DRESS A WHOLE CHICKEN ②

丸鶏は、もも肉、胸肉、手羽先の3つに分けて料理に使います。硬い骨があるので出刃包丁を使っておろしましょう。途中で取り除く軟骨やがらは、だしに使うことができます。

For cooking, a whole chicken is divided into legs, breast and wing tips. You need"Deba knife"to cut bones. Gristles and bones you remove can be used for making soup stock.

1
手羽を切り、関節から手羽先と手羽元に分ける。
Cut wings out and divide it into wing tips and wing sticks at joint.

5
首から両親指を差し込み、背側と胸側に分ける。
Insert both thumbs in neck and divide it into back and breast.

2
両もものつけ根に切り込みを入れ、後ろに曲げて折る。
Cut in both leg bases, bend them backward and break.

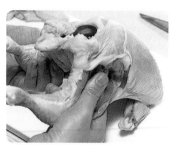

6
肉からはみ出た脂、内側の内臓や白い脂を取り除く。
Remove clutterd fat, gut and white fat.

3
背を上にして置き、十字の切込みを入れる。
Place chicken on its back and make a cross-shaped cut.

7
包丁の背の上から押し、胸の骨に沿って半分に切る。
Cut it into halves along with breast bone by pushing the kitchen knife spine.

4
もものつけ根にある筋を切る。ももを引っ張って取る。
Cut gristles at leg bases and take legs off by pulling them.

8
胴体をぶつ切りにし、4のもも肉も食べやすい大きさに切る。
Cut body and legs into bite-sized pieces.

第4章
Part 4

サブになるおかず
Side dishes

If you learn how to cook these two typical omelet, you can do anything !

代表的なふたつの
作り方を覚えれば
怖いものなし！

卵焼き2種

Tamagoyaki

料理のポイント
Cooking tips

1 半熟状態で仕上げ、余熱で火を通す。
Make half-cooked omelet and
cook through with residual heat.

2 卵焼き器は十分に熱してから使う。
Ensure the omelet pan heated enough.

3 巻きすで形を整える。
Shape it with a bamboo mat.

関東風卵焼き
Kanto style omelet

Time required
所要時間
20分
20 minutes

材料（2人分）

卵	4個
みりん	大さじ1
砂糖	大さじ3
薄口醤油	小さじ1
塩	ひとつまみ
サラダ油	適量

※大根の薄切りを甘酢に漬けたものを添えてもよい。

Ingredients (for 2 people)

4 eggs
1 Tbsp mirin
3 Tbsp sugar
1 tsp light soy sauce
pinch of salt
some cooking oil
※It can be served with thinly sliced Japanese radish pickled in sweet vinegar

ときほぐした卵にみりん、砂糖、薄口醤油、塩を入れて混ぜ合わせる。

Add and mix mirin, sugar, light soy sauce and salt with the beaten egg.

1

卵液をざるでこす。

Sift egg mixture with a strainer.

2

3

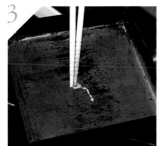

熱した卵焼き器にサラダ油をぬる。卵を少し落とし、軽くジュンと音がするくらいの温度にする。

Grease heated omelet pan with cooking oil. Drip in a little bit of egg and adjust the temperature to make a sizzling sound.

4

1/4量の卵液を流し入れ、全体の厚みが均一になるように広げる。

Pour in a 1/4 of egg mixture and spread to even the thickness.

5

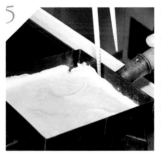

表面にぷくぷくと気泡が現れ、動かなくなったら、菜箸で四隅を切る。

When bubbles begining to appear on the surface and egg mixture is not runny, then cut the corners with cooking chopsticks.

6

半熟になったら菜箸で軽く支え、鍋の反動を使い手前に向かって卵を折りたたむ。

Once it's half-cooked, hold it lightly with cooking chopsticks and fold the egg towards the near side, using a tossing movement of the pan.

7

空いた部分にサラダ油をひく。卵を奥に移動させ、手前側にもサラダ油をひく。

Grease the empty space with cooking oil. Move the egg to the far side and grease the near side with cooking oil.

サブになるおかず

Side dishes

171

手前に残りの卵液の1/3量を流す。7の手前を持ち上げ、全体に卵液を広げる。

Pour 1/3 of the remaining egg mixture into the near side. Lift up the near side of 7 and spread egg mixture over all the surface.

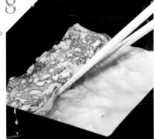

8を2回繰り返す。表面が乾いてから巻くとくっつかない。

Repeat 8 twice. If the surface of the omelet is too dry, it will not stick together.

全部巻きこんだら、空いたところにサラダ油をひき、両面にこんがり焼き色をつける。

Once all the egg mixture is rolled, grease the empty space once more and brown both sides.

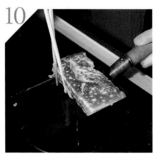

卵がやわらかい半生状態で、卵焼き器から直接巻きすにのせる。

Place the omelet on a bamboo mat from the pan, while it is still soft and half-cooked.

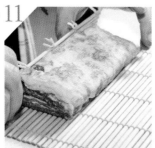

巻きすで巻き、そのまましっかりと押さえて、四角く形を整える。

Wrap with a bamboo mat and press hard over the mat into a rectangular shape.

だし巻き卵
Soup stock flavor omelet

Time required
所要時間
20分
20 minutes

材料（2人分）

卵	3個
薄口醤油	小さじ1
みりん	小さじ1
塩	ひとつまみ
だし汁	75cc
サラダ油	適量

※大根をおろして水気を絞り、濃口醤油をかけたものを添えてもよい。

Ingredients (for 2 people)

3 eggs
1 tsp light soy sauce
1 tsp mirin
pinch of salt
75cc soup stock
some cooking oil
※It can be served with grated and squeezed Japanese radish dressed with dark soy sauce.

ボウルに卵を割り入れ、菜箸でよくときほぐす。

Break eggs into a bowl and beat with cooking chopsticks.

卵に薄口醤油、みりん、塩、だし汁を入れて混ぜ合わせる。

Add light soy sauce, mirin, salt and soup stock to the beaten egg, and mix.

ざるで卵液をこす。

Sift egg mixture with a strainer.

卵焼き器にサラダ油をひく。少し卵を落とし、ジュンと音がするまで温める。

Grease the omelet pan with cooking oil. Drip in a little bit of egg and adjust the temperature to make a sizzling sound.

1/4量の卵液を全体に広げ、表面がぷくぷくしたら手前に向かい反動を使って巻く。

Pour in a 1/4 of egg mixture and spread entirely. When the surface bubbles, roll it toward the near side, using a tossing movement of the pan.

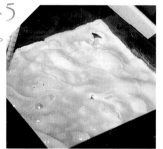

奥に油をひき、焼いた卵を奥に移動させ、空いた手前側にも油をひく。

Grease the far side and move the egg there, then grease the near side with cooking oil.

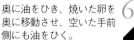

さらに1/4量の卵液を流し、焼いた卵を持ち上げて卵焼き器全体に広げる。

Pour in another 1/4 of egg mixture, and lift up the omelet to spread egg mixture over all the surface.

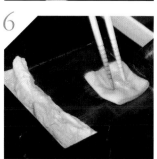

流した卵が半熟になったら巻く。これを3回繰り返す。

Once egg mixture is half-cooked, roll it. Repeat this 3 times.

サラダ油をひき、表面を少し焼く。卵焼き器の端に寄せて形を整える。

Grease with cooking oil and cook surface lightly. Move it to the edge of the omelet pan and shape it.

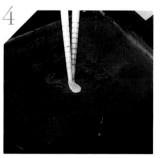

熱いうちに卵焼き器から直接巻きすに取り出す。

Place the omelet on a bamboo mat directly from the pan, while it is hot.

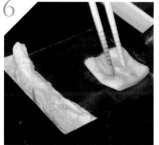

さっと四角く形を整える。

Quickly shape it into a rectangle.

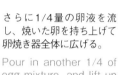

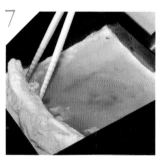

巻きすで巻き、しっかりと手で押さえ、2～3分おく。

Wrap with a bamboo mat and press with hands firmly, and leave it for a few minutes.

サブになるおかず

Side dishes

173

Hijiki no nimono

Presenting a seaweed recipe
containing plenty of
fiber and minerals.

ひじきの煮物

食物繊維と
ミネラル分が豊富な
海藻料理の代表選手

**Time required
所要時間
60分
60 minutes**

材料（2人分）

長ひじきまたは芽ひじき（乾燥）	15g
鶏むね肉	60g
油揚げ	1枚
にんじん	10g
絹さや	7枚
サラダ油	大さじ1
Ⓐ 酒、みりん	各大さじ1/2
Ⓑ ┌ 濃口醤油、砂糖	各大さじ1·1/2
└ だし汁	100cc

Ingredients (for 2 people)

15g dried hijiki seaweed
60g chicken breast
1 deep-fried bean curd
10g carrot
7 snow peas
1 Tbsp cooking oil
Ⓐ 1/2 Tbsp sake and mirin
Ⓑ 1·1/2 Tbsp dark soy sauce and sugar
  100cc soup stock

174

料理のポイント
Cooking tips

1 ひじきは手でつぶれる程度に戻す。
Reconstitute hijiki seaweed until it is soft enough to be squashed by hand.

2 ひじきはたっぷりの水で戻す。
Reconstitute hijiki seaweed with plenty of water.

ひじきは軽く洗ったあと、たっぷりの水に約30分浸して戻す。

After washing hijiki, soak it in plenty of water for about 30 minutes.

ひじきが戻ったらざるにあげる。流水で洗い、砂などの汚れを落とし、軽く絞る。

Once hijiki is reconstituted, drain in a colander. Wash it with running water and clean off dirt such as sand, then squeeze lightly.

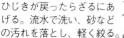

絹さやの筋を取り、大きければななめ半分に切る。約2分塩ゆでしてざるにあげ、冷ます。

Remove strings from snow peas and if large, cut them in half. Boil them in salted water for about 2 minutes, drain in a colander and allow to cool.

油揚げを約10秒ゆで、ざるにあげる。粗熱が取れたら、水分を取り5mm幅の短冊切りにする。

Boil a deep-fried bean curd for about 10 seconds and drain in a colander. Once it cooled a little, remove liquid and cut it into 5mm width rectangles.

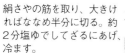

鍋にサラダ油を熱し、2cm角に切った鶏肉を中火で焼く。

Heat cooking oil in a saucepan, add 2cm chicken cubes and cook at medium heat.

鶏肉が白っぽくなったら、短冊切りにしたにんじんを加える。にんじんが透き通ってきたら油揚げを加える。

Once chicken turns white, add carrots cut into rectangles. Add the deep-fried bean curd, once the carrots have turned clear.

しんなりしてきたら、十分に水気をきったひじきを加え、炒め合わせる。

Once tenderized, add well drained hijiki and saute to mix.

ひじきの香りが出てきたら、Ⓐを加えて混ぜ、アルコール分がとぶまで炒める。

When hijiki is aromatic, add Ⓐ and mix, saute until the alcohol is cooked out.

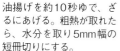

Ⓑを加え、落としぶたをして汁気がなくなるまで煮つめる。器に盛り、絹さやを飾る。

Add Ⓑ and cover with a drop-lid. Simmer till sauce has cooked down completely. Serve it on a plate and decorate with snow peas.

サブになるおかず

Side dishes

Crunchy distinctive texture is
the most important.
The time of reconstitution is the tip.

切り干し大根の煮物

Kiriboshidaikon no nimono

コリコリとした
独特の食感が命
戻し時間がポイントです

Time required
所要時間
40分
40 minutes

材料（2人分）

切り干し大根	……………………	30g
干ししいたけ	……………………	2個
にんじん	……………………	50g
油揚げ	……………………	1/2枚
Ⓐ ┌ だし汁	……………………	300cc
│ みりん、砂糖	……………………	各大さじ1
└ 濃口醤油	……………………	大さじ1・1/2
サラダ油	……………………	小さじ2

Ingredients (for 2 people)

30g dried shredded Japanese radish
2 dried shiitake mushrooms
50g carrot
1/2 deep-fried bean curd
Ⓐ ┌ 300cc soup stock
　 │ 1 Tbsp mirin and sugar
　 └ 1・1/2 dark soy sauce
2 tsp cooking oil

料理のポイント
Cooking tips

1 煮汁が残る程度に煮つめる。
   Cook down until some sauce is left.

2 煮すぎず程よい食感を残す。
   Do not overcook to keep some texture.

干ししいたけは軸を下にして水に浸し、半日おく。

Soak dried shiitake mushrooms in water with stem side to the bottom.

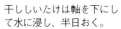

干ししいたけが戻ったら、ぎゅっと絞り、軸を落として5mm幅に切る。

Squeeze reconstituted shiitake mushrooms and cut off stems, and cut into 5mm width.

切り干し大根はさっと洗ってから、たっぷりの水に約10分浸して戻す。

After roughly washing, soak dried shredded Japanese radish in plenty of water for 10 minutes.

切り干し大根が戻ったらざるにあげ、両手でぎゅっと絞り、余分な水分をきる。

Once dried shredded Japanese radish is reconstituted, drain in a colander and squeeze it with both hands to remove excess water.

油揚げは約10秒ゆで、水気をきる。粗熱が取れたら、半分に切って5mm幅に切る。

Boil a deep-fried bean curd for about 10 seconds and drain. Once it's cooled a little, cut in half and cut into 5mm width.

にんじんも5mm幅の短冊切りにする。

Cut carrot into 5mm width rectangles.

鍋にサラダ油を熱し、2、4、6を中火で炒める。油分が少なくなったら具をよけて油（分量外）を足す。

Heat cooking oil in a saucepan and saute 2,4 and 6 at medium heat. If oil becomes too little, move the ingredients aside and add extra oil.

具材全体に火が通ったら、5を加えて炒め合わせる。Ⓐを注いで、沸騰するまで強火で煮る。

Once all the ingredients are cooked, add 5 and saute. Pour Ⓐ and simmer until it's boiled at high heat.

沸騰したら弱火にし、アクをすくいながら、煮汁が1/5量になるまで約15分煮る。

When boiled, reduce the heat to low. Simmer for about 15 minutes until cooking sauce is reduced to 1/5, while skimming the scum.

サブになるおかず

Side dishes

Simple, convenient and quick
for when you need another dish.

ほうれん草の
おひたし

Hourensou no ohitashi

もう1品欲しいときに
簡単で便利な
クイックメニュー

Time required
所要時間
15分
15 minutes

材料（2人分）

ほうれん草 ………………… 1/2束（100g）
Ⓐ ┌ 濃口醤油、だし汁 ………… 各大さじ1
　 └ 酒 ……………………… 大さじ1/2
削り節 …………………………… 適量

Ingredients （for 2 people）

1/2 batch spinach (100g)
Ⓐ ┌ 1 Tbsp dark soy sauce
　 │ and soup stock
　 └ 1/2 Tbsp sake
some shavings of dried bonito

料理のポイント
Cooking tips

1 ほうれん草はたっぷりの湯でゆでる。
  Boil spinach with plenty of water.

2 巻きすを使うと絞りやすい。
  It's easy to squeeze with a bamboo mat.

ほうれん草を盆ざるにあげ、すぐにうちわであおいで冷ます。

Drain spinach in a strainer tray and fan to lt cool down.

ほうれん草は調理前に水にさらしてシャキッとさせる。

Soak spinach in water before cooking to freshen.

1

Ⓐを混ぜ、かけだしを作る。

Mix Ⓐ and make soup stock sauce.

6

根元から軸に十字の切りこみを入れ、根元を中心に水の中でふり洗いする。

Make cross incision from the root to stem. Immerse in water and shake it to wash concentrating on the roots.

2

ほうれん草が完全に冷めたら巻きすで包む。

Once spinach has completely cooled down, wrap it with a bamboo mat.

7

たっぷりの湯で塩ゆでする。塩（分量外）は湯の1％。

Boil in plenty of salted water. Salt（extra）should be 1% of water.

3
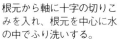

軸から葉に向かって全体をぎゅっと押さえて水気をきる。

Press whole firmly from stems to leaves to squeeze out water.

8

軸を入れて約10秒たったら全体を入れる。約1分して軸がやわらかくなったらゆであがり。

Immerse stem first for about 10 seconds, then put in the rest. After about 1 minute and when the stems are soft, it is cooked.

4

軸に切り目を入れて株を分け、3cm長さに切る。器に盛って6をかけ、削り節を飾る。

Cut stems to divide the batch and cut into 3cm length. Serve on a plate, pour 6 on top and sprinkle with shavings of dried bonito.

9

さや いんげんに
ごまの香ばしさが
からみます

Savaingen no gomaae

さやいんげんの
ごま和え

The string beans are
dressed with the aroma of sesame seeds.

材料（2人分）

さやいんげん	……………………	100g
白ごま	……………………	大さじ4
Ⓐ 濃口醤油	……………………	大さじ2
砂糖、みりん、だし汁	………	各大さじ1

Ingredients (for 2 people)

100g string beans
4 Tbsp white sesame seeds
Ⓐ 2 Tbsp dark soy sauce
1 Tbsp sugar, mirin
and soup stock

料理のポイント
Cooking tips

1 たっぷりの湯でゆでる。
  Boil with plenty of water.

2 ゆでたさやいんげんを水に落とさない。
  Do not drop boiled string beans in water.

さやいんげんは先端部分をつまみ、そのままひきおろして筋を取る。

Pinch the tip of the string beans and strip down the strings.

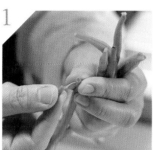

たっぷりの湯を沸かし、塩を1％（分量外）加えて、約4分ゆでる。

Boil plenty of water with 1% salt (extra) and cook them for about 4 minutes.

1本食べてみて、やわらかければ盆ざるにあげ、あおいで冷ます。ななめに2等分する。

Eat one and if it is soft, take them out on a strainer tray and fan to cool. Cut diagonally into halves.

別の鍋に白ごまを入れて強火にかける。

Put white sesame seeds in another saucepan on high heat.

5

鍋が熱くなったら弱めの中火にして、鍋を回しながらじっくり煎り、香ばしくする。

Turn the heat down to low-medium, once the pan is getting hot. Roast the seeds to bring out the aroma by swirling around the pan.

6

白ごまをすり鉢に移し、すりこ木でする。すり鉢の下に絞ったぬれぶきんを置くとすべりにくい。

Put white sesame seeds in a mortar and grind with a pestle. Place a wet cloth underneath the mortar to stop moving.

7

ごまの香りが出たら、Ⓐを入れて、すりこ木で混ぜる。さやいんげんを加え、和える。

Once sesame seeds are aromatic, add Ⓐ in and mix with a pestle. Add string beans and toss.

ごまのすり方
How to grind sesame seeds

ごまをするとき、すりこ木を両手で握ると、先端が鉢の中ですべってすれません。片方の手のひらをすりこ木の上に置き、そこを支点としてもう一方の手で下のほうを回すように動かしましょう。力を入れなくても均等にすることができます。

If you use both hands to hold a pestle, when grinding sesame seeds, the tip of a pestle will slip. Place a palm on top of the pestle as a support, and use the other hand to swirl the lower part. This enables even grinding without effort.

サブになるおかず

Side dishes

Kinpiragobo

きんぴらごぼう

Crispy burdock root simmered sweet and hot is best in a supporting role for rice.

しゃきしゃきごぼうを
甘辛く炒め煮した
ごはんによく合う名脇役

材料 (2人分)

ごぼう ······························	70g
にんじん ····························	10g
豚ロース肉 ·························	15g
赤唐辛子·························	1/4本
サラダ油 ····························	大さじ1
ごま油 ······························	小さじ1
Ⓐ みりん ·························	大さじ1/4
酒、薄口醤油、砂糖 ······	各大さじ1/2

Ingredients (for 2 people)

70g burdock
10g carrot
15g pork loin
1/4 chilli
1 Tbsp cooking oil
1 tsp sesame oil
Ⓐ 1/4 Tbsp mirin
1/2 Tbsp sake, light soy sauce and sugar

料理のポイント
Cooking tips

1 ごぼうは煮ずに、炒めて歯ごたえを残す。
Saute but don't simmer burdock to leave some texture.

2 最後にごま油で香りづけを。
Give it a flavor with sesame oil to finish.

豚肉は5mm幅の棒状に切る。

Cut pork into 5mm wide sticks.

赤唐辛子は種を取り、約10分水に浸してやわらかくする。

Remove seeds from chilli and immerse in water for about 10 minutes to soften.

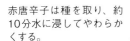

赤唐辛子がやわらかくなったら、2mm幅の輪切りにする。

Once chilli is soft, cut into 2mm wide rings.

ごぼうは泥つきの場合はたわしで洗う。細切りにして切ったはしから、酢水（分量外）につけてアクを抜く。

Wash burdock with a scrubber if it's muddy. Cut in thin strips and soak in water with vinegar (extra) to refine.

にんじんは細切りにする。ごぼうと大きさを合わせるように切る。

Cut carrot into thin strips. Match the size with burdock.

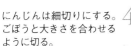

鍋にサラダ油を熱し、ごぼうとにんじんを炒める。透き通ってきたら豚肉を加えて炒める。

Heat cooking oil in a pan, and saute burdock and carrot. Once the color is clear, add pork and saute.

鍋底が焦げそうになったら、少量の水で焦げを落とす。7〜8分炒め、野菜に火が通ったらⒶを加えて混ぜる。

If the bottom of the pan is getting burned, remove burnt deposit with a little water. Saute for 7-8 minutes and once vegetables are cooked, add Ⓐ and mix.

続いて赤唐辛子も加え、大きく炒め合わせる。

Add chilli next and stir-fry.

仕上げに、香りづけのごま油をたらす。さっと混ぜてから器に盛り、好みで白ごま（分量外）をふる。

Drip on some sesame oil to add aroma. Toss before serving on a plate and sprinkle white sesame (extra) on top.

五目白和え

Gomoku shiraae

A dish that satisfies you
with the subtle sweetness of tofu.

ほんのりとした
豆腐の甘みが
たまらない一品

Time required
所要時間
50分
50 minutes

材料（2人分）

木綿豆腐	1/3丁 (100g)
生しいたけ	1個 (15g)
にんじん	20g
こんにゃく	40g
銀杏	6個
絹さや	6枚 (12g)
白ごま	大さじ1
Ⓐ だし汁	250cc
└ 薄口醤油、砂糖	各小さじ1
Ⓑ ┌ 薄口醤油	小さじ1
│ 塩	少々
└ 砂糖	大さじ1・1/2

Ingredients (for 2 people)

1/3 tofu (100g)
1 fresh shiitake mushroom (15g)
20g carrot
40g konjac food
6 ginkgo nuts
6 snow peas (12g)
1 Tbsp white sesame seeds
Ⓐ 250cc soup stock
  └ 1 tsp light soy sauce and sugar
Ⓑ 1 tsp light soy sauce
  some salt
  └ 1・1/2 Tbsp sugar

料理のポイント
Cooking tips

1 豆腐の水気をしっかりきる。
Drain tofu's water completely.

2 仕上げはくずれないように混ぜる。
Mix together without breaking to finish.

木綿豆腐はキッチンペーパーに包み、まな板などで重しをして、20〜30分（重量が2/3になるまで）おいて、水気をきる。

Wrap tofu with a kitchen roll, and press it with a cutting board for 20-30 minutes to drain water (until the weight goes down by 2/3).

銀杏はとがった部分を金づちでたたいて殻をむく。鍋に入れ、ひたひたの湯を注ぎ、お玉で転がし、薄皮をむく。

Hammer the pointy part of ginkgo nuts to remove the shell. Put them in a saucepan and cover with hot water, roll them around with a ladle to remove the skin.

絹さやは筋を取り5mm幅、生しいたけは軸を落とし5mm幅、にんじんは5mm幅の短冊切りにする。

Remove strips of snow peas and cut into 5mm width. Cut off stems of fresh shiitake mushroom and cut into 5mm width. Cut carrot into 5mm wide rectangles.

こんにゃくは5mm幅に切り塩（分量外）をふる。水分が出たら洗い、約30秒ゆで、盆ざるにあげる。

Cut konjac food into 5mm wide rectangles and sprinkle with salt (extra). Once liquid is gone, wash it and boil for 30 seconds. Place on a strainer tray.

鍋に○A、にんじん、生しいたけ、銀杏、こんにゃくを入れ、中火で約3分煮て絹さやを加える。

Add ○A, carrot, fresh shiitake mushroom, ginkgo nuts and konjac food to a saucepan, and cook for about 3 minutes at medium heat, then add snow peas.

約2分たったら鍋の中身をざるにあげる。水気をきりながら、あおいで冷ます。

After about 2 minutes, place the ingredients from the saucepan to a strainer tray. Drain water and fan to cool.

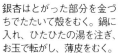

白ごまを煎り、すり鉢でする。木綿豆腐をくずしながらすり鉢に加え、すり合わせる。

Toast white sesame seeds and grind with a mortar. Add tofu pieces to a mortar and grind to mix.

すり鉢に○Bを加えてすりこ木で混ぜる。

Add ○B and mix with a pestle.

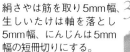

よく混ざったらざるにあげた具材を加え、ゴムべらで和える。

Once they are well mixed, add ingredients from the strainer tray and toss with a rubber spatula.

Simmered taro and pumpkin

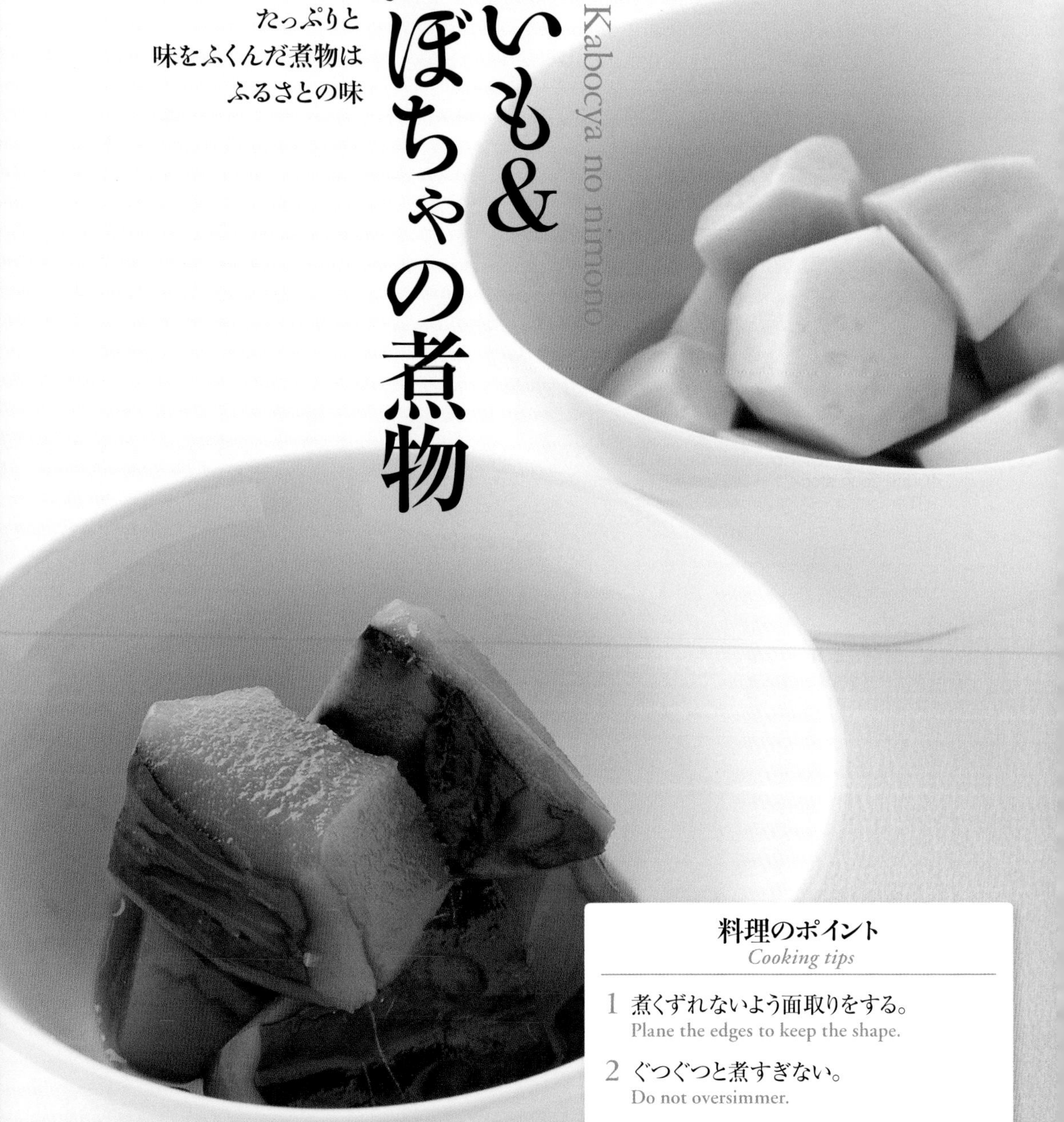

さといも&かぼちゃの煮物

Satoimo & Kabocya no nimono

たっぷりと
味をふくんだ煮物は
ふるさとの味

Flavorful,
simmered dish offers a taste of
hometown cooking.

料理のポイント
Cooking tips

1 煮くずれないよう面取りをする。
Plane the edges to keep the shape.

2 ぐつぐつと煮すぎない。
Do not oversimmer.

3 味は漬けこんでしみこませる。
Let it absorb the flavor by marinating.

さといもの煮物
Simmered taro

サブになるおかず　Side dishes

Time required
所要時間
60分
60 minutes

材料（2人分）
さといも ……………………………	正味250g
煮汁の材料	
だし汁 ……………………………	400cc
砂糖 ……………………………	大さじ1
みりん ……………………………	50cc
酒 ……………………………	大さじ2
薄口醤油 ……………………………	小さじ1
塩 ……………………………	小さじ1/2

Ingredients (for 2 people)
250g (actual weight) taro
Ingredients for cooking sauce
400cc soup stock
1 Tbsp sugar
50cc mirin
2 Tbsp sake
1 tsp light soy sauce
1/2 tsp salt

1

さといもはたわしを使い、ため水の中で皮を洗う。水気があるとすべって皮がむきにくいので、盆ざるにあげて乾かす。

Immerse taros in water and wash skin with a scrubber. Dry on a strainer as it is hard to skin when wet.

2

さといもが乾いたら皮をむく。まず頭の部分を落とす。

Skin the taro once they are dry. Cut the top off first.

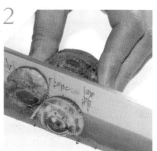

3

次に、縦に皮をむく。

After that, peel skin vertically.

4

皮をむいたさといもを半分に切る。

Cut peeled taro in half.

5

水にさらしてアクを抜く。

Soak in water to refine.

6

米のとぎ汁（分量外）で約10分下ゆでする。

Boil them for about 10 minutes with water used to wash rice (extra).

7

落としぶたを置き、流水を当てるようにして水にさらす。

Cover with a drop-lid and immerse in running water.

さといもを入れた鍋に薄口醤油以外の煮汁の材料とだし汁を加え、火にかける。

8

Add soup stock and all the ingredients apart from light soy sauce to the pan with taros, and turn the heat on.

竹串がすっと通ったら火を止める。

9

Turn the heat off, once a bamboo skewer can pierce through the taro smoothly.

さといもだけをボウルに取り出し、乾燥しないようぬれぶきんをかけておく。

10

Remove taros to a bowl and cover with a wet cloth, so that they don't get dry.

煮汁に薄口醤油を加え、味見して少し濃いぐらいに煮つめる。

11

Add light soy sauce to the cooking sauce. Taste it and simmer it down till it's a little salty.

10に11の熱い煮汁を入れ、ときどき上下を返し、味をふくませる。

12

Pour hot cooking sauce from 11 into 10, and turn them around upside down to absorb the flavor.

かぼちゃの煮物
Simmered pumpkin

Time required
所要時間
40分
40 minutes

材料（2人分）

かぼちゃ ……………………………… 正味250g
煮汁の材料
だし汁 ………………………………… 400cc
砂糖 …………………………………… 大さじ1
みりん ………………………………… 50cc
酒 …………………………………… 大さじ2
薄口醤油 ……………………………… 大さじ3

Ingredients （for 2 people）

250g (actual weight) pumpkin
Ingredients for cooking sauce
400cc soup stock
1 Tbsp sugar
50cc mirin
2 Tbsp sake
3 Tbsp light soy sauce

1

かぼちゃは種とわたを取り除き、3cm厚さのくし形に切る。

Remove seeds and stringy inside. Cut into 3cm thick wedges.

2

さらに3〜4cm幅に切る。

Cut again into 3-4cm width.

皮のところどころを包丁でむく。

Peel away some parts of the skin with a knife.

煮くずれないように、面取りをする。

Plane the edges to keep the shape.

かぼちゃを鍋に入れる。

Put pumpkin in a saucepan.

だし汁、砂糖、みりん、酒を加え、ひと煮たちさせる。

Add soup stock, sugar, mirin and sake, and bring them to boil.

沸いてきたら弱火にする。

Once boiled, turn the heat to low.

竹串がすっと通るようになったら薄口醤油を加え、沸いたら弱火にする。

Once a bamboo skewer can pierce through smoothly, add light soy sauce. When it has boiled, turn the heat down to low.

2〜3分煮たら鍋から取り出す。

Remove them from the pan after simmering for a few minutes.

味見して煮汁が少し濃いぐらいまで煮つめる。

Taste it and simmer it down till the sauce is a little salty.

取り出したかぼちゃに煮汁をかける。⦿そのまま煮続けると煮くずれる。

Pour cooking sauce over pumpkin. ⓟ They will lose their shape if they are left to simmer too long.

ときどき上下を返し、室温で冷ましながら味をふくませる。

Turn them over occasionally to absorb the flavor, cooling to room temperature.

サブになるおかず　Side dishes

This refreshing taste is perfect for a side one served between dishes.

さっぱりとした
味わいは
箸休めにぴったり

Kyuri to tako no sunomono

きゅうりとたこの酢の物

Time required
所要時間
30分
30 minutes

材料（2人分）

塩蔵わかめ	40g
ゆでだこ	80g
きゅうり	2本（200g）
しょうが	1かけ
Ⓐ　酢	大さじ3
だし汁	大さじ2
砂糖	大さじ1
濃口醤油	大さじ1
昆布	3cm角

Ingredients (for 2 people)

- 40g salted wakame seaweed
- 80g boiled octopus
- 2 cucumbers (200g)
- 1 piece ginger
- Ⓐ 3 Tbsp vinegar
- 2 Tbsp soup stock
- 1 Tbsp sugar
- 1 Tbsp dark soy sauce
- 3cm square kelp

料理のポイント
Cooking tips

1 三杯酢に昆布を漬けて味を出す。
Bring out the flavor by soaking kelp in sanbai-zu.

2 具は別々に和える。
Marinate ingredients separately.

わかめはさっと湯通しして氷水に取り、絞ってざく切りにする。

Dip wakame seaweeds in boiling water, then place them in iced water and squeeze, cut them coarsely.

器に④を入れてよく混ぜ、昆布を漬けて約10分おき、三杯酢を作る。

Put ④ in a bowl and mix well soaking kelp in it for about 10 minutes to make sanbai-zu.

たこはひと口大のそぎ切りにする。

Cut octopus into bite size pieces.

きゅうりは、表面のイボをこそげ落とし、両端を切り落とす。端から2/3の深さまでななめに細かく切りこみを入れる。

Smooth out the surface of cucumber and cut off both ends. Make small incisions diagonally from the edge to 2/3 depth.

しょうがは皮をむき、薄切りにしてから針しょうがにする。水にさらしてアクを抜く。

Peel ginger and cut in slices, then cut them into thin strips. Soak them in water to refine.

ひっくり返して、裏からも同様に切りこみを入れる。蛇腹切りにしたきゅうりを2cm長さに切る。

Turn it over and make the same incisions from the other side. After completing the incisions, cut cucumber into 2cm length.

きゅうり、わかめ、たこの水気をきり、盛る直前にそれぞれ1/6量の三杯酢で和える。

Drain cucumber, wakame seaweeds and octopus. Marinate them with 1/6 of sanbai-zu each, right before serving.

2%の塩水（分量外）に約20分、しんなりするまで漬ける。

Soak them in 2% salted water (extra) for about 20 minutes to soften.

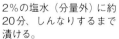

軽く水気をきって盛り、残りの三杯酢をかけ、針しょうがを飾る。

Drain them lightly, then pour on the remainder of the sanbai-zu and decorate with strips of ginger.

サブになるおかず

Side dishes

Chawanmushi

茶碗蒸し

最大のポイントは
卵液の割合と
火加減

The most important tips are
the ratio of egg mixture
and heat temperature.

Time required
所要時間
45分
45 minutes

材料（2人分）

とき卵	……………………………………	75g
えび	……………………………………	2尾（16g）
しいたけ	…………………………	小1枚（40g）
鶏ささみ	…………………………	1/2本（20g）
さといも	…………………………	小1個（50g）
切りもち	…………………………………	1/4枚
銀杏	……………………………………	2個
みつ葉	…………………………………	適量
Ⓐ ┌ だし汁	…………………………	200cc
│ みりん	……………………………	小さじ1
│ 薄口醤油	………………………	小さじ2
└ 塩	…………………………………	小さじ1/5
Ⓑ ┌ だし汁	…………………………	160cc
│ 薄口醤油	………………………	小さじ4
└ みりん	……………………………	小さじ4
Ⓒ ┌ 酒	…………………………………	小さじ1
└ 薄口醤油	………………………	小さじ1

※飾り切りしたゆずの皮を添えてもよい。

Ingredients (for 2 people)

75g beaten egg
2 prawns (16g)
1 small shiitake mushroom (40g)
1/2 tender chicken breast (20g)
1 small taro (50g)
1/4 cut rice cake
2 ginkgo nuts
some honewort
Ⓐ ┌ 200cc soup stock
   │ 1 tsp mirin
   │ 2 tsp light soy sauce
   └ 1/5 tsp salt
Ⓑ ┌ 160cc soup stock
   │ 4 tsp light soy sauce
   └ 4 tsp mirin
Ⓒ ┌ 1 tsp sake
   └ 1 tsp light soy sauce

※Can be served with shaped skin of yuzu citron.

料理のポイント
Cooking tips

1 卵：調味液＝1：3の割合で。
The ratio of egg to seasoning sauce is 1 to 3.

2 蒸すときの火加減に注意する。
Pay attention to the heat level when steaming.

鍋に Ⓐ を入れ、ひと煮たちさせ、塩をとかす。水を入れたボウルで粗熱を取る。

Put Ⓐ in a saucepan and bring it to boil to dissolve salt. Put the pan in a bowl with water to take some heat off.

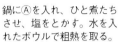

とき卵に1を加え、泡立たないように混ぜる。そのあとざるでこす。

Add 1 into beaten egg and mix without whipping. Sift with a strainer.

半分に切ったしいたけとさといもは3mm幅、みつ葉の茎は3cm、鶏ささみは5mm幅、もちは1cm角に切る。

Cut shiitake mushroom and taro in halves then cut into 3mm width. Cut stem of honewort into 3cm length, chicken into 5mm width and rice cake into 1cm cubes.

塩ゆで（分量外）したさといも、しいたけと、P.185のように処理した銀杏を Ⓑ にしばらく漬け、ふきんで水分を取る。

Soak taro boiled with salt (extra), shiitake mushroom and ginkgo nuts treated (see P.185) in Ⓑ for a while, and remove liquid with a cloth.

5

鶏ささみに Ⓒ の半量を加え、手でもみこむ。

Pour half of Ⓒ on chicken, and massage with hands.

6

えびは背わたを取り、色が変わるまでゆでて殻をむく。Ⓒ の半量で下味をつける。

Devein the prawns and boil until they change color, then shell and season them with the other half of Ⓒ.

7

トースターでもちを焼く。4、5、焼いたもちを器に入れ、卵液を八分目まで注ぐ。

Rice cake is burnt with a toaster. Put 4, 5, and baked rice cake on a bowl, and pour in egg mixture to fill to 80%.

8

せいろに入れ、中火で約2分蒸す。表面が白っぱくなったら弱火にし、15〜20分蒸す。

Steam for about 2 minutes at medium heat with a steamer. Turn the heat down to low, once the surface become whitish, and steam for another 15-20 minutes.

9

竹串でさし、透明な汁が出てきたらOK。えび、みつ葉をのせ、さらに約1分蒸す。

Pierce it with a bamboo skewer and if a clear liquid comes out, it is ready. Put prawns and honewort on top and steam about another 1 minute.

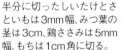

サブになるおかず

Side dishes

Simmer beans and vegetables
with kelp broth
and cook them soft.

Gomokumame

五目豆

お豆と野菜を
昆布だしで煮ふくめ
ふっくらと仕上げます

料理のポイント
Cooking tips

1 大豆はたっぷりの水で戻す。
Reconstitute soybeans with plenty of water.

2 大豆や干ししいたけはじっくりと戻す。
Allow plenty of time to reconstitute soybeans and dried shiitake.

3 調味料はあとで加える
Add seasoning later.

Time required
所要時間
80分
80 minutes

材料（2人分）

大豆（乾）	80g（水煮の場合は200g）
昆布	15cm角
にんじん	80g
ごぼう	70g
干ししいたけ	3個
こんにゃく	2/3枚（125g）
砂糖	大さじ2

Ⓐ
┌ 酒 ………………………… 大さじ2
│ 薄口醤油 ………………… 大さじ2
│ みりん …………………… 大さじ2
└ 酢 ………………………… 小さじ1/4

Ingredients (for 2 people)

80g soybeans (dried) (200g boiled)
15cm square kelp
80g carrot
70g burdock
3 dried shiitake mushrooms
2/3 piece konjac food
2 Tbsp sugar
Ⓐ 2 Tbsp sake
   2 Tbsp light soy sauce
   2 Tbsp mirin
   1/4 tsp vinegar

大豆を洗って5倍の水に半日浸して戻す。大豆は約2.5倍になるので大きめの器を用意する。

Wash soybeans and soak in 5 times more water for a half day to reconstitute. Use a larger size container as soybeans expand 2.5 times the size.

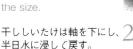

1

干ししいたけは軸を下にし、半日水に浸して戻す。

Dried shiitake mushrooms place in water stem side down and reconstitute for a half day.

2

3

戻したしいたけをぎゅっと握って絞る。戻し汁は捨てずにとっておく。

Squeeze reconstituted shiitake mushrooms. Keep the liquid.

4

しいたけの軸を切り落とし、8mm角に切る。

Cut off stems of shiitake mushrooms and cut into 8mm cubes.

5

戻した大豆をざるにあげて水気をきる。戻し汁は捨てずにとっておく。

Once soybeans are reconstituted, drain with a strainer. Keep the liquid.

6

昆布は固く絞ったふきんなどでさっと表面をふき、キッチンばさみで5mm角に切る。

Wipe the surface of kelp with a tightly squeezed wet cloth and cut into 5mm squares with kitchen scissors.

7

大豆または干ししいたけの戻し汁1カップに昆布を約30分浸す。

Soak kelp for about 30 minutes in a cup of water used to reconstitute either soybeans or dried shiitake mushrooms.

ごぼうはたわしで洗い、表面の汚れや泥を落とす。

Wash burdock with a scrubber and clean the surface.

洗ったごぼうを8mm角に切り、酢水（分量外）にさらしてアクを抜く。

Cut washed burdock into 8mm cubes and soak in water with vinegar (extra) to refine.

にんじんは8mm角に切る。

Cut carrot into 8mm cubes.

こんにゃくも8mm角に切る。具材はなるべく大きさをそろえる。

Cut konjac food into 8mm cubes. Match the size of ingredients as much as you can.

こんにゃくをボウルに移し、塩を全体にまぶし、約10分おいて臭みを出す。水で洗い流す。

Place konjac food in a bowl and sprinkle salt all over, and leave it for about 10 minutes to clean away odors. Wash out with water.

湯を沸かして約1分ゆでる。⦿アク抜き済みの場合は12、13を省く。

Boil for about 1 minute. ⦿Omit 12 and 13 if it's already refined.

鍋を用意し、7をすべて注ぎ入れる。

Ready a saucepan and pour 7 in.

戻した大豆を加える。⦿水煮の大豆を使う場合は21で、砂糖を入れる直前に加える。

Add reconstituted soybeans. ⦿If boiled soybeans are used, add right before putting sugar in at 21.

しいたけ、こんにゃく、ごぼう、にんじんも加える。

Add shiitake mushrooms, konjac food, burdock and carrot.

しいたけの戻し汁をひたひたになるまで加える。

Add enough of the liquid used for reconstituting shiitake mushrooms to cover the ingredients.

強火にかけて、沸騰したら
中火にする。アクが出たら
お玉ですくう。

Put on high heat and
turn it down to medium
heat once boiled. Skim
the scum with a ladle.

ふたをしないで中火のまま、
具材がやわらかくなるまで
約40分煮る。

Cook for about 40 min-
utes until ingredients are
tenderized without a lid
at medium heat.

途中で水気がなくなったら
水やだし汁、残りの戻し汁
を加える。

Add water, soup stock
or remaining liquid from
reconstitution, if the
cooking sauce is cooked
down.

具材がやわらかくなったら
砂糖を加えて混ぜる。

Add sugar once ingredi-
ents are tenderized, and
mix.

2〜3分たったら④を加え、
鍋底から具材を混ぜて、約
5分煮る。

Add ④ after 2-3 min-
utes, mix ingredients
from the bottom of pan
and simmer for about 5
minutes.

大豆が器からあふれた
Soybeans overflow.

乾燥した大豆は水に浸
して戻すと約2.5倍の
大きさになります。器
が小さかったり水の量
が少なかったりする
とばらつきがでるので、
大きめの器とたっぷり
の水で戻しましょう。

Dried soybeans can expand to about 2.5 times
the size when soaked in water. If the container
is too small or the amount of water too little, the
size will vary. Use a larger container with plenty
of water to reconstitute.

豆に味がうまくなじまない
Flavor does not blend well with beans.

豆が硬いうちに調味
料を加えると、豆が
ぎゅっとしまりやわら
かく煮えません。はじ
めはだし汁と戻し汁で
具材を煮こみ、火を通
してから調味料を加え
ます。

If seasonings are added while the beans are still
hard, they will clench and not get tenderized.
Simmer with soup stock and liquids from
reconstitution first. Add the seasoning after they
are cooked.

煮汁が全体にしみて、水分
がほぼなくなれば完成。

Once the cooking sauce
has been evenly ab-
sorbed, and is reduced
to almost nothing, it is
ready.

サブになるおかず　Side dishes

ルウの作り方とポイント
HOW TO MAKE ROUX AND TIPS

ルウとは、薄力粉とバターを1：1の割合で炒め合せたものです。料理やソースに濃度をつけるときの材料として使います。作るときは焦げやすいので常に弱火をこころがけてください。

Roux is cooked from the equal amount of soft wheat flour and butter. It is used as a thickener for sauces, soups and stews. Be careful to cook it over a low heat because it is easy to burn.

材料　INGREDIENT

薄力粉…50g	flour … 50g
バター…50g	Butter … 50g

1

薄力粉はふるって分量を量る。鍋にバターを熱して溶かし、火を止めてから薄力粉を加える。
Sift and scale flour. Melt butter in a pan and add flour after turning fire off.

2

弱火にかけ、薄力粉が色づかないように2～3分炒めるように混ぜる。
Stir flour on a low heat for a few minutes to prevent it from being colored.

3

耐熱のゴムべらですくい、写真のように生地がさらさらになったら完成。
Scoop it with a heat-proof rubber spatula. It is finished when you see it become roux as pictured above.

ホワイトソースにするには
HOW TO MAKE IT WHITE SOURCE

完成したルウに牛乳を加え、再び弱火にかけて全体にとろみがつくまで混ぜると簡単にホワイトソースになります。このときも、色が濁らないように火加減に注意しましょう。
It is easy to make white sauce that you just add milk into finished roux and stir it till thickened again over a low heat. You should be careful at heat condition to prevent it from being colored

第5章
Part 5

ごはん＆汁物＆漬物
Rice & Soup & Pickles

Kinoko no takikomigohan

If you want to burn it
a little, put heat up to high
when finishing.

おこげを作るなら
仕上げの段階で
強火に！

きのこの炊きこみごはん

料理のポイント
Cooking tips

1 米を洗ったら30分おく。
Leave rice for 30 minutes after washing.

2 煮汁と洗い米を同量に。
Cooking sauce and washed rice should be the same amount.

3 炊き上がったら少し蒸らす。
Once cooked, steam the boiled rice a little.

Time required
所要時間
40分
40 minutes

材料（2人分）

鶏もも肉	40g
しめじ	20g
まいたけ	20g
にんじん	15g
油揚げ	1/2枚
米	200cc
だし汁	約200cc
Ⓐ ┌ だし汁	100cc
├ 濃口醤油	大さじ1
├ 酒	大さじ1
├ みりん	大さじ1
└ 塩	小さじ1/4
みつ葉	4g

Ingredients (for 2 people)

40g chicken thigh
20g shimeji mushrooms
20g maitake mushrooms
15g carrot
1/2 piece deep-fried bean curd
200cc rice
about 200cc soup stock
Ⓐ ┌ 100cc soup stock
  ├ 1 Tbsp dark soy sauce
  ├ 1 Tbsp sake
  ├ 1 Tbsp mirin
  └ 1/4 tsp salt
4g honewort

1

米を洗い、ざるにあげる。約30分おき、必要な水分を吸わせ、余分な水気をきる。

Wash rice and drain over a strainer. Leave it for about 30 minutes. Let rice absorb enough water and drain any excess.

2

しめじは石づきを落として小房に分け、2〜3cmの長さに切る。

Cut off stems of shimeji mushrooms and cut to 2-3cm length.

3

まいたけも小房に分ける。

Divide maitake mushrooms into small bunches.

4

にんじんは2〜3mm角の細切りにする。

Cut carrot into 2-3mm wide thin strips.

5

湯を沸かして、油揚げを約10秒ゆでる。引きあげ、盆ざるにあげて冷ます。

Bring water to boil and boil deep-fried bean curd for about 10 seconds. Take it out and cool it on a strainer tray.

6

油揚げの粗熱が取れたら、キッチンペーパーなどで軽く包んで、水気をよく取る。

Once the deep-fried bean curd has cooled a little, wrap it with kitchen roll lightly to remove water thoroughly.

油揚げを5mm幅、5cm長さに切る。

Cut deep-fried bean curd to 5mm wide and 5cm in length pieces.

鶏肉は皮をはがす。脂や筋も包丁で取り除く。

Skin chicken thigh. Remove fat and fibers with a knife.

鶏肉を5mm幅の棒状に切る。

Cut chicken thigh into 5mm width sticks.

鍋に⒜を入れて、中火にかける。

Put ⒜ in a saucepan on medium heat.

すぐに細切りにしたにんじんを加えて、約3分煮る。

Add cut carrot right away and cook for about 3 minutes.

にんじんを味見してやわらかくなっていれば、鶏肉を加えてすぐにバラバラにほぐす。

Taste carrot and once softened, add chicken thigh and break into flakes immediately.

鶏肉の色が変わり、軽く火が通ったら、しめじとまいたけ、油揚げを加える。

Once the chicken is cooked lightly and its color has changed, add the deep-fried bean curd, shimeji and maitake mushrooms.

中火で約2分煮る。

Cook for about 2 minutes at medium heat.

計量カップの上にざるを置く。ざるに14をあけて、具を軽く押さえ、具と煮汁を分ける。

Put a strainer over a measuring cup. Pour 14 over the strainer. Press ingredients lightly to divide ingredients and cooking sauce.

煮汁にだし汁を足して、洗い米と同量にする。Ⓟ米は洗うと水分を吸収し、約1.2倍の240ccになる。

Add soup stock into the cooking sauce to make the amount the same as washed rice. Ⓟ Washed rice absorbs water and will increase in size by 1.2 which is 240cc.

分けた具材を鍋に戻し入れる。水気をきった米も入れる。

Place the separated ingredients back into the saucepan. Add drained rice.

続いて16で調節した煮汁を注ぎ入れる。

Afterward pour in the cooking sauce adjusted in 16.

鍋の中をぐるっとひと混ぜして、具材と米、煮汁をなじませる。

Mix the whole contents of the pan to blend ingredients, rice and cooking sauce.

鍋にふたをして、強火にかける。㊥炊飯器で炊く場合も同じ分量で、すべての材料を入れればよい。

Cover with a lid and turn the heat to high. ⓟIf using a rice cooker, the amounts are the same, just add all the ingredients.

湯気が上がって沸騰したら、弱火にして約10分加熱する。

Once it's steaming and boiling, turn the heat down to low and simmer for about 10 minutes.

失敗しないために　To avoid a failure

ごはんが硬くなってしまった
Rice is too hard.

米を炊く煮汁は洗い米と同じ量が必要。煮汁が足りないと硬くなってしまうので、だし汁や水で調節します。

For cooked rice, the amount of cooking sauce and washed rice must be the same. If there is too little cooking sauce, the rice will be hard, adjust by adding soup stock and water.

炊き上がったごはんがおいしくない
Cooked rice is not tasty.

炊いている途中に鍋のふたを開けると、うまく炊き上がらないことも。途中でふたを取ってはいけません。

If you remove the lid during cooking, it can fail to cook properly. Do not remove the lid while cooking.

火を止めてみつ葉を散らし、再びふたをして5〜10分蒸らす。

Turn the heat off and sprinkle honewort. Replace the lid and steam for 5-10 minutes.

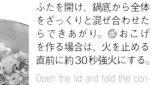

ふたを開け、鍋底から全体をざっくりと混ぜ合わせたらできあがり。㊥おこげを作る場合は、火を止める直前に約30秒強火にする。

Open the lid and fold the contents from the bottom of the pan to finish. ⓟIf you wish to burn it a little, turn the heat up to high for about 30 seconds right before turning off the heat.

ご は ん ＆ 汁 物 ＆ 漬 物

Rice & Soup & Pickles

牛丼

Gyudon

手早く作れてお腹も満足
忙しいときの
お助けメニュー

Quick and filling,
A convenient dish
when you are busy.

材料（2人分）

牛ばら薄切り肉	……………………	160g
玉ねぎ	……………	1/2個（125g）
しょうが	…………………	1/3かけ
にんにく	…………………	1/2かけ
Ⓐ だし汁	…………	100cc
濃口醤油、酒	…………	各大さじ2
みりん	…………………	大さじ1/2
砂糖	…………………	大さじ1
昆布茶	…………………	小さじ1/5
万能ねぎ	…………………	2本
ごはん	…………………	400g
サラダ油	…………………	小さじ2

Ingredients (for 2 people)

160g beef short ribs
1/2 onion (125g)
1/3 piece ginger
1/2 piece garlic
Ⓐ 100cc soup stock
　 2 Tbsp dark soy sauce
　　 and sake
　 1/2 Tbsp mirin
　 1 Tbsp sugar
　 1/5 tsp kelp tea powder
2 stems spring onion
400g cooked rice
2 tsp cooking oil

Time required
所要時間
20分
20 minutes

料理のポイント
Cooking tips

1 調理前に調味料を混ぜておく。
Mix seasoning before cooking.

2 つゆの濃さは好みで調節。
Adjust the richness of the sauce to your taste.

しょうがは、皮をむいてみじん切りにする。

Peel ginger skin and chop finely.

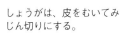

にんにくもみじん切りにする。🅟一度包丁の腹でつぶすと、素早く細かくみじん切りできる。

Chop garlic finely too. 🅟 Squash it once with a knife to make it easier to chop finely and quickly.

玉ねぎは芯を取り外側をはがす。内側はくし形に切り、外側は長さを半分にして1～2cmの幅に切る。

Remove the core and outer layers of onion. Cut inside into wedges and outlayers half in length and 1-2cm in width.

牛肉は4cm角に切る。

Cut beef into 4cm cubes.

Ⓐをボウルに合わせる。
Mix Ⓐ in a bowl.

フライパンにサラダ油を入れ、熱くならないうちに1と2を加える。香りが出るまで中火で炒める。

Pour cooking oil in a frying pan and add 1and 2 before it gets hot. Saute until it's aromatic at medium heat.

香りが立ったら強火にし、牛肉を入れてほぐしながら炒める。焼き色がついたら玉ねぎを加える。

Once it's aromatic, turn the heat to high and add beef. Saute while breaking up the meat. Once it's browned, add onions.

玉ねぎがしんなりしたら5を注いで混ぜる。約3分たったらごはんにかけ、ななめ切りにした万能ねぎを添える。

Once onions are tenderized, pour 5 and mix. After 3 minutes, pour it over rice and place spring onion cut diagonally on top.

つゆをとろっとさせたい場合は、好みの濃度になるまでそのまま煮つめる。

If you would prefer a thicker sauce, simmer it down to the thickness of your liking.

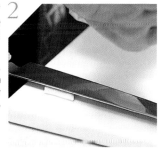
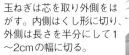

ごはん&汁物&漬物

Rice & Soup & Pickles

親子丼

Oyakodon

If the egg is soft and fluffy, it's highly successful.

とろとろふんわりの
卵になったら
大成功

材料（2人分）

鶏もも肉	……………	1/2枚（140g）
玉ねぎ	……………	小1/2個（70g）
卵	……………	3個
みつ葉	……………	4g
Ⓐ ┌ だし汁	……………	100cc
酒	……………	大さじ2
薄口醤油	……………	大さじ2
└ 砂糖	……………	大さじ1
ごはん	……………	400g
サラダ油	……………	小さじ1

Ingredients （for 2 people）

- 1/2 chicken thigh (140g)
- 1/2 small onion (70g)
- 3 eggs
- 4g honewort
- Ⓐ ┌ 100cc soup stock
- 　2 Tbsp sake
- 　2 Tbsp light soy sauce
- 　└ 1 Tbsp sugar
- 400g cooked rice
- 1 tsp cooking oil

料理のポイント
Cooking tips

1 鶏肉から出た余分な脂を取り除く。
Remove excess fat from chicken.

2 卵は2回に分けて注ぐととろとろに。
Pour beaten egg in two portions to give a runny finish.

玉ねぎは芯を取り、縦半分に切って、5mm幅にスライスする。

Remove the core of the onion and cut it in half vertically. Slice into 5mm width.

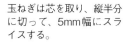

鶏肉は、裏返してみて身からはみ出した皮があれば取り除き、1cm角に切る。

Turn chicken over, remove excess skin and cut into 1cm cubes.

卵をボウルに割り入れ、菜箸で軽くとく。別のボウルに④を合わせておく。

Break eggs in a bowl and lightly beat with cooking chopsticks. Mix ④ in another bowl.

フライパンにサラダ油を熱し、鶏肉の皮目を下にして弱火で焼き、余分な脂を出す。

Heat cooking oil in a frying pan. Cook chicken skin side down at low heat and let excess fat oil out.

出てきた脂をしっかりふき取ると上品な味に仕上がる。

Wipe off fat oil thoroughly for fine flavored finish.

鶏肉から脂が出なくなったら、④と玉ねぎを加え、中火にして煮る。

Once fat oil is all out, add ④ and onion, and simmer at medium heat.

鶏肉の色が変わって火が通ったら、とき卵を2/3程度注ぐ。すぐにふたをして、約1分半火を通す。

Once the chicken changes it's color and is cooked, pour in 2/3 of beaten egg. Put a lid on immediately and cook for about 1 and a half minutes.

ふたを取り、卵に火が通っていたら4cm長さに切ったみつ葉を散らし、残りのとき卵を回しかける。

Remove the lid, and if the egg is cooked, sprinkle on honewort cut into 4cm length, then pour in the remaining beaten egg.

火を止めて再びふたをし、約15秒蒸らす。へらを使ってごはんの上に盛りつける。

Turn the heat off, replace the lid and steam for about 15 seconds. Place it on cooked rice using a spatula.

ごはん&汁物&漬物

Rice & Soup & Pickles

Okowa

おこわ

Perfect for both
a banquet or
a regular meal !

ごちそうにも
普段の食事にも
大活躍！

Time required
所要時間
70分
70 minutes

材料 (4人分)

もち米	480g
ささげ (乾)	80g
Ⓐ 黒ごま	大さじ1
塩	小さじ1
水	大さじ2
酒	大さじ1
塩	小さじ1/3

Ingredients (for 4 people)

480g glutinous rice
80g black eyed peas (dried)
Ⓐ 1 Tbsp black sesame seeds
　1 tsp salt
　2 Tbsp water
1 Tbsp sake
1/3 tsp salt

料理のポイント
Cooking tips

1 ごま塩は水分をとばしてさらに煎る。
   Dehydrate salted sesame seeds and saute.

2 もち米はふっくらと蒸す。
   Glutinous rice should be steamed soft.

もち米を洗って丸1日浸水する。使う前にざるにあげて水気をきる。

Wash glutinous rice and soak for a whole day. Drain over a strainer before use.

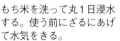

1

ささげは洗ってゆでる。沸騰したら弱火にし、約40分ゆで、ささげと煮汁を分ける。

Wash black eyed peas and cook. Once it has boiled, turn the heat down to low and boil for about 40 minutes, then separate the black eyed peas and cooking sauce.

2

ごま塩を作る。鍋にⒶを入れて、水分を完全にとばし、香ばしくなるまで煎る。

Make salted sesame seeds. Put Ⓐ in a saucepan and dehydrate, and saute till aromatic.

3

フライパンにもち米、酒、2の煮汁250cc、塩を入れて混ぜ、火にかけて水分を吸わせる。

Put glutinous rice, sake, 250cc of cooking sauce from 2 and salt into a frying pan, and mix. Turn on the heat to help absorb the liquid.

4

5

もち米を蒸す間、ささげが乾燥しないようにラップで密閉する。

While steaming glutinous rice, tightly wrap the black eyed peas with clinging wrap.

6

せいろに固く絞った蒸し布をしき、4のもち米を入れて中央にくぼみを作る。

Place a tightly squeezed cloth for steaming on a steamer, then pour on glutinous rice from 4 and make a hollow in the center.

7

蒸し布をかぶせ、ふたをして強火で約15分蒸す。

Cover with a cloth for steaming and place a lid on top, then steam using high heat for about 15 minutes.

8

15分後に箸で持ち上げ、米同士がつながり、モチっとしていたら火を止める。

After 15 minutes, lift out some rice with chopsticks to test if the grains are stuck together and are sticky and soft, then turn the heat off.

9

ささげを加え、ざっくりと混ぜる。器に盛り、3を適量ふりかける。

Add the black eyed peas and mix all together using a cutting motion. Serve it in a bowl and sprinkle 3.

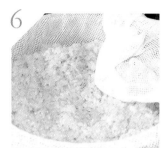

ごはん＆汁物＆漬物

Rice & Soup & Pickles

Assorted seafood on sushi rice

ちらし寿司

Chirashizushi

豪快な盛りつけが
うれしい
お祝い料理

A festive meal that
pleases with gorgeous
arrangement on a plate.

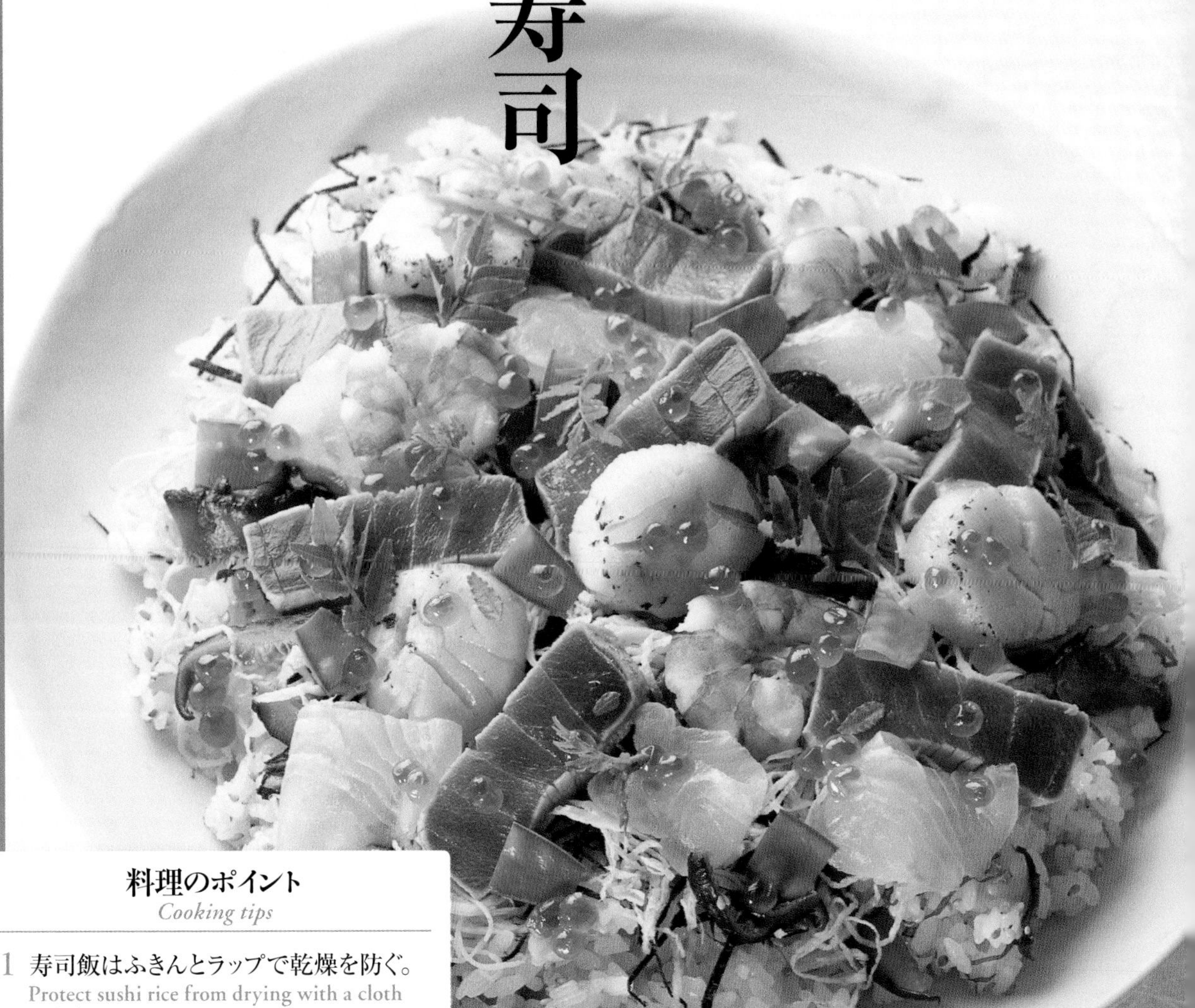

料理のポイント
Cooking tips

1 寿司飯はふきんとラップで乾燥を防ぐ。
Protect sushi rice from drying with a cloth and clinging wrap.

2 全体にまんべんなく具を散らす。
Scatter ingredients evenly all over.

3 緑の野菜は最後に散らす。
Scatter green vegetables last.

Time required
所要時間
120分
120 minutes

材料（2人分）

寿司飯の材料
米	1カップ（160g）
塩	3g
砂糖	10g
酢	大さじ1・1/3
昆布	5cm角

干ししいたけ	2枚
だし汁	3/4カップ（150cc）
砂糖	大さじ2/3
濃口醤油	大さじ1/2
まぐろ	100g
帆立貝の貝柱	2個
えび	2尾
絹さや	4枚
ひらめの切り身	40g
昆布	5cm幅10cm長さ
卵	1個
塩	ひとつまみ
青じそ	2枚
白ごま	大さじ1
きざみのり	大さじ1
いくら	大さじ1
がり	大さじ1
木の芽	適量
おろしわさび	小さじ1（好みで添える）

Ingredients (for 2 people)

Ingredients for sushi rice
1 cup rice (160g)
3g salt   10g sugar
1・1/3 Tbsp vinegar
5cm square kelp

2 dried shiitake mushrooms
3/4 cup soup stock (150cc)
2/3 Tbsp sugar
1/2 Tbsp dark soy sauce
100g tuna
2 scallops
2 prawns
4 snow peas
40g flounder fillet
5cm width 10cm length kelp
1 egg   pinch of salt
2 leaves green perilla
1 Tbsp white sesame seeds
1 Tbsp shredded laver seaweed
1 Tbsp salted salmon roe
1 Tbsp pickled ginger
some buds of Japanese pepper tree
1 tsp green horseradish paste (serve if you prefer)

1　寿司飯を作る。塩、砂糖、酢を泡立て器で混ぜる。昆布を浸し、約10分たったら取り出す。

Make sushi rice. Mix salt, sugar and vinegar with a whisk. Soak 5cm square kelp in it, before removing after about 10 minutes.

2　飯台に水をはり、水分がしみ込んだら水を捨ててふきんでふく。米をといで炊いておく。

Fill a wooden rice tub with water, once it has absorbed water, throw out the remainder and wipe with a cloth. Wash rice and cook.

3　炊けたごはんを飯台に出し、熱いうちに1を回しかける。切るように手早く混ぜる。

Put cooked rice in the wooden rice tub and pour 1 over, while rice is still hot. Mix quickly using a cutting motion.

4　あおいで冷ます。ひっくり返すように大きく混ぜて全体をしっかり冷ます。

Fan to cool it down. Mix roughly as if turning it over to cool the whole down thoroughly.

5　寿司飯を片方に寄せ、ふきんとラップをかけて乾燥を防ぐ。

Put sushi rice together on one side, and cover with a cloth and clinging wrap to prevent it from drying.

ひらめの切り身に塩（分量外）をふって水分を出す。湿らせた昆布ではさんでラップに包み、約1時間おく。

Sprinkle salt(extra) over flounder fillet to extract the water. Hold it with moistened kelp and wrap it with clinging wrap, let it stand for an hour.

干ししいたけは半日水に浸けて戻し、軸を取る。だし汁と砂糖と一緒に紙の落としぶたをして弱火で煮る。

Reconstitute dried shiitake mushrooms for a half day and cut off stems. Simmer at low heat with soup stock and sugar keeping it covered with a paper drop-lid.

煮汁が半分になったら醤油を加える。煮汁がなくなるまで煮こんだら、薄切りにする。

Add soy sauce when cooking sauce is reduced to half. Simmer until cooking sauce has cooked out, and slice them thinly.

まぐろは沸騰した湯にさっとくぐらせ、醤油と酒（分量外）を同量混ぜたものに裏表約1分ずつ漬ける。

Immerse tuna in boiled water quickly. Soak in a mixture of soy sauce and sake (same amount, extra) for about 1 minute each side.

5mm〜1cmの厚さに切る。刃渡りの長い包丁を大きく動かすと切りやすい。

Cut it into 5mm-1cm thickness. It is easier to cut using large movements with a long bladed knife.

帆立貝は貝柱の白く硬い部分を取る。塩水（分量外）に2〜3分さらし、軽く洗って水分をきる。

Remove hard, white part of scallops. Soak in salted water (extra) for a few minutes, wash lightly and drain.

串にさし、コンロの直火で焦げ目がつくまで焼く。氷水にさらし、半分の厚さに切る。

Pierce with a skewer and grill till browned using direct heat from a gas cooker. Immerse in iced water and slice into half of its thickness.

えびは背わたを取り除き、色が赤く変わり、丸まるまでゆでて氷水にさらす。

Devein prawns and boil until they turn red and curl up, then soak in iced water.

十分に冷めたら、殻をむいて水気をふき、半分の厚さに切る。

Once they are completely cooled, remove the shell and wipe off water, cut into half of its thickness.

絹さやは筋を取り、塩水（分量外）でさっとゆでる。冷めたら、1cm幅に切る。

Remove the stringy part of the snow peas and boil in salted water (extra) quickly. After they have cooled down, cut into 1cm width.

ひらめの切り身をそぎ切りにする。再度昆布にはさみ、盛りつける直前までおくとより味がしみこむ。

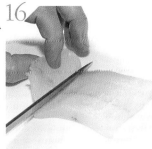

Cut flounder fillet into slivers. Wrap them with kelp and leave until right before serving to let it absorb the flavor.

塩を加えてといた卵をこし器でこす。卵焼き器にサラダ油を熱し半量の卵を薄く広げる。

Sift beaten and salted egg. Heat cooking oil in a omelet pan and spread half of egg mixture thinly.

弱火で卵を焼き、表面が乾いたら裏返す。両面が焼けたら盆ざるにあげて、もう1枚焼く。

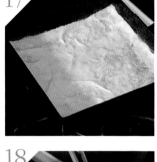

Cook beaten egg at low heat and turn it over once the surface is dried. Cook both sides, then place on a strainer tray. Cook another one.

薄焼き卵をラップで包み、冷蔵庫で冷やす。2枚の薄焼き卵を重ねて1〜2mm幅のせん切りにする。

Wrap thin egg omelets with clinging wrap and cool them in the fridge. Pile 2 thin omelets and cut them thinly into 1-2mm width.

青じそは細いせん切りにし、水にさらす。ふきんに取り出し、絞って水気をきる。

Julienne green perilla and soak them in water. Take them out on a cloth and squeeze them to remove the water.

あおぎながら寿司飯を混ぜてはダメ
Do not mix and fan sushi rice at the same time.

熱いごはんに寿司酢を均一に混ぜ、ご飯を広げてあおぎます。あおぎながら混ぜてはいけません。混ぜるのは水分のあるうちだけです。

Evenly mix sushi vinegar and hot cooked rice, then spread to fan. Do not fan while mixing. You can only mix rice, when there is liquid from vinegar present.

寿司飯に8のしいたけ、20の青じそ、煎った白ごまを加えて切るように混ぜる。

Add shiitake mushrooms from 8, green perilla from 20 and roasted white sesame seeds in sushi rice. Mix using a cutting motion.

21を盛り、きざみのり、卵を散らす。一か所に固まらないように散らす。

Put 21 on a plate, and sprinkle shredded laver seaweed and eggs on top. Scatter them evenly.

そのほかの材料を色よく盛る。わさび醤油をかけていただく。

Place other ingredients colorfully. Serve it pouring soy sauce with green horseradish paste over.

A representation of
traditional
Japanese food.

Nigirizushi & Hosomakizushi

握り寿司＆細巻き寿司

日本の
伝統料理の
代表格

料理のポイント
Cooking tips

1 ネタは新鮮なものを用意。
  Prepare fresh ingredients.

2 寿司飯は乾かないよう注意する。
  Ensure that sushi rice does not become dry.

3 手早く握り、すぐ食べる。
  Mold sushi fast and eat right away.

握り寿司
Nigiri sushi

<table>
<tr><td>

Time required

所要時間
60分
60 minutes

</td></tr>
</table>

材料（2人分）

寿司飯（P.211参照）	300g
手酢の材料	
水	100cc
酢	大さじ1/2
握り寿司のネタ	
えび	2尾（100g）
まぐろ、サーモン	各40g
たい、いか、たこ	各30g
レモン	少々
いくら	大さじ2
卵焼き	2切れ
煮穴子（市販品）	1/2尾
焼きのり	1/4枚
おろしわさび	適量
醤油	適量
しょうがの甘酢漬け	適量

Ingredients (for 2 people)

300g sushi rice (see P.211)
Ingredients for hand vinegar
100cc water
1/2 Tbsp vinegar
Ingredients for nigiri-sushi
2 prawns (100g)
40g tuna and salmon
30g sea bream, squid and octopus
some lemon
2 Tbsp salted salmon roe
2 pieces of omelet
1/2 cooked conger eel (store-bought)
1/4 roasted laver seaweed
some green horseradish paste
some soy sauce
some pickled ginger in sweet vinegar

1

P.211の要領で寿司飯を用意し、ぬれぶきんとラップをかけておく。

Prepare sushi rice as shown on P.211. Cover it with a wet cloth and clinging wrap.

2

えびは背わたを取り、腹部に竹串をまっすぐさして熱湯でゆでる。氷水で冷まして水気をふき取り串を抜く。

Devein prawns and pierce the belly straight with a bamboo skewer, cook with boiling water. Cool them in iced water, then wipe off the water and remove the skewer.

3

尾以外の殻をむき、腹を開く。包丁の腹で押さえて平らに広げる。

Remove shell apart from the tails, then open the belly and press down with the side of a knife to open flat.

4

手に水と酢を混ぜた手酢をつけ、寿司飯を約20g取り、握り寿司の形に軽く握る。

Moisten your hand with hand vinegar, mixture of water and vinegar, then take 20g of sushi rice and mold lightly into nigiri-sushi shape.

5

右手の人差し指でわさびを適量取り、えびの内側につける。

Scoop some green horseradish paste with right index finger, and put it on the inner side of the prawn.

ごはん&汁物&漬物

Rice & Soup & Pickles

4で作った握りを5のネタの上に重ねて、人差し指で中央を押さえて空気を入れる。

Put nigiri rice on top of the topping from 5, and press the center with index finger to let the air in.

ひっくり返して、ネタを押さえ形を整える。

Turn over and press on topping to shape it.

ネタと握りが一体になるように、全体を軽く握る。

Squeeze together lightly so that the nigiri rice and topping integrate.

卵焼きには細く切ったのりを巻き、穴子にはかんぴょうを煮た汁を煮つめたもの（P.217参照）をぬる。

Wrap laver seaweed strip around omelet with sushi rice and brush cooking sauce from simmering dried gourd (see P.217) on conger eel.

3cm×18cmに切った焼きのりを4の寿司飯に巻きつけ、その中にいくらを盛りつける。サーモンにはレモンをのせる。

Wrap sushi rice from 4 with 3cm x 18cm roasted laver seaweed, and put salted salmon roe in it. Place small lemon slice on salmon.

ネタの準備
Preparation for toppings

さくやかたまりのネタを切って準備する。

Prepare by cutting toppings.

まぐろ、たい、いか、たこ、サーモンは同じ大きさにそぎ切りする。

Cut tuna, sea bream, squid, octopus and salmon into slivers of the same size.

いかは、かのこ状に切りこみを入れてから、そぎ切りする。

Make dapple incisions on squid and then cut into slivers.

そぎ切りしたサーモンには、いちょう切りしたレモンをのせる。

Place quarter round slices of lemon on top of salmon slivers.

卵焼き（関東風卵焼きP.171参照）は約7mm厚さに切る。

Cut omelet (see P.171 eastern omelet) into 7mm thick slices.

細巻き寿司
Thin sushi roll

Time required
所要時間
50分
50 minutes

材料 (4本分)

寿司飯 (P.211参照)	200g
焼きのり	1枚
おろしわさび	適量
濃口醤油	適量
手酢 (P.215参照)	適量
きゅうり	1/2本 (50g)
白ごま	小さじ1/2

かんぴょうの甘辛煮の材料

かんぴょう	13g
濃口醤油	大さじ2
砂糖	大さじ2
酒	大さじ1
だし汁	200cc

Ingredients (for 4 rolls)

200g sushi rice (see P.211)
1 roasted laver seaweed
some green horseradish paste
some dark soy sauce
some hand vinegar (see P.215)
1/2 cucumber (50g)
1/2 tsp white sesame seeds
Ingredients for simmered salty sweet gourd strips
13g strips of dried gourd
2 Tbsp dark soy sauce
2 Tbsp sugar
1 Tbsp sake
200cc soup stock

1

P.211の要領で寿司飯を用意し、ぬれぶきんとラップをかけておく。

Prepare sushi rice as shown on P.211. Cover it with a wet cloth and clinging wrap.

2

水で戻して約10分下ゆでしたかんぴょうに、調味料とだし汁を加えて、ゆっくり煮つめ、そのまま冷ます。

Put seasoning and soup stock in a pan with the gourd strips that have already been reconstitiuted and boiled for about 10 minutes, simmer slowly then let it cool down.

3

のりは半分に切り、巻きすにのせる。手酢をつけ、手前5mm奥1cmを残して寿司飯を広げる。

Cut a laver seaweed in half and place it on a bamboo mat. Spread on sushi rice leaving a 5mm space at the near side and 1cm space at the far side, on hands before spreading rice.

4

かんぴょうの甘辛煮を軽くねじって中央に置く。

Twist simmered salty sweet gourd strips lightly and place them in the center.

5

手前から巻き、最後に巻きすでグッとしめる。6等分にする。

Roll the bamboo mat from the near side and press to finish. Cut into 6 pieces.

6

寿司飯の上にわさびをぬり、白ごま、せん切りにしたきゅうりの順にのせる。5同様に巻き、6等分にする。

Put green horseradish paste, white sesame seeds and julienned cucumber on sushi rice in order. Roll in the same way as 5, then cut into 6 pieces.

ごはん&汁物&漬物

Rice & Soup & Pickles

カリフォルニアロール

Western style sushi
that can be eaten
like a salad.

サラダ感覚で
食べられる
洋風お寿司

Time required
所要時間
40分
40 minutes

材料 (1本分)

寿司飯 (P.211参照)	300g
焼きのり	1枚
手酢 (P.215参照)	適量
白ごま	大さじ2
えび (ブラックタイガー)	4尾
スモークサーモン	3枚
アボカド	1/4個 (75g)
サニーレタス	1/2枚
紫玉ねぎ	1/4個
チャービル	少々
プチトマト	3個
Ⓐ チリソース	5g
ケチャップ	15g

Ingredients (for 1 roll)

300g sushi rice (see P.211)
1 roasted laver seaweed
some hand vinegar (see P.215)
2 Tbsp white sesame seeds
4 prawns (black tiger)
3 smoked salmon
1/4 avocado (75g)
1/2 leaf sunny lettuce
1/4 red onion
some chervil
3 cherry tomatoes
Ⓐ 5g chilli sauce
　 15g ketchup

料理のポイント
Cooking tips

1 くずれないようしっかり巻く。
Roll tightly so that it will not break.

2 切るときはラップをつけたまま。
Cut with clinging wrap on.

5 具を芯にして、しっかり押さえながら一気に巻く。
Use ingredients as the core and roll in one move pressing hard.

えびは殻をむいて背わたを取り、串をさしてまっすぐにゆでる。サニーレタスは細切り、アボカドは縦1cm幅に切る。
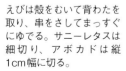
Shell and devein prawns, pierce straight with a skewer and boil. Julienne sunny lettuce and cut avocado vertically in 1cm width.

6 巻きすの上から両手でつかみ、しっかり押さえて巻きじめを下にして形を整える。
Hold the bamboo mat tightly with both hands and press to shape keeping the end of the mat underneath.

巻きすの上に焼きのりをしき、寿司飯をのせ、手酢をつけて広げる。
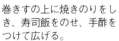
Place a roasted laver seaweed on a bamboo mat and place sushi rice on top, put hand vinegar on hands before spreading rice.

7 ラップをしたまま8等分にし、切ったあとにラップを外す。
Cut into 8 pieces while clinging wrap is still on, then remove clinging wrap after cutting.

白ごまを全体にまぶし、ラップをのせて平らに押さえる。
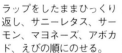
Sprinkle white sesame seeds all over, put clinging wrap on top and press flat.

8 Ⓐを混ぜてソースを作り、絞り出し袋に入れる。
Mix Ⓐ to make sauce and put it in a squeeze bag.

ラップをしたままひっくり返し、サニーレタス、サーモン、マヨネーズ、アボカド、えびの順にのせる。

Turn over with clinging wrap on and put sunny lettuce, salmon, mayonnaise, avocado and prawn on top in order.

9 薄くスライスして水にさらした紫玉ねぎをしいた上に、7と半分に切ったプチトマトを飾り、8をかける。
Decorate using 7 and cherry tomatos cut in half placed on red onions that have been thinly sliced and immersed in water, and pour 8 on top.

219

稲荷寿司

Inarizushi

Harmony of
salty sweet deep-fried bean curd
and sushi rice.

甘辛い油揚げと
寿司飯の
ハーモニー

Time required
所要時間
50分
50 minutes

材料（10個分）

寿司飯（P.211参照）	500g
黒ごま	小さじ1
油揚げ	5枚
煮汁の材料	
だし汁	200cc
砂糖	大さじ3
みりん	大さじ2
濃口醤油	大さじ2

Ingredients （for 10 pieces）

500g sushi rice (see P.211)
1 tsp black sesame seeds
5 deep-fried bean curd
Ingredients for cooking sauce
200cc soup stock
3 Tbsp sugar
2 Tbsp mirin
2 Tbsp dark soy sauce

料理のポイント
Cooking tips

1 油揚げは絞りすぎない。
Do not squeeze deep-fried bean curd too much.

2 ごはんはつめすぎない。
Do not overfill rice into a pouch.

油揚げは、沸騰した湯で
さっと湯通しする。

Dip deep-fried bean
curd quickly in boiled
water.

湯からあげ、ふきんに包み、
たたきながら水分を取る。

Take them out from wa-
ter and wrap them with
a cloth, remove water by
patting.

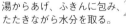

開きやすいように菜箸を転
がして、横半分に切り、袋
状に開く。

Roll cooking chopstick
over it for easy opening,
cut it horizontal in half
and open like a pouch.

鍋に煮汁の材料を入れて沸
かし、油揚げを入れる。

Put cooking sauce in-
gredients in a saucepan
and bring it to boil,
place deep-fried bean
curd into the pan.

沸騰したら弱火にし、落と
しぶたをして、煮汁が少な
くなるまで煮つめる。

Once it's boiled, turn
the heat down low and
cover with a drop-lid,
simmer until sauce is re-
duced.

バットに取り出し、そのま
ま冷ます。

Take them out and
place on a tray, leave
them to cool.

P.211の要領で寿司飯を
作り、黒ごまを全体にふり
さっと混ぜる。

Make sushi rice just like
P.211, and sprinkle
black sesame seeds
and mix quickly.

6を軽く絞る。●絞りすぎ
ると味気がなくなるので軽
く絞ること。

Squeeze 6 lightly. ●If
it's squeezed too much,
it looses flavor, so
squeeze lightly.

寿司飯を50gずつつめる。
折って口を閉じて、俵形に
し、閉じ目を下にして置き、
黒ごま（分量外）を飾る。

Fill each with 50g sushi
rice. Fold and close the
mouth. Mold it to a bar-
rel-shape, place on a
plate mouth side down
and decorate with black
sesame seeds (extra).

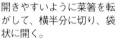

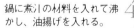

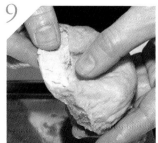

Onigiri

おにぎり

手軽に食べられて
お弁当に
ぴったり！

Easy to eat
and perfect for
a lunch box !

Time required
所要時間
30分
30 minutes

材料（6個分）

米	320g
水	洗い米と同量
えびの天ぷら（市販品）	2本
赤味噌	大さじ2
酒	小さじ1
青じそ	2枚
塩ざけ	1/4切れ
高菜	20g
焼きのり	適量
塩	適量

Ingredients （for 6 balls）

320g rice
same amount of washed rice water
2 prawn tempura (store-bought)
2 Tbsp red miso
1 tsp sake
2 leaves green perilla
1/4 salted salmon
20g mustard leaves
some roasted laver seaweed
some salt

料理のポイント
Cooking tips

1 ふっくらと握る。
Mold softly.

2 ごはんが熱いうちに握る。
Mold while rice is still hot.

ごはんを炊き、3等分する。そのうちのひとつにみじん切りにした高菜を混ぜる。

Cook rice and divide into three. Mix finely chopped mustard leaves in one of them.

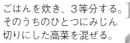

1の半量のごはんでおにぎり1個分。手を水で軽くぬらし、転がしながら、三角形に手を作りふんわり握る。

Half of each makes one rice ball. Moisten your hands with water. Mold softly balling in your hands and forming a triangular shape.

えびの天ぷらを半分に切り、塩をふる。えびの上半分を真ん中に入れ、三角形に握る。

Cut a prawn tempura in half and sprinkle salt. Put top half of the prawn in the center of rice and form into a triangular shape.

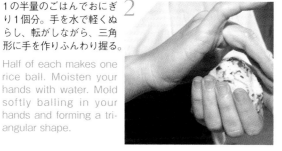

頂点に軽く指で穴をあけ、尾側をつきさし、形を整える。

Lightly make a hollow on the top with your finger, push in the prawn tail side up and shape it.

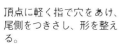

塩ざけを焼いて、軽くほぐし、ごはんの中につめて三角形に握る。

Grill and flake the salted salmon. Make into a filling in the center of rice and mold into a triangular shape.

酒でときのばした味噌をぬって魚焼きグリルで焼く。少し焦げ目がついたら裏返して味噌をぬり、再び焼く。

Brush miso paste diluted with sake on rice and broil with a fish griller. Once it is a little burnt, turn it over and brush miso paste, and grill again.

焼きのりをおにぎりの大きさに合わせて切る。

Cut a roasted laver seaweed into the correct size for rice balls.

2をのりで巻く。4はお雛様の着物のように巻きつける。

Wrap 2 with a laver seaweed. Wrap 4 like the photo.

味噌をぬった青じそを6にはりつける。

Place green perilla brushed with miso paste on 6.

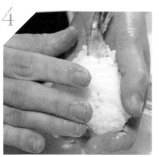

ごはん＆汁物＆漬物

Rice & Soup & Pickles

223

Sake chaduke

さけ茶漬け

最後のしめは
やっぱり
お茶漬け

For the perfect
ending to dinner, it has to be
rice with green tea.

Time required
所要時間
30分
30 minutes

材料（2人分）

塩ざけ	……………………	大1切れ（120g）
焼きのり	…………………	1/2枚
みつ葉	……………………	2本
白ごま	……………………	大さじ1
ごはん	……………………	280g
あられ	……………………	大さじ1/2
塩	…………………………	適量
おろしわさび	……………	小さじ1
せん茶	……………………	400cc

Ingredients （for 2 people）

1 large salted salmon fillet (120g)
1/2 roasted laver seaweed
2 stems honewort
1 Tbsp white sesame seeds
280g cooked rice
1/2 Tbsp arare Japanese crackers
some salt
1 tsp green horseradish paste
400cc green tea

料理のポイント
Cooking tips

1 お茶は食べる直前にかける。
   Pour tea immediately before eating.

2 わさびは目立つ位置に置く。
   Place green horseradish paste on the high spot.

弱火の直火であぶった焼きのりをちぎり、乾いたふきんに包んで、軽くもむ。

Directly roast a laver seaweed over a low flame, break into pieces and wrap in a dry cloth, then massage lightly.

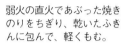

塩ざけは魚焼きグリルで両面を焼く。皮目にこんがり焦げ色がつくまで火を通す。

Broil both sides of salted salmon on a fish griller. Cook till skin is burnt.

塩ざけは皮や骨を取り、身を大きめにほぐす。

Remove skin and bones from salted salmon and flake the meat into large chunks.

みつ葉を2cm長さに切る。

Cut honewort into 2cm length.

たえず鍋をゆすりながら、白ごまを弱火で香ばしく煎る。

Roast white sesame seeds while shaking a saucepan at low heat until they are aromatic.

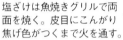

器にごはんを盛り、塩ざけの身をのせる。中央に小さく高く盛るとよい。

Put rice in a bowl and place salted salmon flakes on top. Heap salmon in the middle.

あられ、半量のみつ葉、のり、白ごま、塩を散らす。

Sprinkle Japanese crackers, of honewort, laver seaweed, white sesame seeds and salt on top.

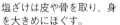

わさびを目立つ位置に置く。

Add green horseradish paste on the high spot.

食べる直前に、熱々のせん茶を注ぐ。残りのみつ葉をのせ、わさびを好みでとかしながらいただく。

Pour boiling hot green tea right before eating. Put the remaining honewort on top and melt green horseradish paste while eating if you like.

関西風うどん

Kansaihu udon

生地を足で踏んで
コシを出す
なかなか楽しい作業です

Stamp feet on the dough
to make it semihard.
It's a fun procedure !

料理のポイント
Cooking tips

1 打ち粉をしてはりつきを防止。
Sprinkle flour to avoid sticking.

2 生地はねかせてから使う。
Use dough after letting it stand.

3 ゆでたら水でしめる。
Put in water to firm-up after boiling.

Time required
所要時間
180分
180 minutes

材料 (2人分)

中力粉	150g
塩	7g
水	65cc
とき卵	大さじ1
油揚げ	1枚
万能ねぎ	3本
かまぼこ	30g
わかめ	5g
Ⓐ みりん	大さじ2
薄口醤油	大さじ2
だし汁	600cc
削り節	5g
Ⓑ だし汁	100cc
砂糖	大さじ2
薄口醤油	大さじ1

Ingredients (for 2 people)

150g all purpose flour
7g salt
65cc water
1 Tbsp beaten egg
1 deep-fried bean curd
3 stems spring onion
30g boiled fish paste
5g wakame seaweed
Ⓐ ┌ 2 Tbsp mirin
  │ 2 Tbsp light soy sauce
  └ 600cc soup stock
5g shavings of dried bonito
Ⓑ ┌ 100cc soup stock
  │ 2 Tbsp sugar
  └ 1 Tbsp light soy sauce

生地を作る。塩を水とかし、中力粉を入れたボウルにとき卵を入れ、フォークで混ぜる。

Make dough. Dissolve salt in water and pour beaten egg in a bowl containing all purpose flour. Mix with a fork.

1

2

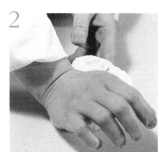

生地が混ざったら、台の上に取り出し、手でこねる。

Once dough is mixed, take it out, and place on a board and knead with hands.

3

打ち粉 (分量外) をして、生地を回転させながら、なめらかになるまでしっかりこねる。

Sprinkle flour (extra) and knead dough rolling until it is smooth.

4

なめらかになった生地を厚手のビニール袋に入れる。

Put smoothed dough in a thick plastic bag.

5

床に布をしき、4をのせ、上に布をかぶせて足で踏む。

Lay a cloth on the floor and place 4 on it, cover it with another cloth and stamp with your feet.

6

踏みながら、かかとを中心に体を回転させる。

While stamping, rotate your body centering the heel.

体をゆっくり回転させ、生地を外に広げるように丸くのばしていく。約2分、生地に弾力が出るまで両足で踏む。

Rotate body slowly and spread the dough round and outwards. Stamp with both feet until dough has body for about 2 minutes.

生地をビニール袋から取り出す。生地が袋にはりついていたら打ち粉をする。

Take dough out from the plastic bag. Sprinkle flour if the dough is stuck in the bag.

上下と両サイドを折って重ねる。再びビニール袋に入れ、同様に2～3分足踏みし、1時間ほどねかせる。

Fold top and bottom, and both sides to layer. Put it back in the plastic bag and stamp on it for 2-3 minutes in the same manner, then let it stand for about 1 hour.

打ち粉をし、ねかせた生地を置く。左右に均等の力を入れ麺棒でのばす。

Sprinkle flour and put the stood dough on top. Roll it out with a rolling pin using even force on left and right sides.

四隅の角を出し、2～3mm厚さの長方形にする。

Form four corners and make a rectangle with a thickness of a few mm.

手前と奥の生地を中央で合わせ4つ折りにする。

Take the near side and far side of the dough to the center, then fold the center to make four layers.

打ち粉をしたまな板にのせ4mm幅に切る。麺同士がくっついていないか確認する。

Put it on flour spread board and cut into 4mm width. Check that noodles are not stuck together.

関西風うどんつゆを作る。鍋に④を入れ、中火にかける。

Make Kansai style noodle soup. Put ④ in a saucepan on medium heat.

東西で異なるうどんのつゆ

Wheat noodle soup varies depending on if its from the East or West of Japan.

うどんのつゆは関東地方と関西地方とでまったく異なります。醤油をたっぷり使う関東風のつゆは色が濃くて甘く、薄口醤油を使用する関西風のつゆは薄い色で、だしの香りが際立ちます。関東ではうどんよりそばが普及しました。

Wheat noodle soup is entirely different depending on its origin from the East or West of Japan. Eastern style soup uses lots of soy sauce is dark in color and sweet, western style soup uses light soy sauce is light in color with the aroma of soup stock. Buckwheat noodles became more popular in the eastern region than wheat noodles.

ひと煮たちしたら削り節を
加え、再沸騰したらアクを
取り、火を止める。

Once boiled, add shav-
ings of dried bonito and
bring to boil again skim-
ming off the scum, then
turn off the heat.

約10分して削り節が沈ん
だら、キッチンペーパーを
しいたざるでこす。

Once shavings of dried
bonito sink after about
10 minutes, sift over
kitchen roll placed in a
strainer.

鍋に⑧を沸騰させ、湯通し
して三角に切った油揚げを
入れる。

Bring ⑧ to boil in a
saucepan, add deep-
fried bean curd
blanched and cut into
triangles.

再沸騰したら裏返して落と
しぶたをし、約10分煮る。

When it boils again, turn
them over and cover
with a drop-lid and sim-
mer for about 10 min-
utes.

かまぼこを4枚に、わかめ
は水で戻して3〜4cm角
に、万能ねぎは小口切りに
する。

Cut boiled fish paste
into four, reconstitute
wakame seaweed and
cut into 3-4cm squares,
chop spring onion.

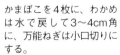

13のうどんを沸騰した湯
で強火で約3分ゆでる。1
カップの水を加え、再沸騰
したら水気をきる。

Boil wheat noodles from
13 at high heat about 3
minutes. Add 1 cup of
water and bring to the
boil again maintaining
high heat, then drain.

20を丼に盛り、かまぼこ、
わかめ、油揚げを上にのせ
て16のつゆをかけ、万能
ねぎを散らす。

Fill a bowl with 20, and
add boiled fish paste,
wakame seaweed and
deep-fried bean curd,
pour soup from 16 and
sprinkle spring onion on
top.

〈冷やしとして〉
冷水でしめ、水気をきって
盛り、つけ麺として食べて
もよい。

〈As a cold dish〉
It can be served as a
dipping noodles by ton-
ing up with cold water,
drain and put in a bowl.

Zarusoba

ざるそば

ひんやりと
冷たくいただく
日本の麺

Japanese noodle
served refreshingly
cold.

材料（2人分）

そば（乾）	180g
ねぎ	20g
針のり	適量
おろしわさび	適量
つけつゆの材料	
だし汁	150cc
濃口醤油	50cc
みりん	50cc
砂糖	大さじ1/2
削り節	2.5g

Ingredients (for 2 people)

180g buckwheat noodles (dried)

20g scallion

some julienned laver seaweed

some green horseradish paste

Ingredients for dipping sauce

150cc soup stock

50cc dark soy sauce

50cc mirin

1/2 Tbsp sugar

2.5g shavings of dried bonito

料理のポイント
Cooking tips

1 麺は芯がなくなるまでゆでる。
Cook until noodles have no core.

2 つけつゆは削り節で旨みを出す。
Add flavor to dipping sauce with shavings of dried bonito.

沸騰したたっぷりの湯に、そばが重ならないよう鍋全体に広げながら入れ、ゆでる。

Place buckwheat noodles in a saucepan with plenty of boiling water ensuring they are evenly spread to avoid piling, and boil.

ねぎは2〜3mm幅の小口切りにし、しばらく水にさらして水気をきる。

Chop scallion into 2-3mm width and soak in water for a while, then drain.

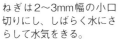

沸騰してきたら差し水をし、湯の温度を下げる。

When boiling, add some water and bring the temperature down.

つけつゆを作る。鍋にみりんを入れて、中火で沸騰させ、アルコール分をとばす。

Make dipping sauce. Add mirin to a saucepan, bring to boil at medium heat and allow alcohol to cook away.

芯がなくなるまでゆでる。そばをちぎり、芯がないことを確認する。

Cook till there is no core. Break a noodle to check there is no remaining hard core.

だし汁、濃口醤油、砂糖を入れる。沸騰したら削り節を加える。

Add soup stock, dark soy sauce and sugar. Once boiled, add shavings of dried bonito.

そばが完全に冷たくなるまで、すぐに流水で洗う。水気をきって盛り、針のりをのせる。

Wash buckwheat noodles in running water until it is completely cold, drain well and put julienned laver seaweed on top.

弱火で煮こみ、アクをとる。火からおろし、しばらくおいておく。

Simmer at low heat and skim off the scum. Take it off the heat and leave it for a while.

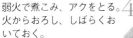

4をキッチンペーパーをしいたざるでこし、器に入れる。ねぎとわさびを小皿に盛る。

Sift 4 through kitchen roll placed on a strainer and put it in a bowl. Place scallion and green horseradish paste on a small plate.

Okonomiyaki

お好み焼き

ソースとマヨネーズの
組み合わせの妙で
やみつきに

Get hooked on
the superb combination of
sauce and mayonnaise.

料理のポイント
Cooking tips

1 生地にやまといもを入れてふんわりさせる。
Add Japanese yam to make dough fluffy.

2 何度もひっくり返さない。
Do not turn over often.

3 焼いている途中で押しつぶさない。
Do not press too hard while cooking.

Time required
所要時間
30分
30 minutes

材料（1枚分）

生地の材料

薄力粉	40g
やまといも	15g
Ⓐ だし汁	50cc
薄口醤油	小さじ1
酒	小さじ1
塩	ひとつまみ
キャベツ	100g
揚げ玉（天かす）	大さじ1
卵	1個
切りもち	20g
豚ばら肉	25g
えび	1尾
ゆでだこ	20g
サラダ油	適量

仕上げの材料

お好み焼きソース	適量
マヨネーズ	適量
マスタード	適量
青のり	適量
削り節	適量

Ingredients (for 1 piece)

Ingredients for dough

40g flour
15g Japanese yam
Ⓐ ┌ 50cc soup stock
　 │ 1 tsp light soy sauce
　 │ 1 tsp sake
　 └ pinch of salt
100g cabbage
1 Tbsp bits of deep-fried tempura batter
1 egg
20g cut rice cake
25g pork ribs
1 prawn
20g boiled octopus
some cooking oil

Ingredients for finishing touches

some okonomiyaki sauce
some mayonnaise
some mustard
some laver seaweed powder
some shavings of dried bonito

1

キャベツを粗みじん切りにする。

Chop cabbage semi-finely.

2

キャベツの水気をよくきる。

Drain cabbage liquid well.

3

Ⓐを合わせてよく混ぜる。やまといもはすりおろしておく。

Put Ⓐ together and mix well. Grate Japanese yam beforehand.

4

薄力粉をざるでふるい、ボウルに入れる。Ⓟふるっておくとダマになりにくい。

Sift flour using a strainer and put it in a bowl. Ⓟ If it is sifted, it's hard to get lumps.

5

中央をくぼませる。くぼみに3のやまといもとⒶを加える。

Make a hollow in the middle. Add Japanese yam and Ⓐ from 3.

ごはん&汁物&漬物

Rice & Soup & Pickles

中央から泡立て器で混ぜる。 6

Mix with a whisk from the center.

ダマができないように、しっかりと混ぜる。 7

Mix well so that there are no lumps.

キャベツ、揚げ玉、卵を入れる。 8

Add cabbage, bits of deep-fried tempura batter and an egg.

9

スプーンを使って約30秒空気を入れながら混ぜる。

Mix with a spoon for about 30 seconds letting air in.

もちを5mm幅に切る。 10

Cut rice cake into 5mm width.

ゆでだこを5mm幅に切る。 11

Cut boiled octopus into 5mm width.

えびは殻をむき、背わたと尾をとり、縦ふたつにスライスする。 12

Shell, devein and remove tail from a prawn, slice vertically into two.

フライパンにサラダ油を熱し、もち、たこ、えび、スライスした豚肉を並べて軽く焼く。 13

Heat cooking oil in a frying pan. Add rice cake, octopus, prawn and sliced pork, cook lightly.

お好み焼きの秘密
Secrets of okonomiyaki

大阪では戦前からお好み焼きの屋台がよく見られ、"洋食焼き"と呼ばれていました。当時は、1枚1銭で売られていたため、"一銭洋食"という名も。これがお好み焼きのルーツで、大阪を代表する味として、多くの人たちから愛されています。

Okonomiyaki stalls were popular in Osaka before the war, it was known as "western bake". It was also called "1 sen western food" as at that time one piece was sold for 1 sen. This is the root of okonomiyaki that has become loved and known by many people as Osaka's typical food.

生地を流し入れ、18cmほどの円形に整える。

Pour dough in and shape into about 18cm circle.

プクプクと泡が出て固まってくるまで約4分焼く。

Cook for about 4 minutes until you see small bubbles from it coagulate.

ひっくり返してさらに3～4分焼く。

Turn it over and cook for another 3-4 minutes.

全体に火が通ったら、いったんふたに生地をあけてのせる。

Once cooked, put the crape on the lid.

そのままくずれないように、ずらすようにして器に盛る。

Move it to a plate by sliding so that it does not fall apart.

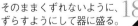

失敗しない ために　To avoid a failure

焼くときに押してはダメ
Do not press when cooking.

お好み焼きを焼くときに、スプーンなどで押しつけると空気が入らず、ふわっと仕上がりません。ひっくり返したときに厚みが違う場合、へらで軽く高さをそろえるぐらいにしましょう。

When you cook okonomiyaki pressing with a spoon, it does not let air in for a fluffy finish. Keep it to light presses with a spatula only to even the thickness.

19

お好み焼きソースとマスタードをのせ、混ぜるようにして広げる。

Add okonomiyaki sauce and mustard to the top, and spread while mixing together.

20

好みでマヨネーズを絞り出し袋に入れて飾る。

Put mayonnaise in a squeeze bag and decorate if you like.

21

削り節と青のりを全体に散らす。

Sprinkle shavings of dried bonito and laver seaweed powder all over.

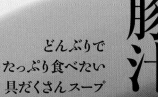

豚汁

Tonjiru

どんぶりで
たっぷり食べたい
具だくさんスープ

Soup with plenty of ingredients
that should preferably be served
in a large bowl.

材料（2人分）

豚薄切り肉	60g
大根	30g
にんじん	30g
れんこん	30g
ごぼう	30g
さといも	小1個 (50g)
こんにゃく	60g
だし汁	400cc
合わせ味噌	30g
ごま油	小さじ1
飾りの材料	
ねぎ	15g

Ingredients （for 2 people）

60g thin sliced pork	
30g Japanese radish	
30g carrot	
30g lotus root	
30g burdock	
1 small taro (50g)	
60g konjac food	
400cc soup stock	
30g blended miso	
1 tsp sesame oil	
Ingredients for decoration	
15g scallion	

Time required
所要時間
40分
40 minutes

料理のポイント
Cooking tips

1 こんにゃくは塩で臭みを取る。
   Remove odor from konjac food using salt.

2 鍋底についた旨みを取る。
   Scrape flavorful bits from the bottom of the saucepan.

さといもとねぎは水に、ごぼうとれんこんは酢水（分量外）にさらす。

Soak taro and scallion in water, and burdock and lotus root in vinegar and water (extra).

こんにゃくは手で細かくちぎる。塩（分量外）をまぶして軽くもみ、2〜3分おいてからゆでる。

Break konjac food in pieces with hands. Sprinkle salt (extra) and massage. Leave it for 2-3 minutes, then boil.

鍋にごま油を熱し、2cm幅に切った豚肉を炒める。

Heat sesame oil in a saucepan and saute pork cut into 2cm width.

大根、にんじん、れんこん、さといもは3mm幅のいちょう切りにする。

Cut Japanese radish, carrot, lotus root and taro into small pieces of 3mm width rectangles.

にんじん、れんこん、ごぼう、大根、こんにゃくの順に加えてよく炒める。

Add carrot, lotus root, burdock, Japanese radish and konjac food in order, and saute well.

ねぎは1〜2mm幅の小口切りにする。

Edge cut scallion in 1-2mm width.

だし汁を入れ、鍋底の旨みをこそげ取ってから、さといもを加えて煮る。

Pour soup stock in and after scraping flavorful bits from the bottom of the saucepan, add taro to simmer.

ごぼうは皮をむかずにたわしで表面をよく洗い、ささがきにする。

Wash burdock with a scrubber without peeling skin and shred.

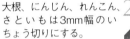

合わせ味噌をざるを使ってとき入れる。器に盛り、ねぎを散らす。

Dissolve blended miso with a strainer. Pour in a bowl and sprinkle scallion.

ごはん＆汁物＆漬物

Rice & Soup & Pickles

237

Shijimi no akadashijiru

しじみの赤だし汁

しじみからだしが出るので
だしは昆布のみと
シンプルに

When cooked the clams
will provide the soup so
to keep it simple use only
kelp for the soup stock.

Time required
所要時間
40分
40 minutes

材料（2人分）

しじみ	100g
水	300cc
昆布	5cm角
赤味噌	小さじ2
酒	大さじ1
万能ねぎ	2本

Ingredients (for 2 people)

100g
300cc water
5cm square kelp
2 tsp red miso
1 Tbsp sake
2 stems spring onion

料理のポイント
Cooking tips

1 しじみは真水で砂抜きする。
   Remove sand by soaking clams in fresh water.

2 沸騰直前に昆布を取り出す。
   Remove kelp immediately before boiling.

万能ねぎは2〜3mmの小口切りにする。

Edge cut spring onion into 2-3mm pieces.

ふきんで昆布の表面を軽くふく。白い粉は旨み成分なのでふき取らない。分量の水に30分以上浸す。

Wipe the surface of kelp lightly with a cloth. Do not wipe away white powder as it refines the taste. Soak and leave it for more than 30 minutes.

1

しじみは、真水に浸して、約2時間冷暗所に置き、砂をはかせる。

Soak clams in fresh water for about 2 hours in the cool dark place to remove sand.

2

しじみの水気をきり、塩（分量外）をまぶす。

Drain clams water and sprinkle salt (extra).

3

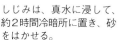

両手でしじみをこすり合わせるようにして汚れやぬめりを落とし、水洗いする。

Use hands to clean dirt and slime from clams by rubbing them each other and wash.

4

6

昆布を浸した汁ごと鍋に入れて、中火にかける。

Pour kelp together with water it was soaked in into a saucepan, place on medium heat.

7

沸騰直前になったら昆布を取り出し、しじみと酒を加える。ボ 沸騰後も昆布を入れておくと、えぐみがでてしまう。

Remove kelp immediately before boiling, and add clams and sake. ℗ If kelp is left after boiling, it will bring a bitter taste.

8

しじみの口が開いたら、アクをすくう。ひと混ぜして、貝殻の内側についたアクも浮かせてから取るとよい。

Once are open, skim off the scum. It is better to mix once to let scum from inside the shells float up, then scoop off.

9

鍋にざるを重ねて赤味噌を落とし、泡立て器で混ぜてとく。器に注ぎ、5を散らす。

Place a strainer over the saucepan, then drop on red miso and dissolve it using a whisk. Pour it into a bowl and sprinkle 5 on top.

ごはん＆汁物＆漬物

Rice & Soup & Pickles

なめことほうれん草の味噌汁

Nameko to hourenso no misoshiru

Add ingredients
that cook fast
after dissolving miso paste.

火の通りが早い
具材は味噌を
といてから加えて

材料（2人分）

なめこ ……………………………… 30g
絹ごし豆腐 ………………………… 50g
ほうれん草 ………………………… 10g
味噌 ……………………………… 大さじ2
だし汁 …………………………… 250cc

Ingredients （for 2 people）

30g nameko mushrooms
50g silken tofu
10g spinach
2 Tbsp miso
250cc soup stock

料理のポイント
Cooking tips

1 なめこのぬめりを取る。
Remove slime from nameko mushrooms.

2 具材を加えるタイミングに注意。
Pay attention to the timing of when to add ingredients.

ほうれん草は3cm幅にざく切りにする。

Cut spinach into 3cm width.

絹ごし豆腐は1cm角に切る。

Cut silken tofu into 1cm cubes.

湯を沸かして洗ったなめこを落とす。

Boil water and add washed nameko mushrooms.

鍋の中をぐるっとかき混ぜて、ひと煮たちするまで待つ。

Mix ingredients in the saucepan and wait until it is boiled.

ひと煮たちしたら、なめこを冷水にとり、水気をきって、軽くぬめりを取る。

Once nameko mushrooms are boiled, remove them and place in cold water, drain then lightly clean off slime.

鍋にだし汁を注ぐ。強火にかけ、沸騰してきたら中火にする。

Pour soup stock in a saucepan. Put it on high heat turning it down to medium once it has boiled.

鍋にざるを重ねて、田舎味噌を落とし、泡立て器でとく。

Place a strainer over the saucepan and drop on the country style miso. Dissolve it using a whisk.

すぐになめこ、絹ごし豆腐を鍋に加える。

Add nameko mushrooms and silken tofu immediately.

沸騰したらはうれん草を加えて、ひと煮たちさせる。火が通りにくい具のときはだし汁で具を煮て、最後に味噌をとく。

Once boiled, add spinach, bring it back up to boil. For ingredients that are hard to cook, simmer with soup stock then dissolve miso last.

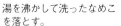

ごはん&汁物&漬物

Rice & Soup & Pickles

Sumashijiru

すまし汁

くずれやすい具を
先に盛ると
キレイな仕上がりに

Put the fragile ingredients
in first for
the best presentation.

Time required
所要時間
20分
20 minutes

材料（2人分）

たけのこ（水煮）	50g
塩蔵わかめ	8g
卵豆腐（市販品）	1個
花麩	2個
木の芽	2枚

吸い地の材料

だし汁	400cc
塩	小さじ1/4
薄口醤油	小さじ1

Ingredients (for 2 people)

50g bamboo shoot (boiled)
8g salted wakame seaweed
1 egg tofu (store-bought)
2 flower shaped wheat gluten bread
2 baby leaves of a Japanese pepper

Ingredients for soup

400cc soup stock
1/4 tsp salt
1 tsp light soy sauce

料理のポイント
Cooking tips

1 具の彩りを考える。
  Consider the colors of ingredients.

2 くずれやすい具は先に盛る。
  Put the fragile ingredients in first.

5

吸い地の材料を温め、たけのこは3〜5分、花麩はさっとゆでて、取り出す。

Warm up the ingredients for soup, boil the bamboo shoot for 3-5 minutes and the flower shaped wheat gluten bread briefly in soup, then remove them both.

花麩は水で戻して、水分を絞っておく。

Reconstitute flower shaped wheat gluten bread and squeeze out the water.

1

6

お玉に卵豆腐をのせ、吸い地の中で温めて取り出し、器に盛る。

Place egg tofu in a ladle and warm it up in soup, remove and put it in a bowl.

たけのこは白いアクがあればボウルにためた水の中で洗い、5mm厚さのくし形に切る。

If the bamboo shoot has white scum, wash in a bowl filled with water, then cut into 5mm wedge.

2

7

わかめを吸い地に入れて温める。

Warm wakame seaweed up in soup.

卵豆腐は器の大きさに合わせて切る。

Cut egg tofu to size depending on the bowl used.

3

8

6に7の吸い地をはる。

Pour soup from 7 in 6.

わかめは塩抜きして、さっと熱湯でゆでて冷まし、3cm角に切る。

Wash off salt from wakame seaweed and quickly cook it in boiling water, then cool and cut into 3cm square.

4

9

たけのこと花麩を飾り、木の芽をあしらう。

Decorate with bamboo shoot and flower shaped wheat gluten bread, and put baby leaves of a Japanese pepper on top.

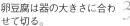

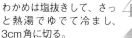

ごはん＆汁物＆漬物

Rice & Soup & Pickles

ぬか漬け

Nukaduke

Pickling bed
needs to be
well maintained.

ぬか床には
ていねいな手入れが
必須です

料理のポイント
Cooking tips

1 生ぬかをしっかり煎る。
  Roast fresh rice-bran thoroughly.

2 ぬかに加える水加減に注意する。
  Be careful about the amount of water to add to
  the rice-bran.

3 ぬか床はしっかり密閉する。
  Seal up pickling bed tightly.

所要時間

Time required
60分
60 minutes

材料（2人分）

ぬか床の材料

生ぬか	1kg
水	1000cc
粗塩	130g
野菜くず（セロリの葉・大根の葉・キャベツの外葉などなるべく水分の多い野菜）	80g
鷹の爪	2本
昆布	10cm角
しょうが	1かけ
水花かつお	3g
きゅうり	1本
にんじん	1本
なす	1本
キャベツ	1枚
やまいも	50g
塩	適量

Ingredients（for 2 people）

Ingredients for pickling bed

1kg fresh rice-bran
1000cc water
130g sea salt
80g bits of vegetables (Vegetables that contain a lot of water such as celery leaves, Japanese radish leaves, outer layers of cabbage)
2 dried red peppers
10cm square kelp
1 piece ginger
3g thin fluffy strips of shredded dried bonito

1 cucumber
1 carrot
1 eggplant
1 leaf cabbage
50g yam
some salt

1 ぬか床を作る。生ぬかをフライパンに広げ、中火で煎る。

Make pickling bed. Spread fresh rice-bran on a frying pan and roast at medium heat.

2 電子レンジで温める場合は、ラップをせずに約1分半温め、表面が熱くなればよい。

If you use a microwave, heat for about a minute and a half without clinging wrap until the surface is just hot.

3 さわってみて熱くなったら、バットに広げて冷ます。完全に冷めるまでおく。

Touch it and if hot spread it in a tray to cool. Leave it until it has completely cooled down.

4 鍋に水と粗塩を入れ、強火にかけ、沸騰したら冷ます。塩がとけるまで混ぜる。

Put water and sea salt in a saucepan over high heat, once it is boiled cool it down. Mix until salt has dissolved.

5 冷めた生ぬかを大きなボウルに入れる。

Put cooled fresh rice-bran in a large bowl.

6 4の塩水を数回に分けて入れ、なじませるようにもみこむ。

Pour on the salted water from 4 over a few times and knead it to blend.

7 軽く握ってだんごができるくらいまで混ぜる。

Mix until it can be made into a ball by holding it lightly.

8 ぬかが入る大きさのふたつきの密閉容器に移す。野菜くずを入れる。

Move rice-bran to a sealable container large enough to hold rice-bran. Add vegetable bits.

9 鷹の爪、昆布、皮つきのしょうが、糸花かつおを入れる。

Add dried red peppers, kelp, ginger with skin and shredded dried bonito.

10 上からしっかりと押さえ、1〜2週間なじませる。

Press firmly on top and leave it for 1-2 weeks to blend.

11 1〜2週間たったら表面にふきんをしいて水分を取り、容器の内側についたぬかをふき取る。

After 1-2 weeks, place a cloth over the surface to let it absorb water and wipe off rice-bran that stuck in sides of inside container.

12 塩をふったきゅうりをまな板にこすりつけ、板ずりしてアクを抜く。

Rub salted cucumber against a cutting board to remove harsh taste.

13 にんじんは葉つきの部分を切って皮をむく。太い部分は縦に切りこみを入れる。

Chop leaves off carrot and peel skins. Make vertical incisions in thick part of the carrot.

ぬか床を長持ちさせるコツ
Tips for keeping pickling bed longer.

ぬか床は一度作れば、何度でも野菜を漬けることができます。ただし、きちんとした手入れが必要です。まず、毎日2回は混ぜてぬかを空気にふれさせること。また、漬けた野菜の水分が出てくると腐りやすくなるので、こまめに水気を取ることが大切なのです。

Once pickling bed is made you can pickle vegetables over and over again, however you have to take care of it. Mix rice-bran twice a day to let air in. The water needs to be removed regularly, because the water from vegetables will make it easily go bad.

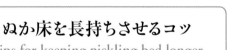

なすはヘタの部分に包丁を入れ、取り除く。

Chop off hull of eggplant.

きゅうり、にんじん、なす、キャベツに塩をまぶす。にんじんは切りこみ部分にもまぶす。

Sprinkle salt on cucumber, carrot, eggplant and cabbage. Make sure to sprinkle into the incisions in the carrot as well.

やまいもはぬめりが出るので、皮がついたまま塩をまぶす。

Sprinkle salt over the skin of yam as yam has slime.

ならしたぬか床に野菜を漬け、ぬかで覆う。

Bury the vegetables in smoothed pickling bed and cover them with rice-bran.

上からふきんをかぶせ、密閉して冷暗所で保存する。

Cover with a cloth and seal the container, store in the cool dark place.

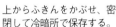
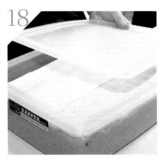

半日おき、味がなじんだら取り出し、ぬかを洗い落とす。

Leave it for half a day and remove them once flavor has blended, wash off rice-bran.

食べやすい大きさに切り、器に盛る。

Cut into bite size pieces and place on a plate.

1か月以上漬けて古漬けで食べる場合は、水にさらして絞り、醤油をかける。

For pickles that have been pickled for more than a month, immerse in water, squeeze them then add soy sauce before eating.

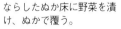

穴あきカップや穴をあけたプラスチック容器で水分を取る。

Remove the water using either a cup or a plastic container with holes.

2〜3週間留守にする場合は表面に塩を散らし、冷暗所に置く。

When you are away for 2-3 weeks, sprinkle salt over the surface and keep in the cool dark place.

ごはん＆汁物＆漬物

Rice & Soup & Pickles

梅干し

Umeboshi

The tip is to dry
thoroughly
in sunlight.

日光でしっかりと
干すことが
ポイント

料理のポイント
Cooking tips

1 容器をきちんと消毒する。
Sterilize a container properly.

2 重しは梅と同じ重さをのせる。
Use a weight that matches that of the
Japanese plums.

3 天気のよい日にしっかり干す。
Dry thoroughly on a sunny day.

材料（2人分）

梅	2kg（完熟したもの）
粗塩	300g
焼酎	大さじ2

赤じその材料

赤じそ	2束
粗塩	大さじ2

Ingredients (for 2 people)

2kg Japanese plums (fully ripened)
300g sea salt
2 Tbsp distilled liquor

Ingredients for red perilla

2 bunches red perilla
2 Tbsp sea salt

3

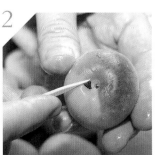 *(image id 4)*

ひとつひとつ水気をふき取り、余分な水気を取る。

Wipe off the water from each of plums to remove excess.

4

ボウルに梅を入れ、焼酎大さじ1をふりかけ、手で全体にまぶす。

Put Japanese plums in a bowl and sprinkle 1 Tbsp of distilled liquor, mix with hands to blend.

5

梅干しを漬ける容器に残りの焼酎を入れて、容器を消毒し、ひとつかみの粗塩をまぶす。

Put the rest of the distilled liquor in the container to be used to pickle the Japanese plums to sterilize it, then sprinkle a handful of sea salt.

完熟した梅をたっぷりの水に約4時間さらしてアク抜きし、水気をきる。

Soak fully ripened Japanese plums in plenty of water for about 4 hours to remove harsh taste, and drain.

1

6

梅ひとつひとつにたっぷり粗塩をつける。

Cover each of Japanese plums with sea salt.

竹串を使って黒い部分（ヘタ）を取り除く。

Remove black parts (hull) using a bamboo skewer.

2

7

容器に入れる。1段並べたら粗塩をかける。これを繰り返す。

Place them in the container. After finishing the first layer, sprinkle sea salt and repeat.

梅を全部入れたら、残りの粗塩をすべて入れる。ぴったりと落としラップをする。

8

Once all the Japanese plums have been put in the container, put in the remaining sea salt. Place clinging wrap to cover the plums completely.

梅と同じ重さの重し（石など）をのせる。1日に1回びんをゆすり、5日間冷暗所に置く。

9

Place a weight (for example, a stone) that matches the weight of plums on top. Shake the container once a day and keep it in the cool dark place for 5 days.

写真のように梅が下がるまでしっかり漬けこむ。

10

Soak well till Japanese plums go down as shown in the right photo.

赤じそは葉の部分だけを使うので、葉だけをむしり取る。

11

Nip out just the leaves of red perilla as only the leaves will be used.

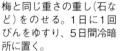

むしった葉を、たっぷりの水で洗う。

12

Wash them with plenty of water.

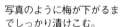

粗塩大さじ1を入れ、押し洗いする。手が荒れるので手袋をして力強くもむ。

13

Put 1 Tbsp of sea salt on the leaves and wash by pressing. Use gloves to massage hard as hands will get rough and dry.

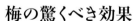

一度出てきた水分を捨て、再び粗塩大さじ1を加えて押し洗いし、水分を絞る。

14

Clear away the water extracted from the leaves, and wash again with 1 Tbsp of sea salt by pressing, then squeeze the water out.

10のラップを取り、赤じそを入れる。びんを動かして梅の漬け汁を赤じそにまぶす。

15

Remove clinging wrap from 10 and add red perilla. Move the container to allow the red perilla to absorb Japanese plum pickling sauce.

梅の驚くべき効果
Astonishing effects of Japanese plums

日本では風邪をひいたらおでこに梅干しをはる、健康のために梅酢を飲むなど、古くから梅を生活に取り入れています。梅にはクエン酸やリンゴ酸がふくまれ、疲労回復や食欲増進といった効果があります。日本人に欠かせない食品のひとつなのです。

Japanese plums have been a part of daily life since ancient times, for example, placing a Japanese plum on your forehead to treat a cold or drinking Japanese plum vinegar for health. Japanese plums contain citric and malic acid, which helps you recover from fatigue and stimulates the appetite. This is one of the vital food for Japanese people.

重しをのせ, ふたをして冷暗所に約1か月置く。

Place a weight on top and keep it in the cool dark place for about one month with a lid on.

梅を取り出し、3日3晩盆ざるに広げて干す。

Remove Japanese plums and dry them on a bamboo strainer for 3 days and 3 nights.

赤じそはカラカラに乾燥するまで干す。

Dry red perilla until it has completely dried off.

梅の漬け汁は1日外に出しておく。虫などが入らないようにふきんで口をふさぐ。

Keep pickling sauce from Japanese plums outside for a day. Cover the mouth with a cloth so that insects and others can't get in.

ときどきびんをゆすりながら、日光に当てる。

Shake the container occasionally and expose to the sunlight.

梅が日光で温かいうちに漬け汁に戻す。乾燥していたものが戻ったら食べられる。

Put Japanese plums back in pickling sauce while they are warm. Once the dried ingredients are reconstituted, they are ready to eat.

しばらく保存する場合は、梅の漬け汁を入れたびんに梅を戻して密閉する。

If they need to be preserved for a while, put Japanese plums back into the container with pickling sauce, and seal.

ゆかりを作る。18の赤じそを細かく切る。びんに入れて保存すれば1年もつ。

Make dried perilla Yukari. Finely Chop red perilla from 18. It can last for up to a year if preserved in a bottle.

失敗しないために　**To avoid a failure**

熟していない梅を使ってはダメ！

Not fully ripened Japanese plums are no good !

梅は十分に熟したものを使いましょう。右と中央のように、まだ緑や黄色で熟していないものは、中まで味がしみこまず、おいしくありません。

Use fully ripened Japanese plums. Like those of the right and center, those still green or yellow are not ripened, and can't absorb flavors to the core and will not taste good.

浅漬け

Asaduke

Mom's taste
that is easy to make
with a simple procedure.

カンタンな手順で
手軽に作れる
おふくろの味

料理のポイント
Cooking tips

1 しっかり重しをする。
Ensure that they are weighted down.

2 冷蔵庫でねかせる。
Let it stand in the fridge.

3 食べる前は水分を絞る。
Squeeze water out before eating.

252

材料（2人分）

白菜	1枚 (150g)
にんじん	15g
きゅうり	30g
昆布	3cm角
しょうが	1かけ
ゆずの皮	1/8個分
粗塩	小さじ1
昆布茶	大さじ1/4
唐辛子	1/2本

醤油漬けの材料

なす	2本 (180g)
小かぶ	2個 (200g)
セロリ	70g
みょうが	3本 (60g)
濃口醤油	350cc
三温糖	200g
酢	200cc
だしパック	1袋
昆布	3cm角
削り節	2g
煮干し	1本
レモンの皮	1/6個分

Ingredients (for 2 people)

1 leaf Chinese cabbage (150g)
15g carrot
30g cucumber
3cm square kelp
1 piece ginger
1/8 worth of yuzu citron skin
1 tsp sea salt
1/4 Tbsp kelp tea powder
1/2 dried red pepper

Ingredients for soy sauce pickles

2 eggplants (180g)
2 small turnips (200g)
70g celery
3 myouga Japanese ginger (60g)
350cc dark soy sauce
200g brown sugar
200cc vinegar
1 soup stock packing paper
3cm square kelp
2g shavings of dried bonito
1 dried sardine
1/6 worth of lemon skin

1

白菜は、硬い芯の部分を取り、5cm幅に切り分ける。芯の部分は包丁をねかせてそぎ切りにする。

Remove hard core part of Chinese cabbage and cut into 5cm width. Cut the core part in slivers by laying down a knife.

2

にんじんは1〜2mmの薄切りにし、ずらして置いてせん切りにする。

Cut carrot into 1-2mm slices, stagger them and julienne.

3

きゅうりは2〜3mm幅の輪切りにする。

Cut cucumber into 2-3mm round slices.

4

水に浸けて戻した昆布、しょうがをせん切りにする。

Julienne reconstituted kelp and ginger.

5

ゆずの皮は内側の白いわたを取り除き、せん切りにする。

Remove white bits inside of yuzu sitron skin, and julienne.

ごはん＆汁物＆漬物

Rice & Soup & Pickles

ビニール袋に切った野菜を
すべて入れ、粗塩、昆布茶、
種を取った唐辛子を入れる。

6

Put all the cut vegeta-
bles in a plastic bag and
add sea salt, kelp tea
powder and red pepper
with seeds removed.

塩と昆布茶がとけるまで、
力強くもみこむ。

7

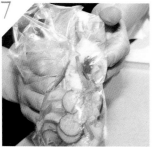

Massage hard till salt
and kelp tea powder are
dissolved.

即席漬物器に入れて重しを
し、冷蔵庫でひと晩おく。

8

Put them in an instant
pickling container, place
a weight on top and
leave in a fridge over-
night.

即席漬物器がなければ、水
入りのボウルを重しにして
冷蔵庫でひと晩おく。

9

If you don't have an in-
stant pickling container,
use a bowl with water
as a weight, and leave
in a fridge overnight.

ひと晩おいたら冷蔵庫から
取り出す。水気を絞り、器
に盛る。

10

Remove after a night.
Squeeze the water out
and place them on a
plate.

醤油漬けを作る。なすはヘ
タを切り落とし、縦半分に
切る。

11

Make soy sauce pick-
les. Cut off the hull of
eggplant and cut verti-
cally in half.

セロリはそぎ切りにして
5mm幅に切る。

12

Cut celery into 5mm
wide slivers.

小かぶは、茎を2cm残し
て切り、皮を厚めにむく。

13

Cut small turnip leaving
2cm of the stem, and
peel skin thick.

˝漬物˝とは？
What is "Tsukemono"?

古くから日本人に愛されている漬物。もともとは収穫
した野菜の余りを長期保存するために考え出されまし
た。材料の水分を取り除き、漬け床や漬け汁の味をふ
くませます。さらに長く漬けることで酵素が働き、漬
物特有の風味が生まれるのです。

Tsukemono pickles are loved by the Japanese
through the ages. The technique was originally
conceived to preserve harvested vegetables
that were not needed straight away. Remove the
water from ingredients and let them absorb the
flavor from pickling bed or sauce. By pickling for
longer an enzyme acts that produces the charac-
teristic Tsukemono pickles flavor.

切り口が八角形になるように縦に6面にむく。

Cut vertically to make six faces, so that slices will be hexagonal.

だしパックに昆布、削り節、わた部分を除いた煮干し、レモンの皮を入れる。

Put kelp, shavings of dried bonito, dried sardine without gut and lemon skin in a soup stock packing paper (small paper bag).

小かぶは水に漬け、竹串を使って葉の間の砂や汚れを落とす。

Soak small turnip in water, and clean sand and dirt between leaves using a bamboo skewer.

18の三温糖がすべてとけたら火を止め、19を入れて冷ます。

Turn the heat off once all the sugar from 18 is dissolved, and put 19 in it and cool.

なす、小かぶと小かぶの葉、セロリ、みょうがを塩水(分量外)に漬ける。

Soak eggplant, small turnips and their leaves, celery and myouga in salted (extra) water.

ひと晩おいた野菜を取り出し、水分をしっかり絞る。

Remove the vegetables after letting them stand overnight, and squeeze out the water thoroughly.

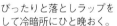

ぴったりと落としラップをして冷暗所にひと晩おく。

Place clinging wrap to cover the ingredients completely, and keep in the cool dark place overnight.

密閉容器に野菜を並べ、20を注ぐ。冷蔵庫でひと晩おき、途中で1回裏返す。

Arrange the vegetables in a sealable container and pour 20 in. Keep in a fridge overnight turning them over once during that time.

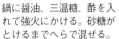

鍋に醤油、三温糖、酢を入れて強火にかける。砂糖がとけるまでへらで混ぜる。

Put soy sauce, brown sugar and vinegar in a saucepan on high heat. Mix with a spatula until sugar is dissolved.

ひと晩おいたら、だしパックを取り出し、野菜を適当な大きさに切り分ける。

After leaving overnight, remove the soup stock packing paper and cut vegetables into bite sized pieces.

著者

川上文代 かわかみふみよ

大阪あべの辻調理師専門学校卒業後、同校職員として12年勤務。2010年より東京・渋谷区にてデリス・ド・キュイエール川上文代料理教室を主宰。

Fumiyo Kawakami

After graduation from Osaka Abeno TSUJI Culinary Institute, she worked in the school for 12 years.
In 2010 she began to run DELICE DE CUILLERES Kawakami Fumiko Cooking Studio in Shibuya-ku Tokyo.

英語で作る 料理の教科書

著 者	川 上 文 代
発 行 者	富 永 靖 弘
印 刷 所	慶昌堂印刷株式会社

発行所　東京都台東区　株式　新星出版社
　　　　台東4丁目7　会社
〒110-0016 ☎03(3831)0743 振替00140-1-72233
URL http://www.shin-sei.co.jp/

ISBN978-4-405-01120-5